ELECTION AND GOVERNANCE IN NEPAL

Election and Governance in Nepal

Edited by

LOK RAJ BARAL

MANOHAR
2005

First published 2005

ISBN 81-7304-598-4

Published by
Ajay Kumar Jain for
Manohar Publishers & Distributors
4753/23 Ansari Road, Daryaganj
New Delhi 110002

Typeset by
A J Software Publishing Co. Pvt. Ltd.
New Delhi 110005

Printed at
Print Perfect
New Delhi 110064

Contents

Preface

This volume on election and governance is the first study of its kind in Nepal. Based on both empiricism and theoretical construct of the subject, the present volume originated from the Nepal Centre for Contemporary Studies' (NCCS) agenda of manpower development in social studies, especially in the field of political science. In view of eleven years' electoral exercises, the Centre singled out elections and democratic governance as one of the key areas of study in a multiparty parliamentary system. During these trying years, a lot of institutional distortions did creep into the system rendering the parliamentary processes not only ineffective but also instrumental in the spread of popular disenchantment with the rationale of the system. Although the overall performance of political parties in general was not up to the expectations of the people, popular inputs were however discernible making the parties and leaders responsive to such disenchantment or even outrage. Conceivably, the political leaders who invariably personalized their respective organizations are now under public pressure to be guided by certain norms of democratic system. This is a positive development in the midst of anger, frustration, and even rebellion (as of the Maoists). The extent to which such frustration had developed in the country has significantly contributed to the spread of the Maoist agenda of People's War. However, it is ironical that the Maoists who have all along been championing the cause of the people's democracy *à la* the Maoist variant seem to be unclear about the suitability of the model in the given Nepali context. Since the Nepalis have apprenticeship in liberal democracy from their very childhood, it becomes difficult for even the Maoists to impose new indoctrination measures. Senior Maoist leaders themselves have admitted this dichotomous situation assuring the Nepalis that their regime would provide no less freedoms than that being granted by the present multiparty pluralistic system. Such vagueness and occasional shifts in their strategies have therefore given grounds for a number of questions about the rationale of launching a violent war. Instead, the Maoists can contribute a lot to making the existing democracy more vibrant and progressive by putting adequate pressure for bringing about socio-economic changes for ameliorating the hardships of the people who are not concerned with new regimes but with those that guarantee a democratic regime based on both constitutional and performance legitimacy. So it has by now been clear that any regime is best judged by its capacity to guarantee political freedom as well as by its capacity to bring about a qualitative transformation in the lives of its citizens.

Our close observations and studies of the decade-long democratic exercises prompted us to single out election and governance as an important aspect of consolidation of democracy in a semi-traditional country. The old mindset is still pervasive in democratic Nepal as the constraints of tradition and history and the unchanged feudalistic and authoritarian political culture of the political elites have affected the conduct of free and fair elections. Politicians lack confidence in elections when there is no control over state resources. How can parties in power fare well has been demonstrated by the two local elections held in 1992 and 1997. The Nepali Congress could win about 60 per cent seats in local bodies in 1992 but the same party when it was in opposition got less than half of the total results. So, the conduct of elections and the problems faced by the National Election Commission have been adequately highlighted in the present volume besides other areas concerning governance and election.

It has also been felt that there has been a neglect of the issue of making democratic governance a participatory process. Our study has shown that no political party is serious about bridging the gaps between precepts and practice. For, most of them have their manifestos that aim at integrating all ethnic, Dalit and other underprivileged sections of society into the democratic process; none seems to be pursuing its own declared agenda of greater accommodation of such groups in the system thus resulting in the continued disparity in society and polity. These dimensions cannot be ignored while trying to encompass the agenda of governance. Unlike other studies on governance, the present volume therefore tries to be as much inclusive as possible despite many constraints for making its size manageable and precise.

Experiences of elections revealed by politicians were no less rewarding as the senior politicians—the chairman of the National Assembly, the minister, and members of parliament and others—found the workshop more appropriate for divulging the intricacies, sources of funding, administrative and political interference, problems of Election Commission and returning officers, and administrators. Disclosures of huge amounts of money spent in some hill districts during the elections were revealing for us prompting us to conclude that such expensive practices in a poor country like Nepal would not help democracy survive. How could a democracy which has become a hostage to manipulators, criminals and money suppliers be able to broaden its base by insuring participation of all sections of society is a major point of examination. Although political parties have taken some initiative to improve the election system and have ac-cordingly formed a high power committee under the chairman-ship of the prime minister, laws and committees' agendas are seldom implemented in their true spirit. Time will only tell how far they would go towards improving the election system.

The second striking feature of the workshop was the involvement of a variety of resource persons—politicians, lawyers, professors, judges, administrators, entrepreneurs and other independent academics who deal with the issues of ethnicity. Of the 28 resource persons, one was drawn from each South Asian country—Bangladesh, India, Pakistan and Sri Lanka—and the rest were from Nepal. The research tools were provided by the experts in the field in addition to the use of archival sources and other forms of information on the subject. On the eve of the workshop, a study-pack containing 33 articles on theory and empirical research in elections was distributed to the fifteen participants who, during the course of the workshop, were required to present their analytical views on the materials read by them. It was interesting to note that all participants seemed to spend their time in reading chapters assigned to them and to report the next morning before beginning of the day's session.

A structured questionnaire was administered to a total of 500 respondents (100 from each sampled district) from across different sections of society. The study tries to balance the gender, age, class, education, occupation and caste/ethnic groups while selecting respondents for filling questionnaires. Among the

500 respondents, 378 were male and 122 female. Youngsters between age 18-35 were 245, middle-aged between age 36-54 were 201 and the elderly between age 55 and above were 54. Class-wise, 12 respondents were from the rich class, 381 from the middle class and 107 from the poor class. Educationally, 61 respondents were illiterate, 127 literate, school level education holders were 191 and highly educated were 121. Among the 500 respondents and taking them occupationally, 204 were agriculturists, 25 labourers, 110 service holders, 82 businessmen, 26 students, 31 housewives, 17 untouchables, and 5 other occupational groups. The caste and ethnic division of the 500 respondents was thus identified: 151 hill caste groups, 134 hill ethnic group, 18 Newars, 20 Terai high caste groups, 68 Terai tribals, 5 Muslims and 46 untouchables. One person remained unidentified during the field trip.

Each sampled district was divided into two clusters—urban and rural. The urban cluster covered all wards of a municipality and the rural cluster consisted of three adjoining village development committees of the sampled district. The study thus administered questionnaires to 101 urban and 399 rural population that constituted the universe of 500 respondents.

By all accounts, the present exercise was both educative and representative in nature. The Election Commission of Nepal deserves our deep appreciation for extending all possible help including sending two participants from the commission itself. Free and frank discussions that took place during the workshop and the manner in which the resource persons drawn from various fields had shown their interest in our effort were commendable. Above all, the trust reposed in us by our donor—the Ford Foundation could enable us to make it a success.

It needs to be made clear that the present volume is not a compilation of articles as is generally seen in edited volumes. Fifteen young social scientists who had undergone rigorous training in research methodology and election exercises were sent out to the field for conducting survey of 500 respondents. Their views have been well tabulated and put into the respective chapters of the book. Although the NCCS has prepared exhaustive annexes of different variables, many of them find space in chapters adding empirical flavour to the book. We admit our limitations and flaws in such an enterprise. Yet, we are rather encouraged by our common endeavour for upgrading political science discipline in Nepal. In fact, the present volume is only a beginning of a series of activities that deal with democracy in its various ramifications. Since our objectives are two-fold—upgrading political science studies in Nepal and helping consolidate the democratic processes, the present study tends to be normative and even value-laden and sanguine. It is due to this reason that we have deliberately involved various persons belonging to politics and other professions as resource person in the workshop on research methodology, democracy and elections. Practical politicians and those involved in conducting elections shared their experiences and limitations suggesting many recommendations for rectifying existing flaws in electoral politics.

This study would not have been possible had the Ford Foundation, New Delhi, not encouraged us to undertake it. The two scholars—Dr. Gowher Rizvi, the representative of the Ford Foundation, and Dr. Mark M. Robinson, Programme Officer—reposed trust and confidence in our team and committed a grant to make it a success. Ford's encouragement has been like a trend-setter in this field. We expect that the NCCS would continue similar activities in the future with Ford's cooperation. We also expect to do some networking activities by developing our contacts with many other centres and institutes of the South Asian region. Such networking and cooperative efforts would definitely promote the spirit of regional cooperation and understanding. At a time when the whole world is having a uniform approach to tackle terrorism which is a menace to democracy and freedom, South Asian countries cannot perennially lag behind in building their own coalition for wrenching the region from the quagmire of habitual conflicts and disorders. The South Asian Association of Regional Cooperation which is in limbo due to conflictual relations between India and Pakistan would from henceforth use the new opportunity to settle their differences. Only by thwarting the menace of terrorism, fundamentalism and secessionism would the spirit of regional cooperation, democracy and freedom prevail. Though such ideas might be dismissed as highly unrealistic in the given South Asian context, the time is not faroff for taking recourse to them. And no government would be able to govern without having such cooperative and secular spirit. So the NCCS is interested in opening series of discourses on democracy and governance at the regional level as well.

We cannot fail to acknowledge the cooperation of the following persons: the chairman of the National Assembly (Upper House) Dr. Mohammed Mohsin, then Minister of State for Social Welfare, Ms. Kamala Pant, Krishna P. Sitaula, member of parliament and the Central Committee, member of the Nepali Congress, and Iswar Pokhrel, member of parliament and the Central Committee, member of the Communist Party of Nepal (Unified Marxist-Leninist) (CPN-UML), the Chief Election Commissioner, Bishnu Pratap Shah, the former speaker and member of the Constitution Drafting Commission, Daman Nath Dhungana, the district judge of Rautahat, Thakur Prasad Sharma, the former chairman of the Federation of Nepal Chamber of Commerce & Industries, Padma Jyoti, the chairman of the Eastern University Service Commission, Krishna Pokhrel, Dr. Krishna B. Bhattachan, Professor Ananta Raj Poudel, Professor Sridhar Khatri and Professor Sushil Raj Pandey, Hari Sharma, Til Bikram Nembang, and Dr. Sabitri Singh, Dr. Birendra Kumar Mishra, former member of the Election Commission, Dhruba Hari Adhikari, journalist, and Dr. Sudhindra Raj Sharma, a researcher, for their participation in the workshop as resource persons. The four scholars—Professor Dilara Choudhury from Bangladesh, Professor Aswini K. Ray from India, Professor Hasan-Askari Rizvi form Pakistan and Dr. Jayadeva Uyangoda from Sri Lanka—contributed to the workshop as resource persons. They came to Kathmandu at short notice and enlightened our young participants with their respective countries' experiences. We appreciate their cooperation for making our programme a success.

The owner of Dhulikhel Lodge Resort, Prem Kumar Shrestha, deserves our appreciation for his cooperation and friendship, shown to us during our weeklong stay at his resort. Thanks are also due to Iswar Kharel, a staff of the NCCS, and Anish Shresthacharya of the Centre for Nepal and Asian Studies, Tribhuvan University, for their cooperation at different stages of the preparation of this book.

LOK RAJ BARAL

Introduction

Lok Raj Baral

The five components of this volume would present a broad picture of the post-1990 Nepali politics in relation to the structures and dynamics of a multiparty system, and constitutional monarchy. All the sections included in the book have a major focus on the co-relationship between the electoral process and numerous other variables such as parties, governance, administration of elections, and voting behaviour, with a background section on the theoretical and practical aspects of political development. Nevertheless, the background section is not loaded heavily with sophisticated theoretical constructs because our purpose in this endeavour is just to identify some of the universally accepted basics of a democratic system and governance. Participation of parties as a crucial variable, issues of legitimacy, parliament in both structural and functional terms, leadership role, etc., constitute the main theme of this study. All these variables have been tested empirically at the local level by using the survey method and personal interviews. Although it is just a miniscule of the whole project because of the size of the district and universe selected for the survey, it has however supplemented our studies of institutions, leadership, parties, interrelationship between the political processes and socio-economic constructs and their impacts on shaping the political culture of the general public.

Elections are one of the integral parts of popular legitimacy in addition to many other issues of political development. Yet, a paradoxical situation develops when elections turn out to be handy mechanisms for perpetuating power and status without internalizing the characteristics of democracy. The manner in which the entire electoral processes are used for petty party and individual interests, to capture power and unaccounted resources, as has been witnessed in many South Asian countries, makes the people lose their faith in parties, leaders and the system. In Nepal, democratic exercises have made the electorate more assertive and conscious of its role, though not to the extent of discarding the corrupt politicians in elections. Yet the process has been able to demonstrate the electorate's preference during the general elections by changing as many as 60 per cent candidates during the 1999 national elections. But the picture was somewhat fuzzy in the local level elections as only the party in power, that too with the home portfolio, seemed to have influenced the local elections considerably. The two local elections have therefore given two opposite results, depending on which party was in power during the elections. If the NC was able to win about 60 per cent local seats in 1992 when the party was in power, the undivided CPN (UML) wrested the same percentage of seats when it was sharing power at the centre with the other two parties, the Rashtriya Prajatantra Party (RPP) and the Nepal Sadbhawana Party (NSP) in 1997.

Despite such circulation of political elites through electoral processes, its impact—on improving the quality of institutions—parliament, executive and parties—is still far-off. So, while opening a discourse on parliament, or on parties, internalization of certain core normative aspects of politics becomes crucial for the system. Thus, representative institutions without having to relate them to cultural patterns and values remain undeveloped. Nepal's eleven years' democratic exercise is thus paradoxical because, on the one hand the country has successfully conducted three national and two local elections, experimented with all types of governments—majority, minority, and coalition between the NC, the RPP, the NSP and the CPN-UML regardless of ideological positions and backgrounds. On the other hand, holding of elections and experimenting with such coalition exercises have turned out to be less tangible for both institution building and for making agile the spirit of the Constitution.

Why Nepal's major events—overthrow of the Rana regime in 1951, the first era of party politics (1951-60), and the restoration of multiparty system in 1990 which were supposed to be trend-setters, have become intermittent, if not abortive, efforts today. It is ironical that even after completing eleven years of a representative system based on the popular concept of sovereignty, political uncertainties haunt the principal parties and their leaders as if transition to democracy is permanent and Nepal's democratic polity is fraught with perennial systematic crises. It can also be called the trajectories of political development, or disjointed pieces of history that need to be put together with great care and confidence on the side of political parties and leaders.

Since Nepal's political development defies incremental trends due to what I prefer to call historical jumps or swings from one end to the other, it is difficult to make a systemically rational evolutionary history. In 1951, a compromise formula was accepted by the forces of change represented by the NC, under whose stewardship the anti-Rana armed movement was successful, and the ousted Ranas prompting King Tribhuvan (then being a participant of the movement) to proclaim a full-fledged democratic government as determined by a constitution to be prepared by a duly elected Constituent Assembly. That declaration was forgotten within a short period of three years with the same king retracting his earlier commitment by investing all powers in himself and issuing decrees for direct rule. His son Mahendra further consolidated monarchical power by 1959 and awarded the Constitution in his terms. Thus, the monarchical consolidation was complete. The same parties that had brought down the 104-year old Rana regime in 1951accepted the Constitution on practical grounds. Yet, the main reason behind such a volte face on the side of parties like the NC and the Communist Party of Nepal was attributed to erosion of their own popularity particularly while bargaining with the king for holding elections to the Constituent Assembly. Its consequences proved to be fatal to them when King Mahendra, after consolidating his power fully through different 'imperatives' of a ruler, staged a coup against the NC-led elected government on 15 December 1960 and dismantled the eighteen month old parliamentary system along with imposition of numerous draconian measures for nullifying the rationale of the party system. And ironically, he used both Article 55 of the Constitution (emergency clause) and the Royal Nepal Army to accomplish his mission. Henceforth, the royal regime (partyless) dominated Nepali politics notwithstanding all forms of opposition—violent and non-violent—resorted to by the outlawed parties. Yet, the mission of eliminating political parties was not accomplished due to built-in contradictions and systemic dilemma on whether or not it should show its liberal face before the world.

So the panchayat experimentation was another twist of Nepali political development, and despite being partyless in spirit, the nemesis of parties permanently worked for exposing the anti-democratic nature of the system. It should nevertheless be accepted that many local level institutional infrastructures and competitive political exercises, despite being confined to the individual level, had prepared an adequate base for today's local institutions. The political apprenticeship received by the people has indeed made a great contribution to the democratic spirit. Given the nature and thrust of the polity exclusively designed for active monarchical rule, the panchayat system was democratic at the lower level and autocratic at the central level. Its exclusionist character and mobilizational pattern had alienated the democratic and progressive parties, driving them to be oppositionists to the hilt. And 1990 proved to be a good year for them for ending the partyless regime.

The Constitution of the Kingdom of Nepal (1990), a product of mass struggle but made out to be a compromise document, is distorted due to the pulls and pressures on the makers of the Constitution themselves. Nor are the movement forces serious about the true spirit of the Constitution thus allowing the retro gressive forces to be more obstructionists against its actual spirit.

Three major trends seem to give rise to systemic vulnerabilities and uncertainties during the eleven years' exercises. First, ideologically, political parties that are the principal agents of democratization and change suffer from institutional incongruities and ambiguities in both ideological and functional terms inter-mixing principles with tactics and strategies. Though a common problem to all, it was/is more evident in the Left parties with many of them changing their ideological positions from time to time. The main opposition party today—CPN (UML)—has different incarnations before it acquired the present form. The CPN (UML) is an amalgam of both extremist and moderate communists, although they still fell uncomfortable with their ideological identity—being at the same time both Marxist-Leninist and liberal democrats, who get ideological inspiration from the Western pluralist democracy. Historical trajectories have demonstrated that all the communist roads, despite some deviations and windings, lead to the multiparty system and pluralism. Yet, political development encounters difficulties when the Left parties pretend that they are first communists and then liberal democrats whose final destination is *janabad* (people's democracy), which is nothing more than an abstraction or rhetoric. The other non-Left parties, especially the NC, one of the oldest moderate liberal party, waver in sticking to their ideological positions allowing themselves to be driven by events and immediate interests. NC's identity has therefore been diluted following the restoration of democracy in 1990. Other smaller parties also followed suit during the post-mid term elections that denied majority to any single party in parliament. Motivated by capturing power by resorting to any means—shifting loyalty, money-power, ministerial post in cabinet, etc.—, most political parties in parliament seem to lower their image before the general people.

So there was hardly any difference between the CPN (UML), the NC, the RPP and the rest with each party's leaders indulging in political trade-offs for power. In the wake of such developments, the prime minister's position was made a hostage as if the democratic process means everything to every politician if it serves an immediate interest. Thus, much damage has been done to the system during this period (1994-9). What is more surprising and intractable is that even an impressive mandate received by a party in the general elections has had neither been able to insure stability nor faster development. The NC, for instance, was/is in power with absolute majority in parliament twice in 1991 and 1999, yet the crisis of governability continues to haunt the country because of the perennial intra-party feuds and interpersonal conflicts between senior leaders. It has thus been proved that majority alone does not guarantee stability and progress if the internal bickering of the ruling party continues unabated. Unreasonable demands and behaviours of opposition parties are no less responsible for promoting extra-parliamentary methods and pressure tactics even during the parliamentary session. The manner in which the entire opposition, particularly the Left-opposition, made parliament a hostage by boycotting the nineteenth session in 2001 on the single issue of the resignation of Prime Minister, G.P. Koirala, for his alleged involvement in a corruption case, and the latter's challenge that he be removed through the established parliamentary procedure either within his own party or in parliament, which the opposition did not accept, wanting/demanding nothing short of his resignation, demonstrated the strains within the parliamentary process.

Second, democracy has been conceived as an electoral mechanism that throws political actors and parties into state-created structures but is not internalized as a political cultural process with which a new orientation of the people at large is possible. In the conventional parlance it is called a way of life and a manifestation of both public power and accountability. In Nepal, however, election, which is used as a tool but not as an essence of the exercise of power through popular participation, has thus given rise to elements of political decay. Normative and institutional distortions have thus crept into the body politick. Its only remedy lies in the seriousness of political leaders.

Contrasted with such negative trends and developments, the overall exercises cannot be berated as futile as many positive aspects are now discernible in the political scene. And the credit goes to the openness of the system that encourages free public debates about all aspects of the polity and its actors. The spectacular latent and patent pressures exerted on changing the role of parties seem to be yielding positive results for the improvement of the system.

Finally, that Nepal's developmental exercises have not become an integral part of a genuine participatory system in which people feel that they are in constant interaction with the various elected units and themselves, demands for both political corrections and socio-economic transformation are being vociferously put before the parties and leaders. Such demands seem to have focused on making the participatory processes more effective and clean. Under the existing electoral arrangement, voters and party workers are active only during elections but as soon as the elections are over, the entire process turns out to be ritualistic. It happens at all levels—village, district and national—notwithstanding the much-touted slogan of local government. Representatives of constituencies return to them for longer duration only during the fresh election campaigns. They can therefore be called absentee politicians who prefer to reinforce the 'centrality' of Kathmandu (capital) that militates against the spirit of decentralization of power or local government. The old historical status of Kathmandu as the nerve centre of Nepali politics and the symbol of modernity remains unchanged in democratic Nepal. How Kathmandu has once again become the hub of Nepali elites can be seen by their temptation to buy land and construct houses keeping their district electoral constituencies as their fiefs. During the Rana time and after, the other Nepalis living outside the valley called Kathmandu 'Nepal'. The unbroken centrality of Kathmandu has its own negative impact on the over-all development of the country, more so in the context of representation. In a real sense, most members of parliament do not represent the aspirations of their voters as they seldom visit their constituencies with a view to serving the people. This is another dimension of the flawed representative system.

Another major concern of the present volume is governance in relation to the overall dynamics of electoral processes. Contrasted with government, governance does not only purvey personnel or political elites that run government but it encompasses all legal and procedural aspects as well. In non-democratic regimes, governance gets a back seat because of the highly personal and familiar or similar parochial trends of a regime. In a democratic system, however, both government and governance become inseparable terms in both nuances and actual practice, because political elites in general are *in* the system through certain defined channels of popular participation. Election is one such important element without which the test of popular legitimacy is not possible. Even if such a channel is flawed, political actors are expected to adhere to the ruler until they correct such flaws later when they realize that the democratic process would itself be undermined as having been devoid of the actual content of popular legitimacy.

Governance is possible only when a government is fully committed to the established process, honours the rule of law, makes institutional behaviour more vibrant and transparent, quickens the process of development, makes the entire political and administrative and other organs of government and polity free of corruption, implements policies and people-oriented programmes with alacrity and greater efficiency, and ensures accountability. Adhering to these elements requires strict conformance to established constitution and procedures. If a government is genuinely committed to these underlined concepts, it inevitably creates efficient and rational governance. On the contrary, no government, more so the democratically elected government, becomes legitimate or democratic if it defies all of the above-mentioned criteria fixed by us. There can be other elements—moral, political and practical—for making a government transparent and accountable.

Given the constraints of tradition and history, all the elements of democratic governance cannot perhaps be put together at a time. Partly such difficulties continue to trouble the ruling and other political elites because of their own lack of confidence, or the established process itself takes its own time to demonstrate a certain degree of maturity. Judged by the behaviour of both the leaders and other activists including the members of civil society, it seems that a stable political culture that shows an orientation towards the political system is still far-off. None the less, the intensity of present political discourse encompassing many institutions hitherto left out of public purveyance, and the apparent slackness being observed in anti-pluralist movements, especially of the Maoist variant, suggests the trend of political stability. People now seem to realize that hype of extreme-radicalism, despite being highly attractive for the time being, would in all probability be neither durable nor practicable in the given context. However, one positive element found in the radical movement is that it has been able to convey the powerful message that unless a society and polity are fully transformed making themselves relevant to all sections of society, particularly the poor, the ethnic and the exploited sections, democracy can never achieve its popular legitimacy. It should therefore not only be broad-based and but also be qualitatively different from the highly stratified society and polity as in the past.

So many points raised by the Maoists are transformatory in nature and can well provide contours for rectifying the maladies of the country. As the Nepali Communist Movement itself has been inextricably linked to the pluralistic movement that was/is underway in the country since its birth in 1949, the *people's democracy* of the Maoist variety, if it at all exists anywhere in the world, may not be a suitable proposition for Nepal. Moreover, all Communist groups of Nepal have been participating in the electoral politics of the country since the first ever parliamentary elections of 1959, contrary to their populist campaign for bringing about *janbad* based on the dogma of Marxism-Leninism-Maoism. So the communists as such cannot be dismissed as anti-liberal forces bent on replicating the abstruse Maoist model, only on the basis of the utterances and the language of assurances of the apex Maoist leaders that the people would enjoy more freedom in their political order than they do in the present multiparty system.[1]

Turning to specific sections of the book, the present study tries to examine the foregoing discourse of political development and of political forces influencing it within an analytical perspective. All the four themes—election and governance, administration of election, parties and election, and voting behaviour—are therefore knit together in order to show how political exercises being undertaken over the years are perceived by both the voters and the agencies involved in conducting such exercises. Since these thematic sections are the products of both fieldwork and analyses based on studies and observations, each section would try to relate it to political developments underway in Nepal.

Nepal's political trajectories, though beset by uncertainties and unpredictable trends, have also laid the foundations of democracy. People are increasingly developing cognitive and evaluative domains making the politicians more accountable and responsive to their demands. The vociferous public debates on reducing social and economic disparity, on improving the election system in addition to implementing the Constitution in letter and spirit have shown the positive aspects of the eleven-year exercises.

Dealing with 'elections and governance', it has been realized that the transfer of power to the people under the present political dispensation is incomplete. Its main reason can be attributed to the behaviour of political parties that fail to prepare legislation and other devices for regulating parties. Though the Constitution has conceived the regulation of parties, their leaders seem to be lackadaisical in implementing it. Moreover, crises of governance are increasingly becoming more rampant and intractable due to violation of the spirit of the Constitution as well as due to the idiosyncrasies of all parties.

The section dealing with 'social structure and voting behaviour' demonstrates the continuity of the traditional class and caste groups in politics. 'All' the major political parties are top-heavy with the high caste groups; representation in the parliament features the same thus leading to the formation of successive cabinets constituted by high caste groups.' Apart from the traditional social structure in which the dominant caste and class groups continue to influence the elections with the help of their inherited status and financial resources, the voting behaviour of the electorate has however shown a certain degree of maturity. It was least attracted by political radicalism of the Maoist as well as by the populism of the CPN (ML). It has also been observed that no ethnic and parochial considerations seem to motivate the voters significantly during the voting. On the whole, voters appear to be more rational than their leaders who, after winning elections, indulge in petty interests and corruption forgetting the spirit of the mandate they receive.

The section 'political parties and election' probes into the dynamics of party politics and tries to draw the conclusion that despite some minimum role of civil society and professional groups, parties are still 'omnipotent and omnipresent' in Nepali politics. In any democratic system, more so in a parliamentary system, parties are an integral part of the day-to-day systemic activities. So they naturally come under the active scrutiny of voters. Generally, parties in Nepal are too casual to address the issues of ethnic groups, Dalit and other underprivileged sections of society. As a result, their representative pattern remains narrow and parochial. All parties, regardless of their backgrounds and ideological moorings, are affected by such trends.

'Election management' relates to the experiences of the Election Commission, general people and other state agencies, and to the empirical tests conducted later by the team. This section suggests a number of measures for the improvement of the flawed electoral processes. Problems have been identified, analytical perspective provided and recommendations advanced in order to urge the politicians for reforms. However, changes in electoral laws, procedures, etc., would hardly matter unless the principal actors—political leaders and their followers—themselves show better examples by changing their attitudes towards the election system. The Chief Election Commission's critique on the role of political parties and on the existing lacunae detected in the conduct of elections seemed to have helped generate public debate on the funding of elections, governmental neutrality and the empowerment of the commission for making free and fair elections a reality.

NOTE

1. Durga Subedi has adequately corroborated my view on the liberal component of the communist movement in Nepal in his recent interview with *The Kantipur* daily. In his opinion, taking up arms against the regime which its antagonists consider as 'oppressive and feudal' alone does not lead to the logical conclusion that the new order to be brought about by the armed movement would be dictatorial. The Nepali Congress, which is the oldest and the main liberal democratic party in the country, had resorted to armed movement thrice, in 1951, and later in the 1960s and the 1970s, following the royal coup of 1960. See Durga Subedi's interview in *The Kantipur* (vernacular daily), 26 September 2001.

CHAPTER 1

Democracy and Elections: Trajectories of Political Development

Lok Raj Baral*

Political development is an amorphous concept and has been selectively used for the Western developed democracies and only partly used as an explanatory tool in general. In the absence of well-articulated concepts and theories in developing countries, the Western scholars' postulates were immediately used as ready-made imports by the scholars of the developing world. Thus, the issues of political development in the developing countries are explained from a hybrid perspective of the West and the developing countries because of the absence of similar formulations in them. India, the laboratory of pluralist democracy in the developing world, could draw the attention of some Western scholars, particularly, Samuel P. Huntington, Myron Weiner, Paul Brass, the Rudolphs, just to mention a few among many, when they, by way of applying their concepts to South Asia, also took note of the context in its wider ramifications. Now much headway has been made in the direction of developing praxis in political development as the recent trends in politics are as much shaped by socio-cultural, ideological, geopolitical and numerous intervening variables as by universalistic ideas and theories. Whether or not a country fits into the category of the developed or developing or underdeveloped groups of nations, institutions, participation, organizations, stability and political order, elite backgrounds and orientation, socio-economic structures (feudal, caste-based, class-based, ethnicity, patron-clientelism and patrimonialism and family inheritance, etc.) have to be adequately dealt with while contextualizing the theories of political develop-

*The author would like to thank the three participants—Ms. Urmila Adhikari, K.C. Khadga and Ram Kumar Yadav—for helping me write this chapter of the book.

ment. So a country's specific environment in which the political dynamics take place does not necessarily provide a uniform theorization for comparative perspectives.

Viewed from such a consciously articulated framework of political analysis, it apparently tries to be country-specific kind of conceptualization, which may or may not be adapted to other situations. However, for making empirically tested and well-grounded theorization and conceptualization, many universally accepted characteristics of political development can be, though selectively, accepted. Such concepts and normative approaches developed in North America and Europe have thus been adapted to all countries regardless of their level of development. And Nepal is not an exception to it as the country's political development has all along been influenced by such Western imports—in both theoretical and practical terms—despite the distinctive indigenous identity of its own. And some new attributes that have invariably worked as both obstructionist and positive factors for political development seem to be an inextricable part of the overall developmental processes of the country.

Whatever the arguments for/against the theories and practices of political development, certain key elements of both modernization and political development cannot be ignored, though modernization and political development are often mistaken as a synonym. Among the meanings and requirements of political development, Lucian W. Pye's list deserves our attention, as many of such elements of political development put forth by Pye are no less relevant to the developing countries. Among such ingredients, economic capability, political development as a part of the modernization process, political development as a nation building process, administrative and legal development, political development as a mass mobilization and participatory process, stability and orderly change, performance legitimacy through the proper mobilization of power, and political development as a multi dimensional process of change are always crucial. Structural and functional differentiation of institutions and roles and equality and capacity (penetration of policies and programmes along with crisis management) are the measuring rods of today's political development. Among the most popularly cited needs of political development are Huntington's analysis of the relationship between 'participation' and 'institutionalization' because the crux of political development depends on the institutional capacity to balance the trends of modernization and change. According to him, political decay easily creeps into the political processes if participatory explosion is not properly balanced through the commensurate development of institutional capacity.[1]

The twin objective of the new democracy project in a country like Nepal is crafting of a legitimate order and of the insurance of performance legitimacy of the government. Democracy minus these two aspects—legal and performance legitimacy, and good governance—is subjected to be perennially threatened either by the anomie observed in the political parties and forces in general or by the powerful impacts of the trends of revivalism. And added to it is the ineptitude of power elites contrary to the clear popular mandate received for governance. But how to insure legitimacy (both legal and performance) and through which mechanisms is the key issue of political development today. So institutions, participation, organizations, elite-structure and behaviour, caste and class backgrounds and the interplay of endogenous and exogenous forces and trends and their immediate impacts on political development need to be examined.

Institutions crafted for insuring both democratic essence and mechanisms play significant role for political development. Above all, structures need to be designed and procedures developed. Constitutions, organizations, parliament, rules and ordinances, bureaucracy, the police and the army, civil society organizations belong to institutional domain. According to the classical approach to the study of politics, only institutional structures were taken as the basis of political analysis or for judging the status of political development. How the country is governed and with what mechanisms and normative principles is a pet theme for analysing the democratization agenda and governance, because both aspects are increasingly becoming significant in today's developmental processes. In the politics of the developing countries, the revolution alone does not democratize the system and elites unless the post-revolution period grapples with the problems of consolidation of the revolution. Thus, it has been said that it is easy to bring about a revolution or change but difficult to transform society and polity in accordance with the spirit of the movement.

If the preponderant characteristics of traditional states continue to influence the post-movement politics as well, political development with a focus on institutions, participation, compatible elite position, resolution of legitimacy crisis, rule of the criteria of achievement rather than ascriptive prescription are diluted. How such normative principles that are universally accepted as the underlined theme of good governance are made an integral part of democratic development? Or are they only selectively making use of institutions for their short run strategies?

And the premise which bases political development in Nepal on some of the components mentioned above becomes significant. A grass roots level understanding of democratic development entails economic development, social reform, change and stability. Based on the five sample districts of Nepal, we have tried to find out peoples' general understanding of the essential components of democracy (see Table 1.1). Although it is only a fraction of the whole, such a field study makes an attempt to correlate it with the national level.

Asked to identify the three main elements of democracy, of the 500 respondents, 51.4 per cent mentioned economic development and conscious people, followed by social reform and change (43.2 per cent), stable government (38.0 per cent), uplift of disadvantaged (37.81 per cent) and independent judiciary

TABLE 1.1: PEOPLE'S UNDERSTANDING OF ESSENTIAL COMPONENTS OF DEMOCRACY

Variables	Total		Sex %		Area %		Party Affiliation %	
	No.	%	Male	Female	Rural	Urban	Member	Non-member
Periodic elections	88	17.6	19.8	10.7	16.0	23.8	25.8	13.6
Stable government	190	38.0	43.9	19.7	37.8	38.6	46.0	34.1
Independent judiciary	120	24.0	28.8	9.0	20.8	36.6	26.4	22.8
Economic development	257	51.4	52.4	48.4	51.9	49.5	46.6	53.7
Social reform/ change	216	43.2	41.8	47.5	42.9	44.6	45.4	42.1
Conscious people	257	51.4	51.1	52.5	51.6	50.5	57.1	48.7
Uplift of dis-advantaged people	189	37.8	38.4	36.1	37.1	40.6	35.6	38.9
Others	21	4.2	4.5	3.3	4.0	5.0	6.1	3.3

(24.0 per cent). The district-wise breakdown of the three major variables is as follows: Dang 73 per cent, Rautahat 58 per cent, Dhankuta 54 per cent, Kaski 38 per cent and Baitadi 34 per cent. On the variable 'conscious people', Dang recorded 66 per cent, Baitadi 65 per cent, Dhankuta 48 per cent, Kaski 45 and Rautahat 33 per cent. On 'Social reform and change', Rautahat recorded 65 per cent respectively followed by Dhankuta 52 per cent Baitadi 39 per cent, Dang 31 per cent, and Kaski 29 per cent.

If one goes by the normative and pragmatic aspects of political development, retaining other attributes such as active participation of people, institutionalization, circulation of power elites on the basis of strict recruitment rules (fair election and common value consensus), political dynamics can develop its own in-built capacity for emancipation from the entrenched norms and values of the past. However, in so doing, the new democratizers do not seem to show an impressive record of their performance. Under the circumstances, therefore, Nepal's political development continues to be traumatic and uncertain, pointing to the fact that the process of transition seem to be a permanently overwhelming trend. Can transition and permanence become one at a time is yet another intriguing question in the present context. Yet, we have some valid reasons for attributing it to the ongoing political exercises in the country.

Construction of Nation State and Political Development

The project of nation state construction and democratic development cannot be separated, though historically democratic churning began in the late 1940s. If one tries to find out which came first, nation or the state in Nepal, it may carry little sense. Culturally, Nepal's unique religious, cultural and ethnic mosaic was not the byproduct of the organization of the present Nepali state by King Prithvi Narayan Shah. Before the conquest of the valley in 1768, a definite cultural setting had existed due to the co-existence of Hinduism, Buddhism and Saivism. Although such a cultural and religious background remained unaffected during and after the crafting of the nation state, nonetheless most state organs except the lower level military personnel became an exclusive prerogative of two high caste Hindu groups—Brahmans and Chhetris. The imposition of Khas language that was gradually popularized as Nepali, notwithstanding the multilingual and multi-ethnic character of the state to which the present Constitution of Nepal has also explicitly mentioned, has become a source of dissatisfaction in today's polity. According to various linguistic and ethnic groups, a particular religion and language might have their origin in specific period of history due to 'conquest, proselytization and immigration', continuity of the same in the new context becomes irrelevant. However, 'even in the most homogenous societies', a variety of social distinctions 'emerge and persist and perhaps unavoidable'. Suggesting some prescriptive measures for managing problems, T.K. Oommen has pointed out that 'when the states are multi-national, they should consciously and systematically foster the policy of linguistic pluralism. This is the essential first step for avoiding the rupture between state and nation and the only sane option for multi-national states.'[2]

Democracy that survives only with the neutral, mediating and balancing role of the state needs to be responsive to a variety of social and political demands put up by the less privileged sections of society. And such demands, which are still confined on the opinion level, would in all probability be articulated and aggregated in a more aggressive manner in the near future. But, on the contrary, if the democratic processes and structures too continue to pursue 'non-secular exclusion' and increase all forms of tensions among and between the state and various ethnic, religious and Dalit communities and political elites of all parties, democracy would remain a catchword for perpetuating the same old exploitative tradition. Many politicians and other intellectuals still try to take pride in Nepal's distinct capacity for maintaining social harmony due to its civilizational background and social harmony. However, cultural romanticization would do little unless democratic development conflates itself with the emergent realities.

Political participation both as a principle and practice was never accepted by the Nepali State as the basis of the nation-state. Social stratification penetrated into the field of politics during the Shah and the Rana rules. The exclusivist character of the state did not promote the agenda of national construction until the end of the Rana rule in 1951. However, as discussed before, the democratic era beginning 1951 and successive to it also failed to undertake the agenda of nation building despite the political space provided to the people at large.

Historically, the Nepali rulers in general have paid little attention to the nation building agenda because of their major preoccupation with the obscurantist construction of the state. Conceivably, the state and caste became identical. Such an admixture block the prospect of political development despite a few administrative and educational innovations made by the state. Institutionally, power structure remained oligarchic and narrow in nature allowing its values and norms to be less developmental. As a result, the past political culture that demands submissiveness, patronage routes, flattery and *chakari* continues to influence today's politics. Yet, sweeping political developments are of late taking place in the country and how such changes would be helpful for consolidating the multiparty system is not certain. Crisis in monarchy has crept in with the slaughter of the entire family of King Birendra in an unprecedented ghastly massacre on 1 June 2003. Traditionally, the monarchy was considered as the enduring institution of social harmony and stability. Now it seems to face both an intra-monarchical crisis of succession and legitimacy, and an external attack mounted by the Maoists and others for its abolition.

Historical Context

Political development in Nepal has been both chequered and traumatic since the early 1950s and a graphic picture is presented below. One of the principal reasons for such a process can be attributed to the emergence of diametrically opposite forces whose political socialization, ideological position (then) allowed them to be guided by such tactics that were devised only for furthering immediate interests. The post-1960 situation had tried to change such a discordant elite culture by trying to draw a clear boundary between the royal regime's political culture and those of its opponents. With the emergence of a powerful 'Communist' group in the 1970s (Jhapali group or the Maoist) and the marginalization of other Left groups whose commitment to the pluralist process was beyond question despite their rhetorical statements and publications claiming that they were the genuine revolutionaries, Nepal's political development entered a new phase with the moderate NC and the extremist Left groups at the centre stage. The Jhapali plus some other radical Communist groups were believed to have influenced the results of the national referendum for choosing either the panchayat system with reforms or a multi-party system. It could be corroborated by the publications and tactics of these groups who worked on their own pet hypothesis that the revival of the multiparty system amounted to the coming of the NC to power after elections and hence the need of thwarting such an eventuality in the politics of the country. However, the political landscape in 1989 changed with the same groups isolating the royal regime following the unilateral Indian decision to terminate the trade and transit treaties and imposing what the general Nepali called 'economic blockade' against the regime. Later, when the NC gave a call for a mass movement against the regime, all parties cobbled together to mount an anti-regime movement in February 1990 that eventually lent legitimacy to the Left combine resulting in its induction into the coalition government formed after the successful movement for the restoration of democracy.

Thus, with hindsight, it could be considered as a success of democracy because of the integration of disparate forces of the country. Later developments have also demonstrated that the inclusivist polity did put these parties and their leaders to a severe test during the eleven-year exercises. All parties and leaders have invariably enjoyed the spoils of power but none of them came out of it unscathed. Given the opportunity, all leaders tend to be myopic with greater proneness to the canker of corruption and feudalistic culture as has been handed down to us from history.

Juxtaposed to the ruthless exposures of parties and leaders is the lurking danger emanating from a variety of sources—revivalist, extremist and systemic parties themselves. Now the political development in the liberal democratic context is frayed as if the future of the system is likely to slide into the abyss.

Nepal's democratic developments have a curious amalgamation of both trauma and excitement. Democratic evolution is characterized by both imponderables and uncertainties because of the failures of political forces that have initiated the transition process against the background of the struggle for establishing a pluralist democratic order in the country. Judged from the historical perspective, such movements that aimed at a new democratic beginning have invariably proved abortive despite the increase of awareness of the people in general. Yet, such public consciousness matters little unless it manifests in an institutionalized form entailing the basics of democratic governance. In 1951 and 1990, the same parties and others became apparently successful in changing respectively the structures of the Rana oligarchy and the absolute monarchical partyless regime, but such changes turned out to be cosmetic keeping in view the old political culture and even power that remained intact, inevitably resulting in making the processes perennially traumatic. So even after covering a long distance of political development, the same old struggle continues pointing to another period of uncertainty of multiparty system based, however spuriously, on the premise of the much touted 'constitutional monarchy' and sovereignty of the people.

Nepal's political developments are not unilinear, running on the same pattern and continuum as are evidenced in India. In India continuity had never been disrupted except once, during the emergency that Mrs. Indira Gandhi imposed in order to stem the emergent political crisis that was likely to affect her own status as prime minister. Whatever the British raj had initiated for providing minimum political apprenticeship in democratic exercises had prepared some sort of an infrastructure for the future. Moreover, the movement leaders themselves became the destiny makers following the transfer of power in 1947 thus enabling themselves to frame a constitution based on the spirit of the independence movement and pluralist democracy as learned by them. And no intermediary force existed between them and the British after the latter left India for good.

Judged from this perspective, Nepal's history of political development that entails all the ingredients of the modern liberal system, i.e. periodic elections based on universal adult franchise, accountability of power to the people, recognition of opposition within and outside parliament, procedures and practices to be established for governance, and above all, acceptance of a multi-party system both as the vehicle and essence of democracy, did not progress along the intended line. And its causes were both historical, behavioural and socio-cultural owing to the totally different setting of Nepali politics and society.

Due to both the absence of a sustained struggle for democracy and freedom within the country and the very weak penetration of liberal values due to geographical isolation with which the family of the Rana oligarchy could insulate itself from the waves of freedom struggle then underway across the world, Nepali democratic development was devoid of a well internalized ideology. Even countries then fiercely involved in liberating themselves from the yoke of colonialism set their agendas accordingly, thus first trying to end colonial rule and then to move on to the path of political development. The Indian case was, as stated before, somewhat different in that British colonial rule had also laid the minimum physical and democratic infrastructures on which the leaders of independent India could construct the edifice of a parliamentary system, though leadership role and orientation became crucial for putting Indian democracy on the right track in the future. In contrast, Nepal was not colonized, nor did it benefit from colonial rule. Yet, it was a backwater of British colonialism as the rulers of Nepal were then under constraints for having a good relationship with the British raj in India. How comfortable the Ranas were till the end of British rule in India could be corroborated by the later developments that not only proved difficult for the native Rana rulers of Nepal but also led to collapse of their power after the end of British rule in India.

Surprisingly, however, Nepal's anti-Rana movement, that was heavily influenced by the Indian nationalist movement led by Mohandas Karamchand Gandhi, did not follow the Gandhian peaceful method for ending the Rana rule in Nepal. On the contrary, the Nepali Congress (NC), a combination of the two parties formed in India—the Nepali National Congress and the Nepali Democratic Congress—adopted violent method by hurriedly mobilizing the ex-soldiers and other activists, and plunged into action. The prominent leaders of the party, who were believed to have been socialized in the Gandhian peaceful method of change, made a significant departure from it by taking up arms. And how the leaders of independent India lent their moral and diplomatic support to the movement had been adequately highlighted by the movement leaders themselves. Such violent articulation of the anti-Rana movement was immediately transformed into *satyagraha* and other peaceful methods after the end of the Rana rule in February 1951. Thus, the new democratic era had begun with some new agendas for change, but they turned out to be abortive as it failed to make a departure from the entrenched values of the Rana regime. Despite the apparent changes in structure, the construction of democratic Nepal too began on the same value premise as the old regimes of the Shah and the Ranas. Conceivably, the traditional values and norms reminiscent of court politics were resurrected in the post-1950 Nepal and which the so-called democratizers accepted as part of Nepali political culture. Yet, despite some 'democratic innovations' this period also continued engendering democratic spirit and freedom.

The politics of a partyless regime (1960-90) cannot lend support to our project of political development because of the quite opposite nature of the polity. Nevertheless, many experiments made during the thirty years' life of the regime, especially the exercises in elections at various levels—village to national—and the subsequent contradictions that exposed the limitations of a personalized regime for crisis management were worth emulating. Such contradictions were further heightened following the announcement of the national referendum in 1979 whereupon political forces working underground surfaced to campaigning for the termination of the partyless nature of the regime, contrary to the continued legal ban on political parties. Contradictions between the much liberalized political atmosphere on the one hand and the informal permission granted to the outlawed parties plus the inner contradictions intensified by the changed processes helped accelerate the pace of the anti-regime movement in the 1980s on the other. Moreover, myopic decisions and their repercussions on maintaining the strategic balance in the region and the manner in which the regime was hounded by the international community on the grounds of violation of human rights and democracy emboldened the NC and other parties to work together for the final assault on the monarchical regime. And in April 1990, the panchayat regime that had already lost its national and international legitimacy collapsed like a pack of cards paving the way for a multi-party system. The Constitution of the Kingdom of Nepal, 1990, drafted under the auspices of the Interim Government composed of the main movement parties' nominees and of the Palace incorporated into it the sovereignty of the people, the constitutional monarchy, the multi-party system and the inalienable freedoms of the people. Direct election to the Lower House of parliament and other features *a la* British model were accepted.

Election Systems

During the last phase of the Rana regime, the concept of an unicameral non-partisan legislature was visualized in the Government of Nepal Act, 2004 Sambat (1948) (*Nepal Sarkarko Baidhanik Kanoon*, 2004) but it could not see the light of the day because of the changed strategy of the new prime minister in the years preceding the fall of the Rana regime itself in 1950. However, in the intervening period prior to the anti-Rana movement, the Nagar Panchayat and Gram Panchayat elections, which, in essence, were only the trappings of elections, made some local level electoral exercises. Nor did the Rana regime move upwards for composing the national legislatures as underlined by the Act, even the most liberal Rana, Prime Minister, was constrained to speak of the evils of the party system, as can be read in these lines: 'It is not the intention of the government that the country should be thrown into the vortex of the party system, and the government will never lend its encouragement to the habit of bringing about the election of any candidate by the strength of party machinery rather than by his own ability and eligibility.' Although the Rana constitutional arrangement had not shown an iota of sharing of power with the people, in the given historical context, 'it was an important landmark' in the country. According to Gupta, with the introduction of a constitutional system, checks on the Rana rule, however inchoate and insufficient it might be, were introduced; the provision for a two-chamber legislature, the principle of representative rule for the elections of Nagar and Gram Panchayats, certain fundamental rights granted to the people appointment of an auditor-general to audit the account of the state; and the public service commission for 'the purpose of selecting qualified candidates to all civil posts under the Government'.[4]

The Interim Government of Nepal Act, 1951, that came into force following the termination of the Rana regime, declared in its preamble that it was necessary that the 'administration of the country should function according to a constitution and certain rules and principles' until the framing and promulgation of the country's Constitution. The Interim Government of Nepal Act therefore was replete with various provisions of parliamentary system despite the absence of elections for recruiting political elites. Yet, without having to go for elections due to the unsettled political environment created by the struggle between the Ranas and the NC leaders immediately after the inauguration of the Interim Rana-Congress government, some elements of democratic infrastructure were inserted in the Act. The idea of an Election Commission, the Public Service Commission, comptroller and auditor-general, general electoral roll, and adult franchise were visualized in the Act.

Notwithstanding such innovations made in the direction of political development and for a genuinely crafted system of governance, the spirit of popular legitimacy was soon forgotten giving rise to the politics of revival that vested all powers with the monarch. Politics during the 1951-9 period were not shaped by periodic elections because of a number of intervening factors such as the progressive decline of political parties in general and the concomitant revival of traditional forces represented by the monarchy. By the time the Constitution of the Kingdom of Nepal was promulgated by King Mahendra in February 1959, much water had already flown in the Bagmati River. During the interregnum of 1951-9, politicians were invariably stripped of their bargaining power due to the attrition of political parties in the post-Rana political development. The royal agenda for restoring all his lost powers during the 104-years Rana rule was accomplished within this period. King Mahendra promulgated the Constitution in 1959 declaring 'in the exercise of the sovereign powers of the Kingdom of Nepal and prerogatives vesting in US in accordance with the traditions and custom of our country'. He enacted and promulgated the Constitution. According to the preamble, the Constitution insured the 'establishment of an efficient monarchical form of government responsive to the wishes of the people'.

Thus, although apparently it looked like that there were two power centres—the king and the elected government headed by a prime minister—it was quintessentially a monarchy with sovereign and discretionary powers vested with the monarch.

The prime minister used only those powers that didn't interdict the core power of the king. Prime Minister B.P. Koirala, whose party had received two/thirds majority in the House of Representatives (Lower House), had allegedly aired his severe constitutional limitations so much so even for minor administrative appointments, the prime minister had to confront the king by way of defending his own list of persons whom the king considered unqualified for the said jobs. Misunderstanding between the king and the prime minister came into the open with the former dropping hints at resorting extreme actions in the name of 'national interest' and the prime minister showing his helplessness if that extreme situation developed forcing the king into action.[5]

The precarious position of the prime minister vis-à-vis the monarch could be easily read into the clauses of the Constitution. Article 26(2) specifically empowered the king to reject while acting in his discretion, a recommendation of the prime minister to summon or dissolve parliament. Taking it as an affront to the spirit of cabinet government, Gupta is of the opinion that 'if an exigency arose when the king rejected the recommendation of the prime minister, then the latter had no choice but to resign'.[6] So the caveats could be observed in the workings of the 1959 constitution.

The first caveat was the lack of electoral precedents that could provide apprenticeship in elections, though a tiny section of the Nepalis were cognizant of developments taking place in their neighbourhood, particularly India. The other caveats were the physical features and difficult terrain that consist of snow-peaked Himalayas, the high mountains, the hills, the inner-Terai and the Terai along with diversities of people of the country. Thus, the election, started on 18 February 1959, ended only after the snow started melting in the Himalayan region allowing the new government to take office in May.

Borrowed from the British and the Indian election systems, the House of Representatives was composed of the 109 members elected directly from each electoral district by secret ballot. The electoral districts were delimited by a Delimitation Commission appointed by the king at his discretion in such a manner that 'each shall contain as nearly as may be practicable an equal number of electors, account however being taken of boundaries of administrative districts, the density or scarcity of population, transport facilities, physical features and community or diversity of the inhabitants'. Interestingly, a large number of candidates for contesting 109 seats and the average turnover of about 43 per cent of the electorate were marked features of the elections. Since it was based on the first-past-the-post system with winners taking all, any party that could get a bare majority was declared a winner. In the given context, the Nepali Congress (NC) won 74 of the 109 seats with 37.2 per cent popular vote and formed the government. It was a landslide victory (two-thirds), a rude shock for both the obscurantist elements and the other smaller parties that envied the NC's emergence. Despite the alleged moves for splitting the votes into several groups in order not to allow a party to form a government on its own strength for which 34 per cent candidates were independents, the election result dismayed many. Political leaders whose roles had remained unchallenged over the years in the post-Rana political development but who had been successful in playing counter-roles to the NC were sidelined in the elections. On the very first day of the elections, some of them lodged a complaint before the king for quashing the elections on the grounds of corruption, rigging and mismanagement.[7]

One important feature of the 1959 elections was the emergence of the NC as the largest organization. But the percentage of votes—37.2 and the 74 out of 109 seats gained by the NC—were indicative of the flaws of first-past-the-post system. Such a dichotomy continues to haunt Nepal, since Nepal has not been able to assess as yet the plus and minus points of such a system. If one compares the 1959 House of Representatives (HOR) with the three general elections of 1991, 1994 and 1999, the picture is not substantially different. As can be seen in Table 1.2 in 1991, the NC won 110 out of 205 seats but received 37.75 per cent votes. In 1994, the CPN (UML) displaced the NC by winning more seats (88) but received only 30.85 per cent popular votes, i.e. 3 per cent less than that of the NC. The third party was/is the RPP that won 20 seats in the 1994 elections but had gained only 17.93 per cent votes.

In the 1999 HOR, the NC won 114 seats out of 205 but it has not increased the popular vote, which is below 40 per cent. In the 1999 HOR, the combined Left votes of the CPN (UML), ML, Rashtriya Jana Morcha, Samyukta Jana Morcha, Nepal Majdoor

TABLE 1.2: PARTIES' POSITION IN GENERAL ELECTIONS 1991, 1994 AND 1999

Parties	Seat			Percentage		
	1991	1994	1999	1991	1994	1999
NC	110	83	112	37.75	33.38	36.14
UML	69	88	70	27.98	30.85	30.74
ML	-	-	0	-	-	06.38
RPP	04	20	11	11.94	17.93	13.46
NSP	06	03	05	4.10	3.49	3.13
NPF	-	-	05	-	-	1.36
NeWPP	02	04	01	1.25	.98	.54
UPF	09	0	01	4.35	1.32	.83
CPN (Democratic)	02	0	0	2.43	.38	.05
Independents	03	07	0	4.17	6.18	2.83
Other parties	0	0	0	6.04	5.49	4.54
Total	205	205	205	100	100	100

Sources: Election Commission, *House of Representative Members, 2048 (1991): Final Results; House of Representative Members, 2051 (1994): Election Results;* and *House of Representative Members, 2056 (1999): Election Results;* Pancha Narayan Maharjan, 'Local Elections in Nepal, 1997' (CNAS Professional Paper), Kathmandu: CNAS, 1998.

Kishan Party cross 40 per cent, surpassing the votes of the NC. However, the combined non-Communist votes of the NC, the Rashtriya Prajatantra Party (RPP) and the Nepal Sadbhawana Party (NSP) maintain the lead both in seats and in popular votes.

One of the important trends set by the three general elections is the stable status of the two major parties—the NC and the CPN (UML). Although the RPP also emerged as a third force following the 1994 mid-term elections, its overall context and performance have not helped to alter its position. Its presence in the first parliament was only symbolic in-as-much as the RPP was split into two at its birth. One RPP led by Surya Bahadur Thapa won one seat and another former Panchayat Prime Minister, Lokendra Bahadur Chand, won three seats. Later, after the merger of the two RPPs on the eve of the mid-term elections in 1994, it became a third party in parliament. Nevertheless, the meteoric rise of the RPP cannot be visualized in the given context of both dynamics and electoral arithmetic. Taking the results of the three general elections and examining the mobilizational capacity of the RPP, it can be maintained that the party will continue to be a mismatch for the two major parties—the NC and the CPN (UML)—unless the latter's electoral politics would remain undisturbed by the rapid rise of the CPN (Maoist). Whether or not the UML can ward off any threat posed by the Maoist depends on how the party would be able to strike a balance between the radicalizing trend of politics and the parliamentary process which, in the opinion of the Maoist, is a decadent system. And the manner in which the elections have been conducted, and the way the system and its actors are made corrupt can hardly improve the system. Such failures would only lend credence to the Maoists, despite their shifting stands on vital issues. If the Maoists also change their line and join the system, the existing popular base of the UML is likely to be eroded at least for one or two elections, because, the UML also comes from similar Maoist background, then known as the Naxalite group, and had cashed in on its revolutionary activities and postures. Now it has become one of the progenitors of the present Constitution.

The trend of a two party dominant system is evident in the results of the three general elections. The percentage of seats won and the popular votes gain by the NC and the UML establish the fact that their dominance would not be disturbed. It is more so in the case of the NC because of the failure of other non-Left parties to emerge as an alternative to the NC. Identified with the former regime supporters and ministers, the RPP encounters both psychological and symbolic difficulties. It acted as a balancer or even as a 'wild card' during the heyday of cabinet instability following the fractured mandate received by the parties in the mid-1990s, thus enabling the smaller parties to increase their bargaining power vis-à-vis the two major parties.[8]

Such an electoral phenomenon is not new in Nepal alone as countries having similar election systems and multiplicity of parties face a wide discrepancy between actual votes and seats distribution. In India, which is treated as the laboratory of the Third World multi-party democracy, the gap between parliamentary seats and the vote percentage is always evident. In the 1989 general elections, 'despite the Congress winning 39.5 per cent of the vote', it lost heavily in terms of seats. Under the first-past-the-post system, 'there is no simple or uniform relation between the proportion of votes a party wins nationally and the proportion of seats it secures in the Lok Sabha'.[9] The 2000 presidential elections of the United States faced for the first time the gap between popular votes and the electoral college as Al Gore polled more votes than George W. Bush but failed to overtake the latter in the electoral college. After a prolonged debate on who should be the actual winner, the Court's verdict favoured Bush for receiving more votes from the electoral college. It shows how democracy is confronted with such a dilemma and eventually compromises on procedures rather than on essence. Yogendra Yadav has described the election phenomenon in these words: 'Elections are not a mirror of political reality. As a representational device, elections are better compared to a camera: in a sense it merely records what is "out there", but it all depends on who holds it, in which direction and with what focus . . . elections go much beyond recording the political reality; in a way, they create a reality of their own in that life is led for the sake of representation.'[10]

The way elections are being conducted in Nepal since the restoration of the multiparty system seem to prove the statement that elections can 'create a reality of their own' and fail to show a systemic compatibility between the conduct of elections, representations in parliament, and the behavioural trends to be set by them for the consolidation of the system. Used more as a political ladder rather than an opportunity for correcting systemic aberrations, the election is used for recycling of elites of upper caste and class backgrounds. It does not mean that elections have not brought about changes in society, but the manner in which they are used for perpetuation of the same categories of elites tends to lose their purpose. On the one hand, the elections held periodically make us believe that they are increasingly becoming integrationist in nature given the enthusiasm of people in the process, on the other such exercises have failed to inject innovative trends for making parliament more representative and businesslike. Each year parliament is weakened with both the government and opposition parties developing a deliberate tendency of avoiding parliamentary route.

The representation pattern in three parliaments—1991, 1994 and 1999—have demonstrated how political parties and the king were inclined to distort the spirit of the Constitution during the selection of candidates, nomination to the National Assembly and also while operationalizing the various provisions of the Constitution. In a nutshell, it can be maintained that the sociological aspects of representation in the national parliament do not fundamentally differ from the partyless panchayat regime. The nature and composition of the Rashtriya Panchayat or RP (a unicameral legislature) and the two Houses of today's parliament continue to be dominated by the high caste Brahmins and Chhettris followed by other ethnic groups (see Table 1.3). The RP was pre-dominantly a Chhetri dominated legislature, the Brahmins have replaced the Chhetris dominance in today's parliament. The three parliamentary elections have thus put the Brahmins on the top with 37.6 per cent Brahmins, 18.11 per cent Chhetris, 22 per cent hill ethnic groups, 21 per cent Terai groups, 8.3 per cent other ethnic groups from the Terai and 2.4 per cent Muslims in 1991 HOR. An increase in the representation of the Brahmin and concomitant decrease of other communities seemed to be a running trend through all the general elections. In the 1994 elections to the HOR, the Brahmins had 44.4 per cent, the Chhetri 18.5 per cent, Newar 6.3 per cent, Hill ethnic group 11.7 per cent and Terai 18.5 per cent. Others (that include Dalits) had 0.5 per cent.

In the 1999 parliamentary elections, such a trend continued by increasing the percentage of Brahmins in the HOR by 46.3 per cent followed by the Chhetris with 17.1 per cent. The total strength of hill ethnic groups was 11.7 per cent and the combined Terai groups including the Muslim could get 18.5 per cent. The Newar, which is a distinct category with 5 per cent population, has a more or less stable representation pattern of about 6 per cent in all elections.

However, the percentage distribution in all the elections is dependent on the candidate selection criteria of a party. If more candidates are selected from a certain community irrespective of the composition of the electoral constituencies, chances will be high for being elected from the platform, though in some constituencies, ethnic and regional considerations and mobilization may also influence the electoral prospects. Since a party's primary objective is to capture power by increasing as many seats in the HOR as possible, local, regional and ethnic aspects of elections cannot be ruled out. Other factors such as popularity test, status, mobilizational capacity, resources, both monetary and administrative, are equally significant for winning the elections.

TABLE 1.3: CASTE/ETHNIC COMPOSITION OF MEMBERS OF THE HOUSE OF REPRESENTATIVES, 1991, 1994 AND 1999

	NC %			UML %			RPP %			Others			Total		
	1991	1994	1999	1991	1994	1999	1991	1994	1999	1991	1994	1999	1991	1994	1999
Total seats	110	83	110	69	88	72	4	20	11	22	14	12	205	205	205
Hill Caste Groups:															
Brahmin	42.7	48.2	47.3	42.02	52.3	54.2	50.0	20.0	-	9.1	7.1	33.4	39.0	44.4	46.3
Chhetri	20.0	18.1	17.3	13.04	12.5	11.1	50.0	35.0	45.5	9.1	35.7	25.0	17.1	18.5	17.1
Newar	5.5	2.4	5.5	8.7	10.2	5.6	-	-	18.2	9.1	14.3	8.3	6.81	6.3	6.3
Others	0.90	1.2	1.8	-	-	-	-	-	-	-	-	-	0.5	0.5	1.0
Hill Ethnic Group	8.2	8.4	10.0	26.1	13.6	18.0	-	15.0	9.1	31.8	14.3	-	16.0	11.7	12.2
Terai Group	22.7	21.7	18.2	10.2	11.4	11.1	-	30.0	27.3	40.9	28.6	33.3	20.0	18.5	17.1
Total	100	100	100	100	100	100	100	100	100	100	100	100	100	100	100

Source: Tabulated from the Election Commission's Results.

The gender representation in all the three parliaments shows a uniform trend with women only marginally inducted. The male domination, which is the characteristic of Nepali society, is also reflected in parliament. Even despite having a mandatory constitutional provision for at least 5 per cent women representation in parties and parliament, no departure from the rule could be noticed. In the 1991 elections, out of 1,345 candidates for the HOR, only 5.87 per cent were female and the party-wise breakdown of female candidates was as follows: NC—11, CPN (UML)—9 out of 168 candidates, RPP—17 out of 301, other Left parties—25 out of 186 candidates, and others—12 out of 348 candidates. Altogether only eight candidates could get into the HOR, among whom five were from the NC and three from the CPN (UML) thus amounting to 3.9 per cent. In 1991 National Assembly, a house of 60 members, 26 were Brahmins, 9 Chhetris (including Thakuri), 2 Dalits (Kami and Sarki). From amongst the hill ethnic groups (Gurung, Limbu, Magar and Newar), 13 could come to the Upper House, while the Terai group composed of Terai Brahmin, Kayastha, Marwari, Yadav and others got 8 members. Among the Terai ethnic groups, the Tharu community had 2 members in the 1991 upper house.[11] The National Assembly had only 3 female members.[12]

The women's presence remains as usual with the political parties in general trying only to fulfil the constitutional requirement of 5 per cent. Of 37 women candidates in the five national parties, the NC had 12, the CPN (UML) 9, the RPP 12, and the United People's Front, 6. In 1994 HOR, only seven women candidates (3.41 per cent) from these parties could win. In the 1999 parliament, there were altogether 21 women members (12 in the HOR and 9 in the NA) including the nominees of the king. It is interesting to note that one odd woman member had got the berth of minister of state in a jumbo cabinet of 37 ministers despite having her credential of winning elections twice from a western hill district. The fact that political parties treat the other half of the national population as simply a vote bank can thus be observed in the representation system.

Although mere nomination or selection of candidates would not help reduce such a gender disparity, even the minimum gesture is not shown towards encouraging women in politics. Moreover, whoever comes to parliament are picked up ascriptively rather than on the grounds of achievement. Relatives of leaders, persons with a high social status, etc., are the obvious beneficiaries of such constitutional arrangements thus depriving others of such opportunities. It has been said that the Dalits have about 16-20 per cent of the total population in Nepal but their representation is almost zero.

The multiplicity of parties that particularly sprout during the registration period but fail to survive afterwards has not substantially affected the domination of big parties. In 1994 general elections, 65 parties were registered by the Election Commission but of them only 24 participated in the elections. It is surprising to note only four were recognized as national parties because, according to the constitutional provision, only a party having polled at least 3 per cent vote is needed for parliamentary recognition. In 1999, of the 100 parties registered, only 39 contested the elections. The mushrooming of political parties on the eve of elections seems to have become very common in all elections, but of the total 65.79 percentage votes cast in the 1999 elections is only marginally split into such political non-entities. Even a large number of independent candidates could not win a single seat showing a peculiar but a definite trend of Nepali electoral politics.

Elections as a crucial variable for political development with specific reference to participation have some distinct features in Nepal. The three national elections held within a period of ten years have certain characteristics, i.e. secularization of politics, the preponderant party factor, a broad integration of forces through the instrumentality of election, etc. It has been observed throughout that linguistic, religious, tribal or caste affiliations did not seem to have played an effective role for political mobilization during election campaigns. Parties formed along communal and sectarian lines were rejected by the people thus providing political space to different social groups through the parties. How the major parties would be able to continue such universally accepted principles of participatory democracy in the absence of a well thought out plan of action for greater representation of the underprivileged groups of society is a matter of the future.

Elections in Nepal are also fraught with a variety of negative trends and dangers. They are increasingly becoming violent, criminalized due to the nexus established between politicians and underground mafias. Money, muscle and manipulation or three Ms loom large in determining the outcome of elections. The presence of three Ms is now a necessary condition for winning elections across the country. The Election Commission, which is the overall in-charge for conducting elections is helpless because of a tendency to defy the code of conduct recommended for parties and candidates. The code of conduct 1996 aims at making elections 'fair, free, riggingless, less expensive, free from undue competition and misuse of power and ostentation'. Underlining the objective of the Commission, it lays down some norms to be observed by everyone involved in elections.

An election expense prescribed by the commission becomes a mere formality, as parties and candidates know that without huge financial investments in their constituencies their chances of winning seats would be remote. And hence the mobilization of the three Ms is a major resource for election. According to a booklet published by the Election Commission, constituencies have been classified into four types on the basis of size, location and needs, and candidates of such classified constituencies are accordingly allowed to spend ranging from Rs. 1,15,000 to Rs. 2,75,000. It has been felt that given the expensive electoral practices that defy all rules and codes, no candidate expects to win elections. It is not only some notorious Tarai districts like Rautahat and Sunsari, etc., but also the hill districts with their numerous constituencies where a huge amount of money is being spent during elections. A candidate admitted that about Rs. 27 lakhs was spent while another candidate from yet another district disclosed that Rs. 30 lakhs was spent but lost. How the money was generated and what was the source, they did not divulge.

One of the major criticisms against the code of conduct is that political parties are not transparent in their election expenses, nor do they ever audit or publish accounts. Even the principal office bearers of the party are ignorant of the sources of funding of elections as a top leader individually handles most expenses. All these trends only demonstrate that all candidates and party functionaries violate rules governing elections.

Paradox of Parliamentary Institutions

Paradoxes abound in Nepali politics. On the one hand, the politics of the latter part of the twentieth century is replete with democratic struggles and intermittent experiments with democratic governance; on the other, the Himalayan kingdom has not been able to bring about basic changes in the traditional mindsets, formalities and in all such trends of a traditional polity. But paradoxes observed in Parliament are marked by both the acceptance of this institution by various parties committed to it and by the concomitant violation of its conduct by all—the ruling and opposition parties and the king. Theoretically, parliament is the mechanism that fosters tolerance, understanding and appreciation and inculcates a participatory political culture. In practice, parliament insures popular legitimacy through elections and elite accountability as the governing elites in the parliamentary system are created by it. Looked from such theoretical and practical perspectives, parliament as a viable instrument of political development is weakened. Such a sliding trend continues with principal parties paying short shrift to restoring the lost essence of parliament.

It seems that political parties and leaders working as systemic agents of change have turned themselves retrogressive to undermine the august institution. Parliamentary abnormalities that are generally experienced are extra-parliamentary since most agendas of both houses of parliament originate from outside and are only picked up as political ploys against adversaries—government or opposition. Moreover, in the absence of its own parliamentary background that could set precedents and conventions, political parties, coming as they do from opposite backgrounds and orientation, find each move incompatible with their aspirations. Few cases can be presented in order to show some aberrations found within the system. First, the elected government itself violated the spirit of the Constitution while nominating the members of the National Assembly (NA) from the very beginning.

It seemed that the king accepted the advice of the prime minister in the beginning as a constitutional monarch to nominate ten members in 1991. But among them, five were active members of the NC itself. Since the second parliament in 1993, the king allegedly did not follow the advice of the prime minister. On the contrary, he nominated those against whom the prime minister had serious reservations. On both sides, political considerations weighed much rather than the fulfilment of the spirit of the Constitution. And the manner in which the nominated members played antagonistic roles since 1994 reminds us of the roles of the nominated members during 1959-60. They were all bent on obstructing each and every move of the government subsequently became successful in sowing discord between the king and the prime minister. The nominees of the king in 2000 not only became active in forging electoral alliances for and against the government but also defeated the government-backed candidate. Persons who are supposed to be 'distinguished', who have rendered 'eminent service in various fields of national life' became active political players for promoting their own personal ambition. This militates against the spirit of the Constitution.

The NC leaders are no less responsible for such erosion of parliament. Their preoccupation with the seizure of power by deviating from the spirit of parliamentary norms, and the casual manner in which they introduced bills without fully studying their implications, have marred the evolution of parliament. The provisions relating to the appointment of the prime minister under Article 42(1) and 42(2), for instance, came under intense public debate. In the midst of such controversies, which often get currency due to the absence of well established conventions and practices, the Supreme Court came into the picture during the minority government headed by the leader of the CPN (UML) and supported by other major parties including the NC. But, sensing the withdrawal of support of the NC and other parties—who had already asked for the special session of HOR for passing a no-confidence resolution against the minority government as per Article 53(3) of the Constitution according to which the king has to comply with the petition of one-fourth of the total members of the HOR demanding a special session during the recess of parliament—the king acted accordingly and summoned a special session as demanded by once-fourth of the members. Instead of facing the vote of no-confidence, Prime Minister Man Mohan Adhikari of the CPN (UML) advised the king to dissolve the HOR and hold fresh elections under his stewardship. The king then consented to the advice of the prime minister and dissolved the house.

When the issue came before the Supreme Court urging it to determine the validity of the dissolution on the advice of a minority prime minister who was then facing the no-confidence motion in a House whose session had already been fixed by the same king, King Birendra took two contradictory decisions—one by conceding the demand of one-fourth of the members by fixing the date and time of the special session of the house; the other was his acceptance of the advice of the beleaguered prime minister to dissolve the house and declare the date of elections. A former speaker of the House of Representatives, Daman Nath Dhungana, who later argued against the dissolution at the court, said that the 'Prime Minister had chosen the window as an exit rather than the main door'.[13]

Coming as it did in the wake of a highly charged environment, the Supreme Court verdict that went against the dissolution, was interpreted in conformity with the respective party lines. Those who had supported the move of the prime minister saw in the verdict a conspiracy for reducing the prerogative of the prime minister and others supporting for the restoration of the house found it is a positive development for limiting the arbitrary decision of such a prime minister who wanted to avoid the impending no-confidence motion that was certain to be approved by the house. Responding to criticisms of the role of the Supreme Court, Bishwanath Upadhyaya, then chief justice and also the chairman of the Constitution Drafting Commission, said that generally no prime minister, heading a minority government, could advise the king for dissolution. But if a prime minister of the majority government takes such a decision and if there is no scope for forming an alternate government, then the advice of the prime minister can prevail.

The same issue of dissolution figured in 1998 when a three party coalition government headed by the RPP leader, Surya Bahadur Thapa, of course with the combined decision of its coalition partners—the NC and the NSP—advised the king on dissolving the house and ordering fresh polls. In the meantime, sensing that the prime minister had advised the king for dissolution with a view to ending the period of political instability intensified by a high degree of opportunism and individualistic behaviour with members of parliament flouting the party whip and discipline, the opposition members, led by the CPN(UML), once again resorted to Article 53(3) demanding a special session in order to stall the move of the prime minister. Now, instead of accepting the advice of the prime minister, despite the latter being a leader with a clear majority in the house, King Birendra chose to consult the Supreme Court asking for its advice on whether or not he should dissolve the house as per the advice of the prime minister. Taking it as a swipe for his earlier decision for restoring parliament, Upadhyaya, now retired, in his own characteristic manner criticized the king's move as 'unjustified' adding 'if the Prime Minister's recommendation was not constitutional, the responsibility would have belonged to the Prime Minister himself, rather than to his Majesty. . . . It is surprising that His Majesty has held consultations in a manner contrary to the spirit of Article 35(2) of the constitution' that deals with the exercises of executive power on the advice of the prime minister.[14]

The prime minister's prerogative to advise the king for dissolution suffered a setback in 1998 following the Supreme Court's advice that the king should abide by the petition by one-fourth of the members who had demanded a special session, which should get priority over the advice of the prime minister. Although Prime Minister Thapa seemed to have acted in haste because of the imminent threat stemming from within his own party (RPP) to the three party coalition government, he was still a majority leader while he had advised the king for dissolution and for holding fresh elections. Giving the opposite opinion on the Supreme Court advice, some dissenters (judges) argued that 'it would not be appropriate for the Supreme Court to give any opinion to the King because the questions put forward did not touch on "complicated legal questions of interpretation of this constitution or of any other law" as required by the Constitution under Article 88(5)'. According to Upadhyaya, if a prime minister with a majority support recommends for dissolution on the basis of obtainable political conditions, the king could straightaway accept such advice.

Whatever the interpretations, Nepal's parliamentary process no longer embraces the concept and practice of a prime ministerial system as is generally practiced in Britain and India. What was more retrogressive was the pressure exerted on the prime minister by the members of the NC, the main coalition partner, demanding that they would support the prime minister on a specific condition that he step down and allow the NC to head the government after defeating the vote of no-confidence then dangling over the prime minister's head. Normally, the defeat of the opposition's move to stall the dissolution of the House would have been taken as the vindication of the prime minister's advice for holding fresh elections, but here instead of establishing the lost ground of the prime minister, the NC party took a myopic decision for power. Thus, the prime minister's position has since been compromised making him more dependent on the palace than ever before.

How parliament has been used merely as the vehicle for power but not as the legitimate forum for democratic governance is being observed today. And political parties have invariably misused it by abetting the members of parliament to be normless creatures who can go to any extent for personal aggrandizement. As a consequence, shifting loyalties, personal debasement and unparliamentary behaviour reign supreme in the name of democracy. Loss of credibility of parliament is another feature as political parties who swear by parliamentary rules and procedures scramble to violate them. During the period in which the making and breaking of governments was a pastime of members of parliamentary arithmetic, counting of heads was the major agenda of all parties. The parliamentary ratification of a treaty or agreement was defied by the same parties and members by trying to dig up the controversy once it had been buried. It happened to the Indo-Nepal Treaty on the Mahakali River following the ratification in parliament by two-thirds as per the constitutional requirement. The 1996 treaty still exists in its dormant stage as no further works on it have been carried out because of the new controversies generated after the parliamentary approval. The anti-treaty lobbies that transcend some Left parties and the so-called 'nationalists', and others who see the treaty as a sell-out to India have a sense of victory. Surprisingly, however, most parties in parliament had agreed to the signing of the treaty and were anxious to take credit for such an 'excellent treaty' but many of them either retracted their position or kept quiet when the controversy arose about the actual benefits to be accrued to Nepal. The Mahakali Treaty is in limbo today because of the failure of the two governments—India and Nepal—to prepare a detailed project report (DPR) for the implementation of the treaty.

Undermining the parliamentary process has become a regular feature. Parties who pass certain bills today reverse their decisions tomorrow as happened to the Citizenship Bill 2000. All major parties—the NC, the CPN(UML) and the RPP—had passed the bill and sent it to the Upper House (NA) for approval. Meanwhile, some people interested in stalling the passage of the bill objected to its contents particularly to the lineage and birth of a person seeking citizenship. The nominated members in the NA also mobilized opinion against it lambasting it as an affront to Nepal's national existence. The bill was sent back to HOR for reconsideration to face the hostile opposition which had passed it earlier but had now become its foes. In their opinion, the bill that allows any person to acquire the Nepali citizenship if he or she speaks the language and has spent ten years in the country besides accepting descent from a citizen parent would be disastrous for the country. Given the open border and such liberal citizenship laws, Nepal's population is likely to increase significantly and hence the fear of being swamped by the Indians. Thus, the court rendered its opinion on the contents of the bill saying that such provisions contravene the Constitution itself, but it kept quiet on determining the status of the bill. The king has not yet sent it back to the parliament. A new controversy had however arisen regarding the role of the king (then King Birendra) as a constitutional monarch.

From a political perspective, the ruling NC party would have consulted the opposition before sending the bill for royal assent. Second, the bill would not have been signed as a Money Bill by the speaker and sent for assent. Third, the king would not have sought the opinion on the content of the bill. Finally, the king has no other options but to assent to it and return it within 30 days in accordance with the provision of the Constitution. Defying such options, the relationship between the king and parliament seems to become more complex and intractable indicating the gradual loss of importance of parliament. There are many other cases that elude serious parliamentary debates and studies. No government and opposition seems to be interested in upgrading the standards of parliament. Whatever institutional norms were introduced initially are now undermined by the actors involved in the processes.

The working of parliamentary committees is another area deserving our attention. In any legislature, the full house cannot deliberate all issues thoroughly and thus sends them for detailed study and opinions of concerned committees. In the given context, however, some committees are more active just to caution the government while many others think that their activities attract less public attention and hence prefer to be dormant. The Public Accounts Committee (PAC), the Foreign Affairs and Human Rights Committee, and the State Affairs Committee are active. Nevertheless, these committees issue orders to the government to take action against the wrong doers rather than report first to the house. From one angle, these committees feel that parliament serves as an effective check on the freewheeling governmental activities that breed corruption and irregularities, and insures accountability. PAC, particularly, has taken the government to task on various issues and deals. The Lauda Air (an Austrian Airliner) and the China South West Airlines contracts concluded between the nation's flag carrier—Royal Nepal Airlines Corporation (RNAC) and the two foreign airlines have drawn much attention to the crises of governance because of the involvement of some government and other officials including the ministers in scams through commission agents. Now the Lauda deal has not only implicated the minister, the RNAC's senior board members, but also the prime minister for providing foreign exchange to hire the Lauda Air without any prescribed procedure.

Taking the report of the PAC and the finding of the Commission for Investigation of Abuse of Authority (CIAA) as handy for removing the prime minister on charges of corruption, the CPN(UML) and other opposition parties demanded the resignation of Prime Minister Koirala for clearing the Lauda-RNAC deal by sanctioning foreign currency by the cabinet chaired by him. Although the Lauda case was whipped up by the opposition parties long before the findings of the CIAA implicating the prime minister stating that corruption was encouraged under the patronage of the cabinet, the Left opposition parties seemed to be encouraged by the CIAA findings despite the latters' failure to charge him legally for such irregularities. Instead, the CIAA cautioned the prime minister for not repeating such mistakes in the future.

The parliamentary system has suffered a great deal by the extra-parliamentary behaviour of political parties. It could be observed during the ninth session of parliament in 2000 when most of the political parties except the NSP boycotted the entire session on the issue of the prime minister's resignation. If the parliamentary parties do not come to the house and put up their demands through the prescribed channels and procedures but prefer to mount their opposition from the street alone, how can a system work? Since no party moved the no-confidence motion in the house but the political parties have all along been agitating to remove the prime minister whose majority in the House was intact, extra-parliamentary approaches to the resolution of any problem seem to be gaining ground.

That the political parties do not follow the minimum norm and try to impose their own agendas can be seen in the manner in which they take partisan positions on various issues. One such example is the role of the CPN (UML) on the issue of the PAC decision to implicate a Central Committee member in the China South West Airlines (CSWA) case. The PAC had found similar kind of corruption in the Lauda Air deal and had passed strictures against the prime minister. But, rejecting the CSWA case as a half truth and incomplete, the CPN(UML) Standing Committee formed its own committee to investigate as if it was a Kangaroo court of the CPN (UML) put up for exonerating the member. It is even more important to note that the PAC was composed of the CPN (UML)'s senior members as chairman and members of the PAC who had publicly supported the decision of the PAC. CPN (UML)'s dual character and tendency to impose its will on others if certain decisions went against its line faced strong public criticism. A daily wrote: 'If UML can slam Koirala guilty on the Lauda Air case on the basis of PAC's findings, then why is it refusing to acknowledge the same on the CSWA case in which PAC has implicated Bhim Bahadur Rawal, a top UML leader and former Minister for Tourism?'[15]

Such conflicting norms and activities have not helped develop parliament as an institution, nor are the parties in general sensitive to making it vibrant and participatory. Distortions have crept into the parliamentary institution due both to the lack of a strong political commitment from the parties and to the manipulation of the election system by the political parties and their collaborators—the vested interest groups. Thus, reforms in the election system and minimum standard of value-based politics seem to be one of the important aspects of rectification.

Parliaments in South Asia in general, as Kashyap has pointed out, 'do not seem to be performing their legitimate functions. Sometimes they are seen doing things that they are never expected to do and doing nothing about matters that should engage their priority attention. There is a general decline in the quality of parliamentary leadership, in the character and conduct of legislators and in the standards of parliamentary debate.'[16] Although these remarks are equally applicable to the Nepali parliament, it needs to be examined further against the background of Nepal's own political development and the forces working within it.

Such a fleeting discourse on the environment-parliament interface may not be adequate for a total picture of Nepali political development. Yet, it shows how Nepal's parliament confronts heavy odds and political idiosyncrasies that affect the evolution of this institution. Perhaps political developmental theorists might be tempted to describe such trajectories as the symptoms of transition and need not a worry for the future course of development. None the less, political development cannot be crystallized without a normative assurance that the system is based on minimum consensus.

Parties and Political Development

The role of political parties in a democracy cannot be wished away for the simple reason that they work both as the vehicles of mobilization of public support or opposition and as the systemic organs within the political processes. Thus, parties operate outside and inside parliament while trying to conjoin the activities at both levels. Nepal's political development is therefore tantamount to party development because of the role of parties in undertaking multifarious activities at a time—carrying out a revolutionary agenda for the overthrow of a non-democratic regime, mounting a resistance movement against any backlash to be launched by the predatory forces, working as the consolidator of the established system, combining both the role of protector and executioner of the system and putting themselves on guard against their own temptation of being corruptible due to the enormous opportunities during their tenure in government and in other lucrative posts. So political parties in a country like Nepal are at the same time the permanent sentinels of freedom, and paradoxically, the destroyers of democracy and freedom too.

Unlike many other South Asian countries, political development in Nepal is more concentric in nature because the parties are too inchoate and diverse and hardly helps them to be compatible with the values of the system. As the oldest and largest party, NC's style of functioning, its agenda of democracy, its ideological incongruity, lack of vision and commitment to the process and similar other ingredients do not match the aspirations of its own support base, nor is its overall image projection during the ten-year period of multiparty democracy impressive. NC's intra-party conflicts, which have almost become a regular feature, are generated not on the grounds of principles and rationality but on the contrary, the extreme sense of individualism, ego, selfishness, temptation of power and status, motivation for getting rich quick have turned the party into an institution for perpetrating misrule. So the NC's long tenure in government (eight years out of eleven) defies a rational appraisal of its role as a consolidator or as a democratic party, it never having been imbibed with the minimum discipline and coherence. Its track record in governance is marked by absurdity. But, comparing the NC with other parties, particularly the Communist Parties and the RPP which are perennially plagued by divisive trends, the NC continued to prevent itself from a formal division as others did during the 1990-2000 period. However, the NC also split in May-June 2002.

Ironically, however, such a homogeneity which was more apparent than real had prevented a formal split but had allowed it to be permanently conflict-prone. It is said: 'Nepali Congress can neither unite nor divide' conveying the message that the party's unity is fake and has only obstructed the consolidation of the party and democracy. Working as a personality-based party through its historical evolution, the understanding among the top leaders or the designation of a leader by another seemed to have been acceptable to the lower level party functionaries. Thus, elections to the higher level party posts were held in the post-1951 Nepal until King Mahendra outlawed parties after the 1960 coup. For thirty years, political parties either worked from India or engaged in clandestine activities. Regular elections to the party posts were revived after the restoration of democracy in 1990, though the personality factor became stronger in taking decision or in producing conflicts within the party in the new democratic system.

The concept of 'supreme' leader and democratic organization were incompatible, with the former asserting his personality in order to prevail in the party's decision-making process. Ganesh Man Singh, who was the 'commander' of the *Jana Andolan* (Peoples' Movement) in 1990 and had been accepted by all movement forces, continued to play that role in the NC after 1990 thus sparking off inter-personal conflict between Prime Minister G.P. Koirala and Singh. Later, K.P. Bhattarai took the mantle of Singh, though not as supreme leader, and continued creating trouble for the prime minister despite Bhattarai's inability to dislodge Koirala from the covetous party and government posts. It seemed that Koirala was undaunted by any threat from within his own party and continued to wear two hats—party's president and prime minister—despite several attempts made within the parliamentary party and during the election for the post of president to remove him. How long could he manage to avert such pressures and what for? But one thing was certain, that the continued infighting within the party and its inevitable adverse repercussions on governance were proving to be attritive.

NC's democratic credentials were also seriously eroded due to the failure of its senior leaders to keep their house in order. The party had been pursuing a flexible approach to the unpredictable swings of Nepali politics at the cost of its own identity. NC did not work as a revolutionary party and preferred to put pressure on the king for change and be satisfied with the minor compromises offered by the king. This psyche seemed to be prevailing in the minds of its leaders. As a result, even the revolutionary Constitution mandated by the *Jana Andolan* was diluted by the political parties in general, and the NC in particular because of its long record of incumbency. Examined from the NC's perspective, political development in Nepal is characterized by uncertainties, lack of direction and is bereft of leadership. NC's past image and democratic symbol alone which are fast eroding due to new trends creeping into the organization cannot make the process sustainable.

What about the other main parties like the CPN (UML), the RPP and the CPN (ML) and other Left parties represented in parliament. What is the logic behind the high degree of divisiveness within the Communist Party/Parties? Since the 1950s, the seeds of division were sown within the Communist Party of Nepal. And the main reason for such a split was the divergent attitude of its leaders towards monarchy with some supporting the monarchy and others opposing it. The international division in the Communist movement had also its impact on Nepal. More important factors were/are the personality clash, parochialism and regionalism, etc. Coming close on this trail, the Communists today continue to be plagued by similar factors and allow themselves to be manoeuvred by its adversaries. Recently, it was reported that there are altogether 13 Communist groups by the same original name 'Communist Party of Nepal' followed by other names such as CPN(Maoist), CPN (Masal), CPN(Marxist), etc. Among these groups, the Maoist is being reckoned as an emerging force that is likely to affect the status of the CPN(UML) as the mainline Communist Party in case the Maoists decide to join the system.

How do these groups relate to Nepal's political development becomes contextual. The dual character—being both Marxist-Leninst or Maoist or similar suffix and prefix, and being adherents of a multiparty system—seems to have created an identity crisis of these groups.

All Communist groups are full of contradictions and uncertainties. The CPN (UML), which is treated as the mainline Communist group because of its impressive parliamentary status, often gives conflicting signals about its commitment to the established system. Their opportunistic lines paid off in 1990 following the formation of a United Left Front during the movement, whereupon the ULF could propel itself into power after the collapse of the partyless regime. Subsequently, the taste of power brought the two parties together—the ML and the Marxist—making CPN (UML) with Man Mohan Adhikari as its chairman. Such a merger paid rich dividend to the UML in the wake of NC intra-party conflict prompting the prime minister to hold a mid-term election in November 1994. NC leaders including the 'supreme leader' joined the anti-Koirala campaign and polarized the NC votes into two hostile camps causing the defeat of the party and placing the CPN (UML) in the first position in the HOR. As the largest party, the CPN-UML was allowed to form the government, which it did and continued for nine months. Yet, the UML's veiled contradictions for and against the political system often crept into politics, making every one suspect its opportunistic rhetoric. Keeping an eye on the election with which it could stabilize its position in the government, the CPN (UML) retracted its previous stand on the issue of politicization of all institutions and state functionaries, which it had condemned as 'congressization', and resorted to populism. Demonstrating an unprecedented haste in presenting itself as an efficient, fast moving party, the UML government in fact hastened the trend of UMLization. Scared of such activities, the opposition parties then decided to vote this government out by demanding a special session of parliament.

Left parties aside, the RPP played a key role following the midterm election that gave no clear mandate to any party. Always claiming to be experienced politicians vis-à-vis the NC and the Communists, the RPP leaders went on asserting that the key to government lay with them, for without the 20 RPP members, no parties could form a government and hence the wooing of their votes even at the cost of their respective identity. Yet, the RPP, despite its reduced position with 11 members in the 1999 house, is the second largest non-Left party followed by the NSP with five seats. But this status does not carry any sense if its organizational base is not elastic. Being the party of the former panchas, the RPP lacks attraction for the younger and educated people of the country. Its negative contribution to political consolidation also came under fierce criticism during the period of political instability between 1996-8, when the RPP members were successful in using major parties—the NC and the CPN (UML)—for selfish purposes as well as for systemic aberrations. The two major parties went out of their way to court the RPP and also to distort the parliamentary process in an unprecedented manner. Although any rationale can be advanced for generalization, Nepal's parties have multiple responsibilities in keeping politics on the right track. But how the parties themselves are captives of their own conduct has thus been summarized in a study of leadership:

Political parties' leaders are increasingly becoming hostages to the providers of funds mobilized from a variety of sources. The major parties when they are in government make maximum use of governmental channels for resource mobilization. And those who allegedly provide part of such earnings to the party leaders continue to be in government contrary to their public image. If the NC seems to face such a cruel dilemma of making them as both assets and liabilities, the CPN (UML) has institutionalized corruption for generating funds for the party. All political appointees and members of parliament and others who earn by virtue of being the role incumbents are required to pay part of such earnings to the party.[17]

Cleansing of the body politic appears to be a stupendous task due to the erosion of operating norms. Can other institutions and civil society movements arrest the putrescence of political institutions? Mulling over ten years' political developments leads us to strike a balance between the two extreme views. The first view underlines certain positive developments that have helped both social mobilization and political development. When the parties are at the lowest ebb, other non-formal institutions and non-governmental organizations have played no less significant a role in articulating political discontent. Parties are put to the severest test despite having no direct and immediate effects on correcting institutional distortions. When the parties fail to fill the vacuum due to their own internal problems, other non-formal organizations can contribute to developmental processes. In Nepal, the informal sectors are still weak to play such a role but their activities in the post-1990 period seemed to have gained wider acceptability in politics and development.

NGOs and Political Development

Generally, the NGOs are understood as those associations and institutions that devote themselves to philanthropic works and render services to the handicapped and less privileged sections of society. Apart from the government and market sectors, NGOs belong to the third sector. In today's world, NGOs are very significant in social mobilization and political development, because without their direct and indirect indulgence, social change in its wider ramifications is not possible. Any theory of modernization or qualitative change of society, 'social mobilization' as posited by Karl Deutsch, is replete with these elements:

high degree of social and demographic mobility; diversification of occupations; literacy and growth of per capita income; rise in social and political awareness; specialized works or role differentiation based on recruitment of bureaucrats and other elites on achievement criteria and economic change. Politically, change implies wider participation, accountability of power, and institutionalization of political and formal and non-formal sectors.

In Nepal, both theoretically and practically, NGOs seem to begin their role when the state system fails to do so. NGOs are more active in democratic Nepal and have significant contributions in uplifting the underprivileged villagers of the country. People's associations and organizations have been successful in exposing the big gap between the upper/middle class and the poverty-stricken Nepalis in general. Here the caste division alone brings forth the actual issue, as high caste people also constitute the needy section of society. Social stratification cannot be singled out for determining 'class' division which is a universally acknowledged economic concept. Nonetheless, caste as a factor for general stratification that has seemingly been used as a device for perpetuating traditional ascriptive values cannot also be set aside while trying to see some sort of a correlationship between the two.

Political movements and even political development are now intertwined. In the 1990 mass movement for the restoration of democracy, informal groups, professional associations and others had been able to give a new dimension to the flagging movement. When the government cracked down on the meeting of various professional groups, it spurred the movement taking it to a grand finale, i.e. the end of the partyless regime. In the period following the movement, the NGO involvement has compensated the overall failure of government to address the basic needs of the people. Water, health, education, poverty alleviation programmes, gender, Dalits, ethnic groups' agendas and other similar local problems are drawing increasing attention of the NGOs. Numerous advocacy groups are active across the country.

The Social Service National Coordination Council (SSNCC), a government organization, has identified target groups, issues and sectors as follows: Child Welfare, Women Service, Youth Service, Handicapped and Disabled. Among the issues are environment, aids and drugs, education and development. Health and Community Developments are the two sectors as listed by the SSNCC in 1992.[18]

Apart from such works done by the NGOs, they have also helped develop a strong civil society movement, despite it being a more specialized term. However, liberal democracy without civil society movement is like a curry without salt as civil society gives rise to independent associations and 'public communication', both of them a precondition for democracy. 'The stronger (or more dense and vibrant) the civil society, the better the democracy.'[19] Those who tend to make a distinction between civil society and social capital seem to focus on the status of democracy in the developed countries and do not try to find civil society as an inclusive principle and practice in the democratic experiences of the developing world. As both democratic experiments and experiences and civil society movements eventually create social capital (inter-personal trust, cooperation among the people) and keep track of government, democracy is better sustained and matured through such formal and informal means. Human rights groups, Amnesty International, social organizations that specifically deal with the issues of gender, Dalits and ethnic groups, labour unions, Federation of Nepali Chambers of Commerce and Industry, Trade Union groups, Kamaiya Mukti Sangathan (Bonded Labour Organization), Bar Associations and individuals are now actively involved in insuring governmental accountability. Corruption, mismanagement, bad governance, a culture of lack of accountability and political normlessness draw the attention of the concerned groups who regularly interact with politicians and other members of society. The role of the private press has shown an exponential growth both in quality and quantity and has dramatically changed the landscape of the print media in the country. Now Kathmandu has as many as eight or nine daily newspapers and unlimited numbers of weeklies and fortnightly magazines. Opening the floodgates has also brought with them information, aberrations and distortions.

Yet, to the extent that the private papers seem to provide the public with uncensored information, it has created inconvenience for the governing elites whose attitudes and orientations are not yet tuned to the demands of the times. Moreover, the monopoly of the government media is now changed, despite a tendency among the power elites to depend upon their media for propaganda and reliability. Nowhere in the world do democratic governments run their own dailies and weeklies. In Nepal, contrary to their own rhetorical statements, the government has been running the Gorkhapatra Corporation that runs two dailies and a few other periodicals. Democratic governments have invariably failed to take any decision on the issue of privatization of the print media let alone the electronic media. Nor has any government taken the initiative of making a departure from the nature, ritual and practices of the past. As a result, the official media, both print and electronic, are the most ludicrous, unattractive and unimaginative lot that merely reflects the continuity of ethos of the traditional polity.

Local Level Response

How the people express their opinion on the decade-long experience in multiparty democracy could be ascertained in our empirical test in three village development committees and in the municipalities of each of the five districts of East, Mid-Eastern Terai, Western hill, South-Western inner Terai and Far-Western hill district. Five hundred respondents in all have constituted the universe among whom fifty respondents from five districts were surveyed on the basis of personal interview methods.

About the democratic exercises carried out over a period of ten years and asked to show their agreement or disagreement on any three variables out of five, the people said that the present constitution was democratic with Baitadi recording 49 per cent, Rautahat 42 per cent, Kaski 37 per cent, and Dang 33 per cent. How the political parties and their leaders follow the spirit of the Constitution was another option. Respondents recorded their disagreement, with Rautahat 74 per cent, Baitadi 67 per cent, Kaski 57 per cent, Dhankuta 51 per cent and Dang 44 per cent. It means that no party sticks to the spirit of the Constitution.

Considering the elections both as a mechanism and essence of democracy, a straight question—What is Election?—was asked. Seven options were supplied to the participants. According to the total responses recorded in all the five sampled districts,

70.2 per cent indicated election as an exercise of the people's right. The district-wise division was: Dhankuta 74 per cent, Rautahat 71 per cent, Kaski 63 per cent, Dang 84 per cent and Baitadi 59 per cent. Sixty-five per cent of the total respondents replied that an election is an exercise of sovereign right of the people, while 32 per cent took it as a legitimate way of capturing power. Table 1.4 shows how the local people have expressed their choice on various issues concerning elections.

Peoples' feeling about the achievements of democracy during the ten-year period were recorded by giving nine options out of which three were to be selected. Constitution Making, Freedom of Speech and Writing and Decentralization were identified in order of this percentage: Freedom of Speech and Writing 74.4 per cent, Constitution Making 43.4 per cent and Decentralization 32 per cent (see Table 1.5). Among the major achievements made after the restoration of democracy in 1990, 56.6 per cent recorded end of untouchable practice, 54.4 per cent mentioned development of infrastructure and 31.8 per cent indicated the abolition of the *kamaiya* (bonded labourer) system (see Table 1.6).

A question about the principal problems of democracy was asked with nine options. Among the total respondents, 66.2 per cent recorded 'corruption' followed by insecurity 50.0 per cent and unemployment 46.4 per cent. Erosion of leaders' morality was another problem (see Table 1.7).

Asked for suggestions for the consolidation of democracy in Nepal, 98.8 per cent suggested good governance, 40.6 per cent pointed out the need for control of corruption, and 33.0 per cent preferred economic development. Yet, some major achievements cannot be set aside either. Our respondents at the local level were quick enough to show some achievements as listed below (see Table 1.8).

Our overall findings at the local level have rather supplemented the opinion at the national level, though national level methods of study on democracy and the election system were not based on the structured questionnaire method. People in general want an efficient and clean government that can act as a vehicle of change economically, socially and politically.

Our open-ended interviews conducted during the fieldwork have brought forth the problems of development in Nepal.

TABLE 1.4: PEOPLE'S UNDERSTANDING OF ELECTIONS

Variable	Total		Sex%		Area		Party Affiliation	
	No.	%	Male	Female	Rural	Urban	Member	Non-member
Exercise of people's right	328	65.6	69.6	53.3	66.4	62.4	68.1	64.4
Selection of good representative	351	70.2	72.8	62.3	69.9	71.3	73.0	68.8
Choice of party policy/programme	147	29.4	33.6	16.4	28.1	34.7	28.2	30.0
A legitimate way to be in power	162	32.4	36.2	20.5	29.8	42.6	30.7	33.2
A game of elites to reach in power	161	32.2	32.0	32.8	30.6	38.6	33.1	31.8
Others	13	2.6	2.9	1.6	2.8	2.0	3.1	2.4
Don't know	13	2.6	1.1	7.4	3.3	.0	.6	3.6

TABLE 1.5: MAJOR ACHIEVEMENTS OF DEMOCRACY IN POLITICAL SPHERE

Variable	Total		Sex %		Area %		Party Affiliation %	
	No.	%	Male	Female	Rural	Urban	Member	Non-member
Constitution making	217	43.4	49.2	25.4	41.6	50.5	53.4	38.6
Periodic elections	117	23.4	25.7	16.4	24.1	20.8	31.3	19.6
Freedom of speech and writing	372	74.4	76.2	68.9	73.7	77.2	81.0	71.2
Decentralization	155	31.0	33.9	22.1	30.1	34.7	34.4	29.4
Independent judiciary	69	13.8	14.8	10.7	12.8	17.8	15.3	13.1
Change of government in accordance with constitution	70	14.0	14.0	13.9	13.8	14.9	15.3	13.4
Responsible opposition	34	6.8	6.3	8.2	5.5	11.9	8.6	5.9
Others	12	2.4	2.1	3.3	2.3	3.0	2.5	2.4
Don't know	82	16.4	13.0	27.0	17.5	11.9	9.2	19.9

TABLE 1.6: MAJOR ACHIEVEMENTS OF DEMOCRACY IN SOCIAL AND ECONOMIC SPHERES

Variable	Total		Sex%		Area %		Party Affiliation%	
	No.	%	Male	Female	Rural	Urban	Member	Non-member
Infrastructure development	277	55.4	59.5	42.6	55.9	53.5	57.7	54.3
End of duel ownership in land	52	10.4	13.0	2.5	10.0	11.9	14.7	8.3
Uplift of disadvantaged	142	28.4	28.6	27.9	28.6	27.7	32.5	26.4
Decline on untouchability	283	56.6	58.2	51.6	58.6	48.5	57.7	56.1
Land distribution to squatter	124	24.8	23.0	30.3	23.3	30.7	28.2	23.1
Abolition of *kamaiya* system	159	31.8	34.4	23.8	31.8	31.7	39.3	28.2
Respect to minority language	83	16.6	17.5	13.9	14.5	24.8	16.0	16.9
Others	19	3.8	1.9	9.8	3.8	4.0	4.3	3.6

TABLE 1.7: EMERGING PROBLEMS AFTER RESTORATION OF DEMOCRACY

Variable	Total		Sex %		Area %		Party Affiliation %	
	No.	%	Male	Female	Rural	Urban	Member	Non-member
Erosion in party's ideology	120	24.0	27.8	12.3	23.1	27.7	24.5	23.7
Decline of party leaders/workers' morality	229	45.8	47.9	39.3	44.9	49.5	44.8	46.3
Corruption	331	66.2	69.6	55.7	65.4	69.3	68.7	65.0
Unemployment	232	46.4	45.2	50.0	47.1	43.6	49.7	44.8
Insecurity	250	50.0	49.5	51.6	50.6	47.5	60.1	45.1
Excessive politicization	134	26.8	27.2	25.4	25.6	31.7	28.8	25.8
Instability	55	11.0	12.4	6.6	10.8	11.9	9.2	11.9
Others	18	3.6	3.4	4.1	3.5	4.0	3.7	3.6
Don't know	17	3.4	2.1	7.4	3.5	3.0	.6	4.7

TABLE 1.8: PEOPLES' SUGGESTIONS FOR INSTITUTIONALIZING DEMOCRACY

Variable	Total		Sex %		Area %		Party Affiliation %	
	No.	%	Male	Female	Rural	Urban	Member	Non-member
Good governance	494	98.8	99.9	82.8	94.0	99.5	99.5	96.7
Social reform and development	138	27.6	26.7	30.3	31.9	13.9	22.7	27.6
Economic development	165	33.0	33.3	32.0	34.6	26.7	29.4	33.0
Free and fair elections	49	9.8	11.4	4.9	9.3	11.9	14.1	9.8
Uplift of disadvantaged sections	92	18.4	13.8	32.8	18.8	16.8	25.8	18.4
Employment	151	30.2	30.2	30.3	31.3	25.7	21.0	30.2
Control of corruption	203	40.6	42.6	34.4	38.8	47.5	39.9	40.6
Security	138	21.6	31.2	16.4	28.3	24.8	28.2	27.6
Others	17	3.4	3.2	4.1	2.3	7.9	3.1	3.4

Democracy as is being practiced today both at the local and central level has not served the minimum interests of the common people; nor has it injected any faith among the minorities and ethnic groups in the system. Nevertheless, given the leadership quality and dedication of parties to improving the election system, to eradicating corruption, to controlling money and muscle power being used for influencing the elections, the general interviewees still feel that democracy in itself is not bad.

Conclusion

Comparative election studies in South Asia do not remove our premonitions of political development. Elections are regularly held in the region, but they are not necessarily contributing to development. This is particularly so in the context of more participatory explosions rather than maintaining a balance between participation and institutionalization. Nepal has undergone several local, district and national level elections since 1959 but they have hardly enhanced institutionalized behaviour at these levels because of the more active and interventionist role of other factors that outstrip institutionalization. The manner in which the Nepali parliament is used merely as a mechanism for creating governments but not for translating the wishes of the people suggests that participation has simply become a constitutional formality. Since many of its functions have also suffered from erosions and distortions, political parties' behaviour is seemingly divorced from the spirit of parliamentary democracy.

The complaints made occasionally by the Election Commission and the opinion expressed by the ordinary voters during the fieldwork focus on common issues and problems concerning the fairness of elections and efficacy of government. And the governments, regardless of parties in power and opposition, do not vigorously pursue the campaign for correcting the distortions creeping into the system. The gap between political rhetoric and existing reality in Nepali politics is widening as the main political parties seem to be in the wilderness due both to internal crises and to the lack of firm commitment to the political process. Parties are not clear what sorts of election systems should be conducive for Nepal. Yet, all parties agree on electoral reforms and have accordingly formed a high power committee headed by the prime minister, though the report is yet to be implemented.

If election is the most important aspect of political development, other institutions working in tandem are no less significant. Nepal's short exercise in multiparty system and constitutional monarchy and the failure of political parties to introduce timely reforms within such institutions have only precipitated crises within them; the latest example was the assassination of the entire royal family members within the palace on 1 June 2001 and the future of monarchy because of the drastically changed political environment due both to the all time low credibility of the palace and to the Maoist 'People's War' launched since 1996. Political parties are jittery on the Maoist War that is spreading by leaps and bounds across the country. Since it aims to abolish monarchy and multiparty parliamentary system, how will the political parties, whose credibility has plummeted because of their bad performance, manage the Maoist crisis without compromising the basics of the ongoing system?

One of the dominant features of Nepali politics is that the traditional political culture continues to influence the agendas of political development. The so-called change agents have all along been playing more compromising roles than the expectations of the people. Conceivably, the elected governments and party leaders have been unable to govern effectively and set progressive agendas for the country, thus giving ground to extremist trends and violence. Some important institutions like the monarchy, political parties and parliament are not effective due to a variety of internal crises, contradictions, distortions and corruption. Swings within the monarchy, parties and parliament are fraught with uncertainties as if Nepali politics is destined to go nowhere. So our conclusion of Nepal's political development remains elusive even after covering a long distance since the opening up of the country in 1951.

NOTES

1. Lucian W. Pye, *Aspects of Political Development* (Delhi: Amerind Publishing Co., 1972), p. 31. For more understanding of political development, see Myron Weiner, 'Introduction', in Myron Weiner and Samuel P.

Huntington, eds., *Understanding Political Development* (Boston: Little Brown, 1987); Edward Shils, *Political Development in the New State* (The Hague: Mouton, 1962); David Apter, *The Politics of Modernization* (Chicago: University of Chicago Press, 1965) and ibid. *Introduction to Political Analysis* (New Delhi: Prentice-Hall, 1978); and Samuel P. Huntington, *Political Order in Changing Societies* (New Haven: Yale University Press, 1968).

2. See T.K. Oommen, 'Conceptualising Nation and Nationality in South Asia', in S.L. Sharma and T.K. Oommen, eds., *Nation and National Identity in South Asia* (New Delhi: Orient Longman, 2000), p. 17.
3. For a clear perspective of post-Birendra Nepali monarchy, see Krishna Hacchethu, 'Raj Parampara ra Bidhima Byapak Paribartan' (Royal Tradition and Major Changes in Law), *Himal* (Kathmandu), 30 June-15 July 2001, pp. 11-12 and Narhari Acharya, 'Rajgaddi Uttaradhikarika Sambandhama Sansadma Chhalphal Awasyak' (Need for Discussion in Parliament), *Kantipur daily*, 26 June 2001.
4. See Anirudha Gupta, *Politics in Nepal: A Study of Post-Rana Political Development and Party Politics* (Bombay: Alied Publishers, 1964), p. 37.
5. See B.P. Koirala's *Atmabritanta* (Life Story) (Kathmandu: Jagadamba Prakashan, 2055 (1999).
6. See Anirudha Gupta, *Politics in Nepal*, op. cit., p. 136.
7. See Grishma Bahadur Devkota, *Nepalko Rajnaitaik Darpan* (Banaras: 1960), p. 700.
8. See Lok Raj Baral, *The Regional Paradox: Essays in Nepali and South Asian Affairs* (Delhi: Adroit, 2000), pp. 117-18.
9. David Butler, Ashok Lahiri and Prannoy Roy, 'India Decides: Elections 1952-1955', in Partha Chatterjee, ed., *State And Politics in India* (New Delhi: Oxford University Press, 1997), p. 156.
10. Yogendra Yadav, 'Reconfiguration in Indian Politics: State Assembly Elections 1993-1995', ibid., p. 179.
11. For 1991 and 1994 figures, see Harka Gurung, *Nepal: Social Demography and Expressions* (Kathmandu: New Era, 1998), p. 149. For the Upper House of 1991, see Suresh C. Chalise, *Sociology of the Legislative Elite in a Developing Society* (Kathmandu, 1995), Appendix 2 (pp. v-xxii).
12. For a more detailed picture of the representation pattern, see Lok Raj Baral, Krishna Hachhethu, Hari Sharma, *Leadership in Nepal* (Delhi: Ardoit, 2001), pp. 19-56.
13. As cited in Baral, *The Regional Paradox*, op. cit., p. 22.
14. See the interview of Bishwanath Upadhyaya to the *Kantipur daily* of 14 January 1998.
15. *The Kathmandu Post*, 29 May 2001. For the role of the prime minister, see also Narhari Acharya, *Naya Nepalko Prastawana* (Proposal for New Nepal) (Kathmandu: Sambatsar Prakashan, 2001), pp. 173-7.
16. Subhash C. Kashyap, 'Institutions of Governance: the Parliament, the

Government and the Judiciary', in V.A. Pai Panandiker, ed., *Problems of Governance in South Asia* (New Delhi: Konark Publishers, 2000), p. 143.

17. Baral, Hcchethu and Sharma, op. cit., p. 69.
18. See K.C. Khadga, 'The Role of NGOs and Civil Society in The Political Development of Post-1990 Nepal' (unpublished paper), Pokhara: Department of Political Science, Prithvi Narayan Campus, 2001).
19. Olle Tornquist, *Politics and Development: A Critical Introduction* (New Delhi: Sage, 1999), p. 135.

CHAPTER 2

Election Management

Ram Kumar Dahal*

Introduction

The holding of free, fair and competitive elections and their effective management including the impartial counting of votes and declaration of election results plays an important role in strengthening democratic governance. Their successful management practically extends democratic suffrage and enhances the process of democratization. As elections are the people's method of choosing representatives of their choice and preference and an effective technique for forming representative government, their management becomes the heart and soul of a modern democratic polity.

On the basis of Nepal's experience in election management during the last three parliamentary and two local elections held in the post-1990 period, the information obtained from the Election Commission of Nepal (ECN), and the data collected from the fieldwork one can explore the various issues and challenges in the field of electoral administration. As the universe of this research is very small in size and covers only five hundred respondents in five districts in different ecological zones, its results and findings might be too narrow and may not necessarily generalize the picture in national perspective. In spite of these limitations, this section however, tries to depict the picture of the current trends in the field of election management in Nepal and recommends appropriate measures to improve such existing shortcomings.

This chapter is divided into five sections. The first section deals with the election systems and their role in strengthening

*I acknowledge the cooperation of Anju Joshi, Ramesh Shrestha and Lal Bahadur Kunwar for collection of field data.

democratic governance and constitutional provisions of election adopted by Nepal. The second section analyses the key issues of election management in three phases: before elections, during elections and after elections. The third section addresses the principal challenges/problems Nepal is facing in the field of election management, and the fourth section concentrates mainly on recommendations to solve those problems. The last section is the conclusion.

Election System: Concept and Context

It would be better to have a bird's-eye view on the major electoral systems and their relevance to democratic governance. The management of free, fair and competitive elections has become an important part of the universal process of democratization and human rights, and accordingly, representative and popular institutions have become the indispensable instruments of democratic governance. It is the voters who, through elections, control political power and give mandate to the political parties/representatives to rule the country for a certain period of time. Voting in open and competitive elections, thus, becomes the most important form of political participation. In the universal process of democratization, elections form 'the basis for liberal democracy', 'source of legitimacy for the political system and fundamental form of political participation'.[1] Elections are the important instruments of democracy.[2] The voters determine or express their preferences, transfer power and convert their votes into parliamentary seats or government posts through constitutionally guaranteed electoral systems which in turn influence voting behaviour and election results and also shape political representation, the party system and other institutions of democratic governance. They operate within a complex context of multiple factors varying in different political systems and situations.[3] As the sovereign people are the sole determining force in a nation's polity, free and secret casting of ballots and their impartial counting makes elections more democratic in true sense.[4] Elections are also closely associated with the political system and political development.[5] The electoral systems have close relationship with the viability of democracy, its governability and its consolidation, and thus, the probability of free and competitive elections is higher in a democratic system than in authoritarian totalitarian regimes. In democratic governance, elections perform a number of functions depending upon the societal, institutional and political context of the nation (e.g. the structure of society, or the political party system).[6]

Elections have been classified into three types—majority/ plurality system; proportional representation (PR) system; and mixed system, though this classification, is insufficient for some election experts for various reasons.[7] In the majority/plurality electoral system, the candidate or the political party who wins the required majority of the votes cast in the constituencies is declared elected and thus becomes a member of the parliament. One of the important characteristics of this election is that there exists a wide gap between the seats gained by the political parties in parliament and the total percentage of votes.[8] The majority electoral system can be categorized into three types: (*a*) Plurality system in single member districts, as currently practiced in the UK and other parts of Anglo-Saxon influence countries, stresses the principle of majority representation and its 'disproportional effect favours the most voted party'.[9] (*b*) The absolute majority in single member districts, as exercised in France, favours the 'party or alliance of parties with the most votes'. (*c*) The electoral system in small-sized multi-member districts (up to five seats), often known as 'majority manufacturer', stresses on distortion effects on the degree of proportionality.[10]

PR system, as against to plurality system, tries to establish 'a considerable degree of proportionality between votes and seats'.[11] The PR is 'a method of election which seeks to ensure that minorities as well as majorities and pluralities are adequately represented in the legislature, and which distributes seats or units of legislative representation' in accordance with the proposition of the vote recorded in the whole electoral division.[12] It is a scheme 'which seeks to ensure that each faction, group or party in the electing population is represented in the elected assembly or committee in proportion to its size'.[13] The PR can be categorized into three: (*a*) PR in variable multi-member districts of larger than average size or impure PR; (*b*) pure PR; and (*c*) PR with a legal threshold of representation at the national level. The first category, as practiced in Spain and Portugal, may 'produce a considerable degree of disproportionality between votes and seats'.[14] The pure PR, as practiced in Israel and the Netherlands, 'aspires to achieve as exact a proportionality as possible'.[15] Since the entire country is treated as a single constituency and voting takes place for list system, the Israeli voters do not vote for an individual candidate. In countries like Ireland, the voting and allocation of seats is made on a constituency basis with individual candidates.[16] The PR system has become a popular form of election in most parts of today's world including the Western democracies except the Anglo American systems of North America, the UK and the Commonwealth.[17]

The third category, as adopted in Germany and Sweden, makes a provision according to which those 'small parties which cannot pass the legal threshold but still distributes the seats proportionally among the successful parties'.[18] The personalized PR, as practiced in Germany and often known as mixed system, combines the characteristic features of both the personal vote and the system of PR or the mixture of both the majority representation and PR. Each German voter in the election to the bicameral legislature, Bundestag, casts two votes at a time: one for the candidates of political parties in his own electoral districts and the other for the party list. In the first voting, the candidates securing majority of votes are declared elected whereas in the second type, it is determined as to how many candidates/representatives are elected from the respective parties in the Bundestag.[19]

The Constitution of the Kingdom of Nepal, 1990, promulgated after the historic mass uprising, has vested sovereignty in the Nepal people; it intends to 'guarantee basic human rights of the people' and 'consolidate adult franchise'. It makes provision for direct election system based on the concept of adult franchise for the 205-members of the Lower House of parliament (House of Representatives (HOR)), and local bodies (VDCs and municipalities). The 205-members of the HOR are directly elected by the electorate on the basis of one-man one-vote system through secret ballots and accordingly, any citizen of Nepal who has reached the age of 18 is entitled to vote in any one of the election constituencies as specified by law. In the current single-member-constituency system, the country, for this purpose, is divided into 205 constituencies, each of which is to elect one member for the HOR. Out of the sixty members of the Upper House Rastriya Sabha (National Assembly), the thirty-five members, including at least three women, are indirectly elected by the Lower House under the system of proportional representation by means of a single transferable vote. Similarly, fifteen members from five Development Regions (three each) are indirectly elected in accordance with the system of single transferable vote by an electoral college consisting of the chairman and deputy chairman of the Village Development Committees (VDCs), and Municipality and the chairmen, deputy chairmen and the members of the District Development Committes (DDCs).[20] Nepal, thus, is constitutionally experimenting with direct and indirect election and PR system.

Issues of Election Management in Nepal

This section focuses on the key issues of election management in Nepal in three phases—before, during and after elections. The management of the first phase includes: the functional autonomy of the Election Commission;[21] management of electoral laws; of electoral constituencies; of polling stations; of the voters and Voters' Identity Cards (VICs) and of manpower. Management during elections basically involves the administration of polling booths; of physical resources or facilities; of officials deputed in the booths; of security of, and outside the booths; of candidates, voters, election authorities/officials and observers and ballot boxes; and in general creating a favourable environment for peaceful voting. Moreover, it also includes the various forms of rigging; intervention of government in election activities; behaviour of political parties and their attitude and degree of respect to the codes of conduct and a number of factors. The post-election management includes the administration of post-poll appraisal by the ECN, of election offences and of punishment, etc.

The task of holding free and fair elections in any democratic country depends upon the Election Commission whose independence and autonomy is constitutionally guaranteed. Similarly, under the 1990 Constitution of Nepal, the task is entrusted to the ECN which consists of the Chief Election Commissioner (working as the chairman) and other commissioners as members of the commission (Art. 103). The present constitution, however, does not specify the number of commissioners but currently, the commission, including the Chief Election Commissioner, consists of 6 commissioners.

As in other democratic countries, the independence and functional autonomy of the ECN in post-1990 Nepal is constitutionally guaranteed and the commission is entrusted with the important task of conducting, supervising, directing and controlling the election to the Parliament and other local bodies (village, town and district levels). Under the current system, the ECN has the power to announce the date for parliamentary and local bodies' elections and bye-elections; but the date for the mid term polls is fixed by His Majesty the King himself on the recommendation of the prime minister. The commission, for this purpose, prepares the electoral rolls of the voters in all the constituencies (Art. 104) and can delegate some of its powers to the Chief Election Commissioner or any other commissioners or any officer of HMG to proceed with the work according to the conditions specified in the letter of authority.[22] Constitutionally, the commissioners are independent of the government in respect to appointment and dismissal. The Chief Election Commissioner and other commissioners can be removed from office on the same grounds and in the same manner similar to that of judge of the Supreme Court of Nepal (SCN) and are to be retired upon completion of the age of sixty-five even before their term expires. Their term of office is six years and shall be eligible for reappointment. Their remuneration and other conditions of service shall be specified by law and shall not be altered to the detriment of the incumbents. Any person once appointed as the Chief Election Commissioner or an Election Commissioner will not be eligible for appointment in any other government service except that of political research, study and advisory nature. No commissioners can hold their office after the completion of 65 years of age. Their term of office can be terminated by impeachment in the HOR by two-thirds majority votes of Parliamentarians.[23]

The function of holding competitive elections also depends upon the effective management of electoral laws, rules and regulations, and orders governing elections. In order to regularize the electoral process in Nepal and conduct elections at various levels in a free and fair manner, various acts have been passed by the parliament under the 1990 Constitution.[24]

Besides these enactments, the ECN, from time to time, has issued different directives (*Nirdeshika*) regularizing and governing election.[25]

The effective management of electoral constituencies is one of the important aspects of the election management process in the holding of free and fair elections. The 1990 Constitution empowers the Election Constituency Delimitation Commission (ECDC) to determine the number of electoral constituencies in the 75 districts of Nepal. The ECDC, constituted by His Majesty the King on the recommendation of the Constitutional Council, had delimited the constituencies in 1991 for districts. While doing so, the commission had considered the boundaries of administrative districts, geographical conditions, density of population, transportation facilities and communal homogeneity or heterogeneity of the inhabitants (Art. 105). The ECDC is constitutionally empowered to operate freely from the influence of the government and the 1990 Constitution clearly mentions that no question shall be raised in any court of law on the allocation of seats and the delimitation of constituencies made by the ECDC.[26] The task of first electoral districting, under the 1990 Constitution, was completed on 3 January 1991 according to which two districts were given 6 seats; 7 districts 5; 8 districts 4; 21 districts 3; 26 districts 2 and 11 districts one seat each in the 205-member HOR.[27] The clause 3.3 of the Members of the House of Representatives Act, 1990, mentions that the ECDC unless determined by law is empowered to make necessary changes in the membership structure based on the results of the population census,[28] published in Nepal every ten years by the Central Bureau of Statistics (CBS). Accordingly, the redistricting in the electoral constituencies was done in 1994.[29] Some political parties are of the view that if this trend would continue in future, it would create an imbalance in Nepalese politics and legislative power would be concentrated in the southern plains. In such a case, if the population would be considered as the only basis for representation in the HOR, the migrants might control the legislative power.

The third parliamentary elections in May 1999 were held in two phases by the ECN due to security reasons. The discussion between the ECN and the security authorities in 1999 had led to the conclusion that due to security reasons, it would be more convenient and effective to hold the 1999 polls at three phases. But as it would require a minimum period of 30 to 45 days to conduct the election, whereas the ECN thought it better to conclude them within two weeks in two phases so that they could be conducted in a very peaceful atmosphere.[30] Accordingly, elections in 36 districts were held in the first phase and remaining 39 in the second phase. But the holding of the 1999 polls in two phases became a subject of much controversy among the political parties. The big parties including the CPN-UML and the RPP were not in its favour whereas both the government and the ECN were fully committed to hold them in two phases. The former had opposed it on the ground that it would benefit the ruling party and encourage government intervention in elections in a phase-wise basis.

The management of elections starts from the preparation of electoral rolls in each constituency in the districts. The Electoral Laws of Nepal have provided for the annual registration system in the electoral rolls. Under the Electoral Rolls Act, 1996, there is a provision for a single electoral roll system in the country for which the ECN appoints in each district a Chief Voters' Registration Officer (CVRO) who is empowered to register the voters in the district. Under the present system, the Chief District Officers (CDOs) in each district serve as CVROs. The ECN has been planning to establish district election offices in a phase-wise basis and accordingly, 30 such offices (in 5 districts in the first phase and 25 in the second one) were established in 30 districts and is also planning to establish these offices in future in the remaining districts. Under the current system, the enumerators are appointed by the ECN who visit door to door in the constituencies for the compilation of names of the voters. Currently, the secretary (*sachiv*) of the VDC and the Ward Committee of the Municipality work as enumerators in their respective areas. A period of one month is given for enumerating the names of voters and compilation of the rolls. A voter is entitled to cast his/her vote only in the constituency where his/her name has been registered. In order to be registered as voter, he or she (*a*) must be a citizen of Nepal; (*b*) must have attained the age of 18 years on the last date of the Nepalese calendar year specified by the Election Commission; (*c*) must not have been certified by a recognized physician as mentally retarded; (*d*) must have a permanent residence within any constituency; (*e*) must not have been convicted with imprisonment under the Election (Crime and Punishment) Act, 1990 for one year or more and a period of one year has not elapsed from the date of release.[31] Every year, the electoral rolls is updated by adding the names of those who have completed the age of 18 years by the last of Chaitra (the last month of the Nepalese calendar) and deleting the names of those who are dead, have migrated or ceased to qualify as voters.[32] Soon after the completion of the compilation of the electoral rolls, they are published at every VDC's office or at every municipal ward's office. Under the existing laws, opportunities for lodging claims and protests for inclusion or deletion of names in electoral rolls are also given. During this phase, transfer-application of voters name from one place to another is also accepted under certain format. But interestingly enough, very few such applications have been received so far. This is due to non-introduction of a card system in all the districts. Soon after the process of scrutinizing the claims and protests is completed, the final electoral rolls are published in CVRO's office, who has overall charge of registration of voters in the district. The ECN has the sole power to review the final electoral rolls if some severe and massive irregularities are found. But the ECN so far has rarely reviewed them.

In course of reforming the existing electoral process and reducing the irregularities in elections, the ECN introduced, on an experimental basis, the system of voters' identity cards (VICs). The ECN had the programme of introducing the system in five phases throughout the kingdom and had directed the government to implement the programme from the financial year 1997-8. The system was introduced in 13 constituencies in the first phase but due to the non-allocation of budget on VIC system in the financial year 1998-9, the proposed programme for 41 constituencies was postponed.[33]

The selection of polling stations is another important step in the management of elections. There is no extensive legal provision regarding the selection of polling stations in Nepal. Clause 43 of the members of the HOR Elections Act, 1990, simply mentions the process for the selection of booths but other provisions are to be determined by law. As no clear-cut legal provisions have yet been evolved, the controversies and disputes over the selection or determination of booths remain as usual even after the completion of three parliamentary and two local elections. But this state of legal uncertainty, as the opposition parties have stated, has particularly benefited the ruling party in bringing election results in its favour, and, thus, has to be ended immediately.

The guiding principles so far practiced regarding the selection of booths are: booths should not be placed within one km area of the national boundary, booths be placed in public places (e.g. government buildings, VDC/municipality office, government schools, campuses and public fields) not in private gardens; booths should not be close to each other and should be selected for benefiting the general people as accepted by the consensus of political parties. The member of the HOR Act, 1990, and its amendments in 1996 (clause 43) and Local Bodies (Election Process) Act, 1991, have authorized the ECN to determine the number of polling booths. The polling officer, under clause 43 of member of the HOR Act, 1990, and rule 24 of member of the HOR Election Rules, 1990, can increase, after taking the prior approval of the ECN, the number of polling booths and transfer them from one place to another.

The polling booths for the election of the chairman, vice-chairman and other members of the VDC are to be located at the VDC office or any suitable public place; at every wards' office for the election of the municipal authorities; in *illaka* office for the election of DDC authorities and in five regional centres for the election of 15 MPs of the Upper House. There are approximately 16,000 polling stations/booths and sub-stations/sub-booths in the kingdom, a booth for an average for 1,000 to 1,200 voters. If the number of voters increases, there is also provision for additional sub-booths but whose number may not be more than two.[34] In the 1991 polls, there were 8,225 and 6,564 polling stations and sub-stations/booths for the total 1,11,91,777 voters. The average of voters for one booth was 1,360. In 1994, the number of voters were 1,23,27,329 and the booth and sub-booths were respectively 7,411 and 8,192 and the average of voters for one booth was 1,663. Similarly, in 1999, 1,35,18,839 voters were to exercise franchise in 6,821 booths and the average ratio for one booth was 1,982.[35] The ECN, however, is also thinking or planning to determine or select the same permanent booths for the election of the members of the HOR and local elections for the convenience of, if possible, all voters in the areas. The ECN, for this purpose, had also held talks/interactions with the representatives of the various political parties. The reduction of the existing number of booths from 7,412 in 1994 to 6,821 in 1999 (-591 booths throughout the kingdom) became a subject of much controversy between the ECN and the government on the one hand and the opposition parties on the other.

The numbers of polling stations in the 1991 parliamentary and 1992 local elections were different. The polling stations for the 1997 local elections, which were based on the local elections of 1992, was adopted/accepted for the 1999 polls. As the ECN had decided to hold 1999 elections in two phases due to security reasons, the number of booths was reduced. There was, however, 30 per cent increase, as the ECN claimed, in the number of polling stations of 1997 elections on the basis of the increase in the number of voters. The ECN had planned to increase the number of polling stations immediately after 1994 polls and took steps accordingly. But this could not be implemented, as the ECN viewed, because of the compulsion to conduct elections in two phases within a short period of less than two weeks time.[36] But the ECN thinks that the problem of peace and security, especially in those areas where the Maoists were more active, had thus prompted the ECN to reduce the number of existing booths.

The successful holding of impartial and competitive elections largely depends upon the effective performance of the manpower deputed to the booths for the conduct of elections. As large number of personnel (both administrative and security) are involved, the effective management of manpower is, thus, really a challenging job especially in today's Nepalese situation when the civil servants themselves are divided on political grounds. Under the 1990 Constitution, it is the duty of HMG's to provide the ECN with such number of employees and other materials as necessary to carry out its functions (Article 108). Accordingly, the CROs, ROs, POs, and a number of civil and police personnel are involved in elections. Soon after the announcement of the date of elections, they are appointed by the ECN. In case of parliamentary elections, one RO is appointed in each constituency. In those districts where there is more than one constituency, a CRO is appointed among the existing ROs who also acts as an RO for one of the constituencies in the district.

Under the current system, judges and legal and judicial officers are appointed as ROs in parliamentary elections and CDOs as ROs in case of local elections.[37] The current practice is that the ROs have to appoint, if the appointment has not been made directly by the ECN, one Polling Officer (PO) for each booth and other assistant polling officers according to the number of sub-booths. Polling officials are drawn from among the government and semi-government cadres.[38]

In order to acquaint the ROs with the existing electoral procedures, directives of the ECN for holding free and fair elections and to impart practical knowledge of handling election materials (e.g. ballot boxes, indelible ink, etc.), seminar-cum-workshops are organized at all regional headquarters. Moreover, similar kind of training is also imparted to the POs by the trained ROs before they leave for their respective polling stations with materials.[39] In order to watch the conduct of polling and to see whether the voting has been conducted impartially or not, or whether the voters have been properly identified or allowed to cast the vote or not, every candidate has the right to depute his polling agents to every booth.[40] Practically speaking, if he can work impartially and effectively, his role in ensuring peaceful and fair election is no less important.

Immediately after reaching their booths, the POs, with the help of local people, police and administrative personnel, manage the physical resources/facilities there (e.g. construction of tents and huts; management of chair, bench, desk, rope, bamboo and preparation of queue for voters and a secret place for voting); determine the boundary of the booths; keep ballot boxes in proper order; publish notice for restricting campaigning within the booth area and put restrictions on the selling of wine until the election is completed.[41] Before voting starts, they have to open the sealed packets of ballot boxes; sealing the empty ballot boxes in the presence of the agents of political parties; put their signatures in a paper and thus, in general prepare a favourable environment for free and secret voting. Moreover, they have the authority to permit to enter into the booths to only those who are the real voters, agents of candidates, those persons getting permissions from the ECN and those personnel (administrative and security) deputed to the booth.[42] In the 1999 elections, a total of 59,514 officials (including 6,821 polling officers, 6,821 assistant polling officers 29,203 assistants and 16,669 peons) were mobilized. For this, Rs. 19 crores and 25 lakhs were allocated which was more than 50 per cent of the total budget of Rs. 36 crores allocated for conducting elections.[43] Under the current practice, all the materials that are to be used in the elections including ballot boxes are purchased by the ECN at the central level and transported to the districts via helicopters and planes. Some are of the view that if these materials were locally purchased, they would cost less than the transportation cost. The ballot papers are printed only with candidates' election symbols, the number of constituency and the name of the districts, and are dispatched to their destinations under the control and supervision of the ECN. In the parliamentary elections of 1999, nearly Rs. 10 crores (Rs. 9 crores 75 thousands) were spent on transportation cost only.[44] But the ECN is also criticized for the huge amount of money it spends on transporting small and even locally available cheap election materials to the districts especially in the non-remote areas including the Trai belt where these goods are freely available at cheaper rates.

Voting and Non-Voting in 1999 Polls

The Nepalese had voted in national and local elections even in the pre-1990 period, though the form of political participation was different in nature. So, they have been familiar with voting in elections since 1959 when for the first time they got a chance to vote in the 109-member House of Representatives under the Constitution of the Kingdom of Nepal, 1959. Their understanding/perception of voting and level of participation in it is very important in post-1990 Nepal. The percentage of voting in 1999 polls thus was a matter of prime concern for this team of researchers due to many prominent reasons including the academia and the media reporting/creating rumour of less percentage of voting (i.e. voters' negative trend towards election), increasing political apathy among the voters and people's growing dissatisfaction against the functioning of multiparty democracy (MPD). But the survey report defied these rumours and proved that voter's interests in elections have not decreased (see Table 2.1). Nearly 86.6 per cent of a total of 500 respondents had stated that they had voted in the 1999 polls followed by negligible per

TABLE 2.1: REASONS FOR NON-VOTING IN 1999 POLLS

*(Total number of respondents: 500
% based on multiple responses)*

Variables	Total		Area %		Party Members %		Sex	
	No.	%	Rural	Urban	Yes	No	Female	Male
Names not listed in voters' list	15	22.7	20	31.3	16.7	24.1	25.0	22.0
Lack of voters ID Card	4	6.1	6	6.3	0	7.4	6.3	6.0
Proxy voting	2	3	4	0	8.3	1.9	6.3	2.0
Polling centre far from home	11	16.7	16.0	18.8	16.7	16.7	12.5	18.0
Violence and insecurity in polling centres	1	1.5	0	6.3	0	1.9	0	2.0
Lack of proper candidate	4	6.1	8.0	0	0	7.4	6.3	6.0
Election boycotted by his/her party	1	1.5	2.0	0	8.3	0	0	2.0
Others	38	57.6	5.6	62.5	66.7	55.6	55.0	60.0
Don't know	1	1.5	2.0	0	0	1.9	6.3	0

cent of non-voters (13.2 per cent), and do not knows (0.2 per cent). When the 13.2 per cent respondents who had not voted (66 in number) in the 1999 polls, were categorically asked to express reasons for their non-voting, non registration of their names in the electoral rolls topped the list (22.7 per cent) followed by far distance of polling centre (16.7 per cent), lack of voters identity card (VID) (6.1 per cent), lack of proper candidate (6.1 per cent), proxy voting (3 per cent), violence and insecurity in polling centre (1.5 per cent), boycott called by the voter's party/affiliated (1.5 per cent), others (57.6 per cent), do not knows (1.5 per cent).

The cross tabulated data (based on multiple responses) from different variables indicate that the trend of non-voting due to non-registration of names in the electoral rolls was the highest in Rautahat (31.3 per cent) followed by Baitadi (28.6 per cent), Kaski (26.7 per cent), Dang (15.4 per cent), and Dhankuta (13.3 per cent). The percentage of such non-voters was higher in urban centres (31.3 per cent) among labourers (33.3 per cent), in housewives (33.3 per cent) and among non-members of political parties (24.1 per cent). Similarly, it was higher among the Hindus, (25 per cent) and females (25 per cent); among the economically poorer sections of the people (44.4 per cent); and among literates (33.3 per cent); ethnic groups (50 per cent) and the 18-34 age groups (26.3 per cent).

Altogether 16.7 per cent of the total number of non-voters (66) had got no opportunity to vote in the 1999 polls because of the distance of the polling stations from their homes. As the number of the polling stations, particularly in the hill districts, were reduced in 1999, the voters could not exercise their voting rights in the hill districts, and had to walk 4 to 10 miles to reach the booths. It is most inconvenient for the aged, sick and physically handicapped voters. Voices are raised that the members of electoral booths must be increased. The ECN also had planned to increase them in future but it has not been implemented due to security reasons. Respondents of different occupations, religions, caste/ethnic and age groups, urbanites and rural people, male and female, voters of different educational backgrounds and economic status have accepted this factor as the second important reason of non-voting in 1999 polls. But the percentage of such non-voters, as calculated from the cross-tabulated data from different variables, was slightly higher among the urbanites (18.8 per cent) than the rural respondents; more than two-thirds among the housewives (66.7 per cent) than businessmen (23.1 per cent) and agriculturists (15.8 per cent); higher in the NC (50 per cent) than the UML and RPP which recorded no such percentage, and less than double among the Brahmins/Kayastha (40 per cent) than their counterparts—hill tribes (31.3 per cent) and other Terai groups (25 per cent). The percentage was nearly five times higher in above 55 years age group (60 per cent) than 18-35, and 36-54 age groups. But the percentage was equal among the members/non members of political parties with records of 13.2 per cent and 13 per cent respectively.

Lack of voters identity cards (6.1 per cent) and proper candidates (6.1 per cent) stood as the third important reasons for non-voting in the 1999 polls. Among the total numbers of non-voters (66 respondents) 4 per cent respondents said that they had been barred from voting in the 1999 polls due to non-availability of voters' identity cards Baitadi (42.9 per cent) recorded the highest percentage of such non-voting followed by Rautahat (6.3 per cent). As no VIC system had been introduced in Dhankuta, Kaski and Dang during the 1999 polls, these districts recorded no such problem. As most of the people of the lower strata in Baitadi had gone to the neighbouring Indian towns (e.g. Tanakpur, Jhulaghat) in search of jobs when voters identity cards were distributed, they got no opportunity to get the card and hence to vote. As most of the people in Rautahat had got no citizenship certificate, it became difficult for 6.3 per cent voters (out of the total 66 non-voters) to get the VIC. Similarly, 6.1 per cent of the total 66 non-voter respondents had not voted in the 1999 polls due to lack of proper, qualified and competent candidates. This trend was encouraged due to many reasons including the growing factionalism within the political parties: personal rivalries among the candidates and the selection of weak candidates at the central level without any detailed knowledge of the candidate. Finally, the role of personal linkage with the central leadership of a candidate was particularly significant. Dhankuta recorded the highest percentage of such non-voting (13.3 per cent), followed by Kaski (6.7 per cent) and Rautahat (6.3 per cent). Dang and Baitadi recorded no such non-voting.

Rigging in 1999 Polls

Like in three earlier parliamentary and two local elections, rigging had also become one of the challenging problems in the 1999 elections. Almost all the political parties were said to be involved in it in one way or the other, but have blamed each other for such malpractice. But the survey report has shown the opposite trend as is generally believed. When respondents were asked to express their views on rigging in the polls, 73.2 per cent (317 out of the total 433 respondents) answered in the negative followed by 'yes' (25.2 per cent) and 'do not know' (1.6 per cent) (see Table 2.2). In an answer to the question concerning various forms of rigging in the 1990 polls (based on the multiple responses) proxy voting (72.5 per cent) topped the list followed by underage voting (52.3 per cent), use of force and violence (35.8 per cent), vote buying (34.9), partiality by police and administrative authorities (26.6 per cent), unauthorized booth capturing by

TABLE 2.2: FORMS OF RIGGING IN 1999 POLLS

(Total number of respondents: 500
% based on multiple responses)

Variables	Total		Area %		Party Members %		Sex	
	No.	%	Rural	Urban	Yes	No	Female	Male
Booth capture	10	9.2	9.1	9.5	16.2	5.6	4.2	10.6
Vote buying	38	34.9	35.2	33.3	48.6	27.8	29.2	36.5
Use of force and violence	39	35.8	31.8	52.4	29.7	38.9	25.0	38.8
Underage voting	57	52.3	54.5	42.9	40.5	58.3	45.8	54.1
Not allowing agent of other parties	4	3.7	2.3	9.5	8.1	1.4	4.2	3.5
Proxy voting	79	72.5	77.3	52.4	75.7	70.8	66.7	74.1
Partiality by police and adminis-tration	29	26.6	21.6	47.6	32.4	23.6	8.3	31.8
Others	4	3.7	3.4	4.8	2.7	4.2	0	4.7
Total			235.2	252.4	254.1	230.6	183.3	254.1

political parties (9.2 per cent), not allowing the agents to be present in the booths or purchasing the agents of other political parties (3.7 per cent), and others (3.7 per cent).

The cross tabulated data from different variables indicate that proxy voting, as encouraged and practiced by political parties, candidates and their supporters, was considered as the principal form of rigging (as 72.5 per cent of the total 109 respondents viewed) in the 1999 polls by the respondents from different political, economic, socio-cultural, educational, religious, and regional background. The culture of proxy voting, however, was encouraged by the panchayati leaders during 1961-89 elections, which still continues in the post-1990 Nepal. As the cross tabulated data (out of the total 79 responses) suggested, the percentage of proxy voting was higher in the rural area (77.3 per cent) than the urban one (52.4 per cent); higher in labour and student occupational groups (100 per cent) than among agriculturists (75.7 per cent), service holders (71 per cent) and businessmen (70 per cent); and slightly higher amongst party members (75.7 per cent) than non-party ones (70.8 per cent). Similarly, the percentage was higher among the Dalits (91.7 per cent) than the Hill tribes (84.2 per cent), Newars (66.7 per cent) and Terai Brahmins/Kayastha (66.7 per cent); larger in the above 55 years of age (81.3 per cent) than in the 18-35 age bracket (74 per cent) and illiterates (71.4 per cent). The percentage, however, was similar in the three principal political parties of Nepal—the RPP (77.8 per cent), the NC (76.9 per cent) and the CPN-UML (76.9 per cent).

This researcher got the impression after his interactions with the respondents, voters, personnel (both police and administrative), political leaders, teachers, NGO experts and civil society activists that proxy voting largely took place due to many reasons, e.g. non-identification of voters by the election and security authorities, encouragement to proxy voters by the political parties and candidates, negligence shown by the election authorities in voters' identification, illegal contact between the political parties and the election authorities, pressurizing the election authorities not to pay attention to the proxy voters, and undeclared booth capturing in various forms. In order to impart justice to the real voters who came late and whose votes were already cast by proxy voters, the electoral laws of Nepal authorize the former to vote in elections as a voter of different category. The ECN calls it *nibida matpatra* (tender vote) which is polled not in the ballot boxes but in a separate envelope. This vote (kept in the envelope) is not counted in the regular counting process but will be opened only in case of complaint in the Election Tribunal. Respondents of various political, economic, socio-cultural and educational background identified, next to proxy voting, underage voting as the second principal reason for rigging in the 1999 elections. Such a practice was encouraged by the non-party Panchayati leaders (e.g. candidates and their agents) during the 1961-89 elections. That trend still continues in today's multiparty elections especially in those constituencies where the voters' identity card system is not introduced as yet. The root of the underage voting lies in the preparation of electoral rolls (e.g. registration of voters' name) where political parties having influence in a particular pocket area try to pressurize the secretary of the VDC and ward office of the municipality to register their underage voters in the electoral rolls. Once their names are registered in the rolls, the ROs, POs and election authorities are not authorized to check them during voting, even though they know of the presence of unauthorized or underage voters.

The multiple responses drawn out (of total 57 respondents) from the cross tabulated data from different variables indicate that underage voting in the 1999 elections was higher in the rural area (54.5 per cent) than in the urban one (42.9 per cent). The percentage was 100 per cent in ethnic occupation areas, 60 per cent among the businessmen, 54 per cent among the service holders and 48.6 per cent among the agriculturists. The percentage was higher among non-party members (58.3 per cent) than among party members (40.5 per cent). The RPP recorded 55.6 per cent, the CPN-UML 38.5 per cent and the NC 30.8 per cent. The cross tabulated data further demonstrated that underage voting was higher in other Terai ethnic groups followed by Hill tribes (63.2 per cent); among Hill Brahmins (55.2 per cent); and among the above 55 age groups (62.5 per cent). The percentage was slightly higher among educated voters (up to school level) (60.4 per cent) in comparison to illiterates (57.1 per cent); among literates (50 per cent); and among the male (54.1 per cent) as against female groups (45.8 per cent).

The use of muscle power has been pointed out by the respondents as the third form of rigging in the 1990 polls. The use of muscle power (e.g. force and violence) in elections is a chronic problem in Nepal since the panchayati days. In order to get elected a government-backed candidate in the Panchayati elections, both the military and the police force were strictly instructed to vote in a particular booth for a particular candidate. The use of muscle power in the post-1990 Nepal has two forms: one used by the party in power and government and the other used by the opposition political parties and candidates. The first category of force and violence includes direct intervention by the central and local police and administrative authorities (e.g. home ministry officials, CDOs and police and other administrative staff) in getting the candidates of the party in power elected by any means. That's why, each party sharing power, even if in the coalition government in the second half of the 1990s tried to capture the home ministry. In the second local elections, the CPN-UML, which had control over the home ministry declared election results in its favour. The use of muscle power and home made bombs (both by the government and the political parties and candidates) has become a regular phenomenon in the highly sensitive border districts of Terai (Rautahat) where Indian wrestlers and criminals are brought for this purpose.

CENTRAL GOVERNMENT'S INTERVENTION

During the last three parliamentary and two local elections, intervention by the central and local governments in different forms (both direct and indirect) have been experienced in one way or the other. As the 1990 Constitution did not specifically mentioned the elected government for the conduct of free and fair election and entrusts the task to the incumbent government, political parties like the CPN-UML had also demanded the formation of a separate government for electoral purposes (as in Bangladesh) and are also in favour of amending the Constitution to include this provision. As most of the parliamentary parties (larger or smaller) are eager to form such a government during elections, and particularly willing to control the home ministry, a general perception has crystallized among the political parties that the party in power would naturally win the elections misusing the government resources and the home ministry.

Various reports have been published in the media about the misuse of the entire governmental power and resources. The prime minister himself was involved in campaigning in the districts through helicopters. As no democratic and parliamentary culture has evolved in Nepal, political parties, according to their capacity had utilized the local administrative and police authorities (CDO and police) in defeating their opponents. The opposition parties have raised the issue that particularly in the last two local elections, the government had the advantage of special benefits through the CDOs and the police. Moreover, the extreme polarization of civil servants on political grounds into *Sangh*, *Sangathan*, *Manch* and *Parishad* has also provided ample opportunity to the central government to intervene in the elections through government officials.

The Election Code of Conduct, 1996, accepted by the ECN, government, and the political parties, is a self-controlling or self-abiding mechanism, intended to make the elections free and fair. The code is biding on political parties, candidates and HMG simply as a moral rule. The Code of Conduct is to be abided by HMG according to which it has to make the mass media free from its control and also puts restriction on the adoption of particular programmes, means and service by the government for election purposes. The Code of Conduct to be abided to by political parties and candidates include restriction on the propagation that undermines the nationality, independence, integrity and sovereignty, multiparty democracy, and constitutional monarchy. The code also restricts the affixing of any posters, pamphlets or bills, use of enamel for painting on somebody's private house, or use in propaganda, processions, pamphlets or means of transport. Use of loudspeakers, radio, cassette or similar other apparatus for amplifying the human voice was also included in the regulation list. The code also intends to regularize the conduct of the mass media, public meetings and processions.

The Code of Conduct also puts a ceiling on expenditure by the political parties and candidates during election campaigns. One of the characteristics of the Code of Conduct is that it has classified the districts into four categories. 'A' category includes three districts of the Kathmandu valley; category 'B' includes 21 districts of Terai; category 'C' includes 44 Hill districts; and category 'D' includes 7 Himalayan districts. A detailed expenditure limitation list on ten heads totals Rs. 2,75,000; Rs. 2,35,000; Rs. 1,65,000 and Rs. 1,15,000 respectively in four category districts.[45] The difference between class A and D is Rs. 1,65,000 which, as some political parties view, is impractical and inadequate to the current market rates and price-hike in Kathmandu valley. Moreover, the price rate prescribed for vehicles, e.g. jeeps, cars, bus, truck and tractor per day is also not uniform and practical. Candidates in districts of Terai and Kathmandu valley complain that the amount determined on transportation is too low. Interestingly out of the ten heads prescribed for the limits on election expenses (except miscellaneous on which Rs. 10,000; Rs. 8,000; Rs. 6,000 and Rs. 3,000 are allocated for A, B, C and D category districts respectively), there is no separate expenditure-head for lodging and food for the candidates contesting elections. Most candidates contesting elections in the 1999 polls had complained that the limit for election expenses were not adequate to meet their expenditure at the current market prices. In spite of these attempts made by the ECN to regularize the election expenses in post-1990 Nepal, the increasing trend of high expenses is obvious. Practically most political parties and candidates in the 1990 polls have crossed the limits set by the ECN.

When the respondents were asked to express their views on various areas of election expenses of candidates (see Table 2.3), the mobilization of party workers in elections (64.6 per cent) (as based on data drawn from multiple responses) topped the list followed by publicity (55.2 per cent), distribution of money and goods to the voters (53.2 per cent), purchasing the brokers (31 per cent), distribution of development materials (21 per cent), for arms purchase and use of force (19.6 per cent), for

TABLE 2.3: AREAS OF EXPENSES IN 1999 POLLS

(Total number of respondents 500 % based on multiple responses)

Variables	Total		Area %		Party %		Sex	
	No.	%	Rural	Urban	Members	Non Members	Female	Male
Booth capture	10	9.2	9.1	9.5	16.2	5.6	4.2	10.6
Publicity	276	55.2	53.6	61.4	62.6	51.6	55.7	55.0
Mobilization of Workers	323	64.6	65.2	62.4	72.4	60.8	65.6	64.3
Distribution of development materials	105	21	21.8	17.8	20.2	21.4	18.9	21.7
Distribution of money to brokers	155	31	30.8	31.7	32.5	30.3	18.0	35.2
Distribution of money to police and administration	67	13.4	13.0	14..9	19.0	10.7	8.2	15.1
Arms purchase	98	19.6	17.8	26.7	19.6	19.6	9.8	22.8
Vote buying and distribution of goods	266	53.2	53.9	50.5	54.6	52.5	50.8	54.0
Others	2	0.4	.5	0	0	1.2	0	5
Don't knows	35	7	7.3	5.9	.0	10.4	12.3	5.3
Total			263.9	271.3	282.2	257.3	239.3	273.8

buying the police and administrative authorities (13.4 per cent), others (0.4 per cent), don't knows (7 per cent). The percentage, however, differed in various age and regional groups, (rural-urban areas), ethnic, religious, and economic groups (rich, higher middle, lower middle class and poor). On the basis of information collected from a cross tabulation of data from different variables, it was found that the expense was slightly higher in the mobilization of students (76.9 per cent) than the ethnic occupation (76.5 per cent), service holders and farmers (64.7 per cent); in the CPN-UML (79.2 per cent) followed by the NC (77 per cent) and the RPP (64.7 per cent) and in the 36-54 age group (69.2 per cent) followed by 18-35 (61.6 per cent) and above 55 years age groups. The percentage was higher among party members (72.4 per cent) than among non-members in Hill Brahmins, Chhetries and others (77.5 per cent) followed by Hill tribes (64.9 per cent), Newars (61.1 per cent) and Terai Brahmins and Kayasthas (55 per cent).

Expenses, however, differed in different regions (Himalayan, Hill and Terai) of Nepal according to the market price. In order to campaign safely in the nook and crannies of election constituencies (a complicated job in the Hill and the Himalayan districts due to difficult terrain), the candidates in the 1999 polls had both to mobilize dozens of workers for at least a month and to bear the complete cost on lodging, food/dining, smoking, recreation and other expenses of their workers. It usually takes nearly a month for the candidates to move on foot in the wards of the VDCs of particular constituencies.

Publicity in elections came second in rank in the order of priority (55.2 per cent) on which the candidates used to spend their money. The various means of publicity in the 1999 elections in different regions of Nepal included door-to-door campaigns by candidates with their workers in groups in mass meetings, public meetings, corner meetings, use of loudspeakers, radios, cassettes or similar other apparatus for amplifying the human voices. Particularly in the Kathmandu valley and in other municipalities, towns and urban and commercial centres of Tarai, other additional means of publicity, e.g. pamphlets, posters, bills, badges were also used. Pamphlets and posters were two important areas in this direction. The candidates had also spent sizeable amounts of money on the distribution of cash and goods to the voters. As this is highly personal, this is not seen by others, and no evidence remains to prove that someone has given or received a certain amount of money for certain reasons. The money in the 1999 elections was distributed by the candidates through their agents and workers and in some places by the candidate himself, mostly a day before the elections late at night. It sometimes happened that another candidate/his agents/supporters followed him in distributing money (e.g. up to 1,000 for one voter) in the hills and even at a cheaper rate in the Himalayan districts. The amount was also distributed to particular groups of people through the agents of a particular area/VDC, so that they could be distributed to the voters by them but the agents were also found benefiting out of that money and not distributing in fact to the groups and voters. The distribution of individual goods to individual voters included ribbon, *chura* (bangle), *dhago* (thread) of cheaper rates for the female and underwear, handkerchief, caps for the males. Free drinks, dining, smoking were also generally offered to the voters by candidates in public hotels in general and in private locales in particular.

The management of security officials (both police and the military force) or the security system as a whole adopted by the government in elections becomes one of the important parts of the election, which includes activities like securing polling booths, election authorities, voters, election materials (e.g. ballot boxes, stamp pads, ballot papers) and in general, creating an environment for free and fair elections. The security system in elections might be classified into three phases: pre-elections security; security during elections; and post-elections security. The pre-election security includes the security of election materials (e.g. ballot boxes, stamp pad, ballot papers), that of the election authorities before election, preparation of election booths and creating a favourable physical environment for free and fair voting. Security during elections includes the security of voters in queue inside the booths or outside, of the election authorities (ROs, POs and other officials) deputed to polling stations, of election materials and others. In the post-election phase, the security personnel have to secure the ballot boxes while carrying them to the district headquarters from the booths (in case of parliamentary elections) and during the counting phase, and also to provide security to the agents and election authorities till the final declaration of results. The current security system/ personnel can be grouped into four: (1) regular security mechanism; (2) mobile security; (3) striking force; and (4) aerial security based upon conditions in the district and the security and strategic policy adopted at the central level. The regular security system operates as part of the District Security Committee (DSC) which plays a key role in the security of the entire district.

Under the Local Administration Act, 1971 (clause 6.7), the DSC includes the CDO as the chairman, the Local Chief of the Royal Nepalese Army, the Chief of the District Police Office and the Local Chief of the Armed Police as members, and the Chief of the District Office of National Investigation Department as the member-secretary.[46] The regular security personnel operate in all the three phases mentioned earlier. They have also to provide security to the candidates before elections or during their campaigning phase if they request for it and ensure the overall security of the polling booths, polling authorities and materials in all the three phases. The mobile force operates as a reserve force outside the polling stations for security support to the existing regular security personnel who serve/operate outside the booth and are entrusted to protect the voters in the queues inside the booth and outside. According to the current practice, a mobile force generally has to provide security to nearly 4 to 5 polling stations depending upon the situation of the booths in the constituency. They have to play a key role in preparing a favourable environment for free and fair elections. Nearly 3 to 4 mobile forces are kept within one constituency depending upon the situation and the security and strategy/policies adopted at the central level. The striking force, generally two in one constituency depending upon the situation, is to support the mobile force and is always kept ready for any sort of possible disturbance in the constituency. As this force operates in disguise and is kept secret, the people have no idea about it. The aerial security/patrolling was used in some rare districts where the probability of ballot box looting by the Maoists on the way was higher and hence the ballot boxes were transported from the booths to the district headquarters by helicopters. There is also provision for air patrolling of the booths by the army, which are important from the security point of view.

In the 1999 polls, a total of 51,399 police security personnel (25,412 in the first phase and 25,987 in the second phase), 6,721 mobile army and 16,032 regular/permanent army were mobilized in the polling stations. In the first phase, a police force of 16,739 personnel from their own districts was deputed to the booths and 8,673 police personnel were brought from other districts. In the second phase 17,726 police personnel were deputed and the needed additional 8,251 personnel were brought from other districts. A total of 16,924 police personnel (8,673 in the first phase and 8,251 in the second phase) were brought from other districts.[47]

From the security point of view, the election booths, as per the strategy and criteria fixed and accepted at the central level, are categorized into three groups: extremely sensitive, sensitive and ordinary booths and the security personnel are deputed according to the sensitivity requirements. Generally, 15 security personnel are deputed in the extreme sensitive booths, nine in less sensitive and seven in ordinary booths. These personnel work under the guidance of one government official, mostly from the CDO office, and have to secure a written order from the concerned authority or whosoever is authorized by the CDO to give such an order before firing. But in practice, sometimes controversies develop when the police authorities fire and kill people after receiving only an oral order from the concerned authority and when the latter refuses to acknowledge that he had given such an order. This tendency places the police authorities in a false position, which is a common occurence in Nepal.

In the extreme sensitive booths in the Tarai districts like Rautahat where home-made bombs are blasted to terrorize the voters of opposition political parties, even 28 security personnel cannot provide protection to the booth. The number of such personnel, thus, depends on the situation of the booth and the strategy worked out at the central level.

The national level security and strategic policies (while determining the sensitivity of the districts, constituencies and booths and the number of security personnel to be deputed there) are framed at the central level, which are communicated to the concerned district offices (e.g. office of the CDO, police, district office of the National Investigation Department) which have to implement them. The CDO and the in-charge of the police, thus, play key roles in maintaining the security of the district but the police authorities (SP, DSP) have to work under the guidance of the CDO.

As in earlier elections, the army in the 1999 polls had not entered the operational level of facing the public directly (in the booths) but had participated in the mobile and the striking activities including aerial security (particularly transporting the ballot boxes from the Maoist affected booths to the district headquarters in the western hill districts). The army thus operated in the district, in its own way co-ordinating with the District Security Committee (DSC) and inspecting the general security policy in the district.

The observation of elections in present-day South Asia and the world has been a regular phenomenon and the current electoral laws of Nepal have made the necessary legal provisions. In order to supervise and observe elections, Clause 5 of the Election Commission Act, 1990, mentions the appointment of observers by the ECN. The code of conduct and policies regarding observers were accepted in 1999. In the 1999 polls, one international and six national observation teams/agencies had observed the elections which had been certified effective and impartial: 1,493 observers in the first phase and 1,521 in the second phase had observed the elections. The logistics and coordination work for this was handled by the UNDP at the request of the ECN.[48] These observers had taken detailed information about the elections.

The post-election management includes the security of ballot boxes, counting of votes, final declaration of election results, post-poll appraisal by the ECN, management of election offenses, punishment, and the Election Tribunal. Under the current laws, as soon as all the ballot boxes in the district headquarters are collected from all the booths/constituencies, the ROs and POs fix the date for counting of votes as per the instruction of the ECN and begin counting according to the electoral laws (in the presence of candidates and their agents). Soon after the voting is completed, the ballot boxes in the parliamentary elections are taken to the district headquarters. In the Maoist affected areas, for fear of being looted, ballot boxes are transported to the headquarters by helicopter secured by military (aerial security is provided to them). In case of equal votes between two candidates, the POs/ROs decide by lottery (clause 66) and a person who wins an election through lottery is deemed as having one more vote than his nearest rival.

The declaration of final election results is the most important issue in this direction. Under the current practice, the election results are made public as soon as the counting of votes of one constituency is complete. This information is communicated immediately to the ECN through wireless sets, tele-faxes and telephone according to the communication facilities available in the district headquarters. The ECN usually disseminates or broadcasts election results through the electronic media (television, radio) and later publishes through the government controlled print media (Gorkhapatra/Rising Nepal) and its own regular publications (e.g. *House of Representatives Election, 1999 Results*). After the final declaration of election results, post-poll appraisal workshops, meetings and consultations are organized by the ECN where the ROs and POs effectively participate and express their views and opinions regarding improving rules, regulations, management and security of polling booths and effective implementation of the code of conduct. During the last few years, the election commissioners, particularly the Chief election commissioner himself, had effectively participated in brainstorming discussions regarding electoral reforms both organized by the ECN itself and other non-governmental forums such as NCCS. But due to many technical, non-technical and financial constraints, the outcome and the recommendations put forward by election experts were not implemented towards reforming the elections.

Challenges and Problems

Practically a number of challenges and problems have been experienced and faced during three parliamentary and two local elections. And if these challenges remain unsolved or unmanaged, they may become more acute in the future. Therefore, in order to overcome/solve and minimize them and strengthen the process of democratization, it is essential to identify them clearly. On the basis of information collected from personal interviews in five districts with personalities from various walks of life, from findings of the questionnaires, Nepal's experiences in elections in the post-1990 period and from facts provided by the ECN, from the opinions of political parties and candidates, issues raised by the media and academia and the burning issues during elections, the following problems came sharply into focus.

- Currently, the ECN faces a number of challenges in holding of free and fair elections. The temptation of conducting elections for almost all the political parties while they are in power has seriously questioned the impartiality and fairness of elections so far conducted. Reports of electoral rigging and malpractices (conducted both by the government and by the opposition) published by various Human Rights Groups and Election Observation Teams and the re-election of defeated candidate in Nuwakot have weakened the base of legitimacy. A number of difficulties and problems in holding free and fair elections are identified by the commissioners themselves in different public forums. Stress has been given to reforms in existing electoral laws, in consolidation of Election Commission of Nepal itself, and in the Election Code of conduct. The Election Commission of Nepal cannot act as an impartial and efficient body to conduct elections in a free, fair and impartial manner until it is completely independent of HMG in matters of law, money and personnel.[49] Political parties have also raised this issue through a constitutional body: the Commission is handicapped to discharge its functions effectively. The composition of the Election Commission and the quality of members, who are former bureaucrats, is fifty. Even after their term expires, some of them are appointed to political and diplomatic posts by the government. So, they tend to be loyal to the government due to favours dispensed on them.
- A number of problems have also been pointed out by the political parties and election experts in the field of the management of electoral laws. They stress that the current legal enactments and provisions are inadequate, impractical and controversial. Thus, they are not enough to create a favourable environment for free and fair elections. They point out that the subjects like peace and security, election crimes, activities of political parties, and the election observers have not been legally regulated nor are they brought under the area of law. Moreover, the Election Code of Conduct 1996,

prepared by the ECN in consultation with HMG and the political parties, to conduct elections in a healthy manner, is expected to be morally binding on the government, political parties and candidates. Such expectation contrasts with the regular violation of such codes during the elections.

- The present electoral rolls suffer from a number of problems. There is no basis for the identification of voters while preparing voters' list. The voters' list so far prepared by the secretary of the VDC has a number of mistakes, both technical and intentional. Technical mistakes include printing and editing errors (e.g. incorrect names especially in the first and the last one). The intentional mistakes, among other things, include the political biases of the secretary in the preparation of voters' list or non-registration of voters of opposition parties and registration of the names of underage persons below the age of eighteen. As these secretaries easily come under the direct influence of powerful local leaders and authorities, the manifold problems remain multiplied. Practically names of the deceased, migrants or qualified voters continue to be in the list. As most of the people in the remote villages are illiterate and have no knowledge about voters' list, claims and protests become almost meaningless. Moreover, the ECN has rarely reviewed the final rolls despite errors being detected.

- The introduction of the system of VICs had played an important role in conducting elections in a free and fair manner. Improvements have also been seen in the areas of polling station management, security arrangement and process of voting in those areas where the VICs were introduced. But even in those constituencies, a lot of errors and weaknesses (technical and intentional) have been found. The irregularities conducted by the authorities further created problems in the distribution of VICs. As the VICs were issued to those voters whose names were registered in the voters' list, the preparation of the electoral rolls was itself very important in this direction. Under the present system, even underage voters and foreigners receiving these cards cannot be barred from voting in the election. The seeds of the controversies, thus, were sown with the preparation of the electoral rolls itself. Moreover, the process for the distribution of cards so far experienced is not simplified and well managed. The VICs in almost all the constituencies were distributed in a hurry and the photos for the cards were taken in haste, creating a number of problems including mistakes in the names (especially in the first and last one), non-identification of photos, placement of wrong photos (male photos in the cards of females or vice versa), non-matching of names and pictures. A lot of people could not receive cards in time and could not cast their votes in the polls. Moreover, a person has also received more than one card from various constituencies due to the phase-wise distribution of cards. Moreover, cards were also purchased by the candidates a day before the elections and the voters of the opposition parties and opponents were barred from voting in the booths.

- Electoral laws, rules and norms regarding the selection of booths had been violated in different elections. Election booths in the 1999 polls were also placed in private lands and gardens in Rautahat district.[50] The basis for booth-selection, as some political parties believed, was not scientific and practical. In some constituencies, as in Baitadi-1, voters have to walk nearly 7 to 10 km from their homes to go to the booths, which have naturally caused hardships. Thus, the management of the booths by the ECN has to be reviewed in future for minimizing their hardships.

- The reduction of polling stations especially in the western hill districts have become a challenging and controversial issue among the principal political parties of Nepal. Two views, however, were expressed; first, it would be more wise to properly manage the existing booths than to increase them. Increase of booth creates more problems including that of peace and security and is not a solution for the existing problems. A favourable environment for free and fair elections could be created only in manageable booths. The election authorities deputed to the booth should not take shelter with the local influential parties or leader if the law and order is in place. Second, the reduction of the polling stations, as political parties like the CPN-UML believed, is strategically and politically calculated. It has created problems for the old, the sick and the handicapped.

- The management of manpower in the electoral booths is gradually becoming more challenging for the concerned authorities. Political parties have repeatedly stressed that the basis for the selection of CROs, ROs, POs and officials has not been scientific and systematic. The extreme polarization of civil servants along party lines has raised a serious question regarding the impartiality of elections. Such polarized personnel, who work to secure more votes in favour of a political party of their taste, have been found involved in various election crimes and malpractices including among other things, the distribution of ballot papers without signatures, hiding of ballot papers in their bodies (including in pockets, caps and socks), declaring valid votes invalid and vice versa, placement of the *Swastik* symbol on the uncovered plastic ink pad. Though the parliamentary elections are conducted by the judges, the civil servants are placed in the booths or the officials to be deputed in the booths are selected by the CDOs on the basis of political colour under pressure of the government. The CDOs, who are under the Home Ministry, generally follow the orders of their administrative and political bosses (secretary and high ranking administrative officials and minister). Such tendencies have invariably found in all governments regardless of parties. Its example was the 1997 local elections influenced by the then home minister, an UML leader.

- The violation of codes of conduct by all parties particularly by the big ones is a normal practice. The laws, rules and regulations alone, however, are not enough to regulate/ regularize the behaviour of political parties, candidates, concerned authorities and persons. The non-observance of election codes of conduct by the political parties in most cases remain unpunished by law. Only the weak candidates are penalized. Candidates frankly admit that they had spent huge amounts of money, crossing the limit fixed by the Code of Conduct. In order to utilize the facilities given to a candidate by the election code of conduct, the bigger parties use dummy candidates to harass their rivals. The government has misused the power, resource and authority in getting more votes in favour of the party in power. Ministers provide financial allurement. In Rautahat by-election alone, held in 2000, eighteen ministers and fifty-one MPs of the NC had openly violated the norms and codes of conduct.[51]

- The problem of maintaining law and order and security in the electoral booths has become more challenging for the security personnel. The work of the security personnel mobilized in the booths in the remote districts starts from the day the Polling Officers and ROs receive election materials from the ECN. As the security forces have to operate within the general security plan and in close cooperation with the election authorities in the booth in particular and the people in general, they have to become politically/administratively neutral, and abide by certain behavioural and moral rules which include, among other things, not accepting free food and lodging and not residing in disputed places/houses (e.g. the house of the candidates). The crisis management in election booths largely depends on the nature, character, personality and socialization of the security officials. The rational, low tempered, tolerant and determined officials take appropriate decisions. Their activities in crisis management in booths include scolding the wrong doers, blank firing to create fear among them, firing and even killing those who create terror in the booths. With the growing influence of the Maoist activities, particularly in the western hill districts, the country had witnessed a sharply deteriorating security environment.

The current practice of providing security by the election authorities from district headquarters and to their respective polling stations, security of individual candidates throughout the campaign period, and most important of all, creation of a sense of security among the voters by assuring them safe passage up to the polling stations and making them vote in a free and fearless manner were other equally important challenges to the ECN. In order to meet the security challenges, the ECN had held discussions with the commander-in-chief of the Royal Nepalese Army and directed the government even to depute army personnel in the polling stations if the number of police force became insufficient to provide essential security in the booths. As the ECN thought the security of the voters, candidates and poll officials were of paramount importance, it decided to conduct election in two phases.[52] Particularly in most border districts/towns of Terai (Rautahat), the monitoring of polling centres by the security personnel has become the most complicated job. Polling generally is peaceful and smooth till 3 o' clock and most political parties try to bring their committed voters to the booths before this time. But the situation becomes tense when one of the competing parties guesses that it is losing ground in the particular booth or its position is becoming weaker without any committed votes. Then it tries to disturb and frighten the voters by blasting small home-made bombs near the booth. As the voting gets disturbed, the polling officer has no option except to put up a notice stating that the voting has been cancelled until further notice. In such cases, the police cannot do much in helping to conduct the elections smoothly and peacefully.[53]

- Controversies mostly surface during in counting when the agents of two parties fight with the election authorities pressurizing them to declare the invalid votes valid and *vice versa*. The election authorities are also assailed by the political parties for favouring some candidates. The agents of dummy candidates also create unnecessary problems, disturbing the counting process and adding fuel to fire. The bigger parties, according to their capacity, try to politicize the counting process. Controversies in booths also take place when votes are found without the signatures of the ROs and POs; *Swastik* symbol fixed in inappropriate places; votes polled outside the ballot boxes; use of thumb before the name of the candidate and votes polled without *Swastik* symbol.
- Though the 1999 polls had been observed by national and international agencies, and other I/NGOs, they had visited only those areas where there were metalled roads or highways. These observers, even though they were requested to visit the extremely sensitive booths, had not dared to do so. They had reported that elections had been held in a peaceful manner even though the bombs had been blasted and elections had been postponed there.[54] As they had not visited the remote parts, their report was undoubtedly unrepresentative, biased, one-sided, impractical, inaccurate and untrue.[55] Due to the extreme polarization of observers on political grounds (as most of the Human Rights and Election observation groups are affiliated with one or the other of the political parties of

Nepal), the observation had not been politically neutral and impartial. Moreover, most of these observation teams had not submitted their reports to the concerned authorities. These observers had also openly violated their codes of conduct in 1999 and no action had been taken against them.[56]

Recommendations

In order to strengthen the process of democratization, it is essential to recommend appropriate measures for avoiding problems in election management. On the basis of information data collected from the questionnaires and personal interviews, and the issues raised by media and academia, the following recommendations can be put forth:

- It is essential to strengthen and consolidate the ECN in matters of law, money and personnel to reform the electoral process and electoral laws. Restriction on appointment of commissioners in diplomatic and political/constitutional posts after the expiration of their terms should be encouraged. It is better if peace, security, election crimes, activities of political parties and election observers, and code of conduct are brought under law.

It is also essential to prepare, update and publish the electoral rolls impartially, independently and practically. For this, the preparation of the voters' list and the identification of voters must be done on valid grounds, with the concerned authorities correcting both the technical and intentional mistakes in time to avoid repetitions. Names of deceased, migrated or disqualified voters must be removed from the voters' list. The ward office of the municipality and secretary of the VDC must act impartially and remain politically neutral. The distribution of voters' ID cards, by and large, has played a positive role in minimizing the unfair means in the elections. Though many technical and intentional mistakes have appeared in the initial phase, they can be corrected or reformed gradually in the future. Distribution of ID cards be made simplified and the card system introduced in all the constituencies simultaneously so that a person may not take additional cards from other constituencies. The determination or fixing of the booths during elections, particularly in the Terai, has become a subject of controversy among the voters and ECN authorities. It would be better to fix the booths on a permanent basis by the ECN itself after a detailed study of the constituency so that the scope for conflicts in the determination of booths might be reduced or eliminated forever. The acceptance of a code of conduct in the 1999 elections by the political parties, candidates and the government, in comparison with earlier elections, at least in theory, is definitely an important move in the direction of holding free and fair elections. But these codes need to be strictly implemented. The dummy candidates can be discouraged from becoming candidates in elections, and accordingly, the amount of deposit must be fixed at NRs. 1,000. Power and resources should not be misused and parties and candidates must abide by these rules. If the government, the ECN, all political parties and candidates come to a consensus regarding the observance of election rules the election expenses of candidates would gradually and automatically be reduced. The use of vehicles with Indian plates during elections, particularly in the border towns of Terai, has to be strictly discouraged. Political neutrality and impartiality on the part of the election officials in booths is another important prerequisite for making elections competitive, free and fair.

- Rigging of elections in Nepal can be minimized through mumerous measures including the launching of long-term socio-cultural, economic and politico-administrative awareness. The representation of indigenous/minorities or backward communities in the Upper House, as some of the respondents, particularly from the lower strata show it, is partially a solution to the existing problems. If the political parties maintain their discipline, develop the mechanisms and follow the principles laid down by the election code of conduct, elections can be held in a free and fair manner. Thus, corruption, misappropriation of funds and rigging could be reduced to some extent. As the ineffective implementation of election codes of conduct is the principal reason for rigging, they have to be effectively and strictly implemented. The respondents recommended various measures to reduce the state of rigging in elections (see Table 2.4). The introduction of voters ID cards in all the constituencies (58.8 per cent), abiding by election code of conduct (35.8 per cent), impartiality of police

TABLE 2.4: RECOMMENDATIONS TO MINIMIZE RIGGING

(Total number of respondents: 500
% based on multiple responses)

Variables	Total		Area %		Party Members %		Sex %	
	No.	%	Rural	Urban	Yes	No	Female	Male
Voters' list must be based on fact	151	30.2	27.1	42.6	29.4	30.6	27.0	31.2
Election commission be strengthened	125	25	24.6	26.7	33.7	20.8	14.8	28.3
Effective implementation of election code of conduct	179	35.8	35.8	35.6	41.1	33.2	31.1	37.3
Introduction of voters' identity cards in all constituencies	294	58.8	58.6	59.4	68.1	54.3	49.2	61.9
Effective management and security of polling centers	156	31.2	33.6	21.8	24.5	34.4	28.7	32.0
Discouragement to use of money and muscle power	227	45.4	45.4	45.5	44.8	45.7	42.6	46.3
Impartial use of police and administration	173	34.6	34.3	35.6	42.9	30.6	30.3	36.0
Others	15	3	2.0	6.9	3.7	2.7	1.6	3.4
Don't knows	29	58	6.0	5.0	1.2	2.7	1.6	3.4
Total			267.4	279.1	289.4	260.2	226.9	280.8

Note: The cross tabulation of data from different variables indicate that the introduction of voters ID Card would be one of the principal possible measures to introduce in future elections. This view was shared by many respondents from various political, socio-cultural, economic, educational, religious and ethnic background. This opinion was shared by respondents from ethnic occupation (94.1%); students (65.4%) and peasants (60.8%). The percentage was higher in party members (68.1%) than non-members (54.3%) and also higher in Hill Brahmins, Chhetri and others (72.8%) followed by Dalits (65.2%) and Newars (61.1%). The percentage for male was slightly higher (32%) than the female (28.7%); and higher in lower middle class in economic status (63.8%) followed by the rich (58.3%) and the higher middle class (51.2%).

and administrative authorities (34.6 per cent), security management of polling centre (31.2 per cent) and empowerment of the ECN (25 per cent) came in order of respective priority.

CONCLUSION

The ECN has so far conducted three parliamentary and two local elections in a free and fair manner, which has undoubtedly strengthened the process of democratization in the post-1990 Nepal. Numerous improvement measures have been introduced including the formation of a high power commission headed by the prime minister himself. The ECN itself has undertaken a number of corrective measures including the introduction of the voters identity card system in some constituencies on a phase-wise basis. Yet political parties do not seem to show their changed attitude towards implementing the reform agenda. The ECN has some problems with its relations with the government and the former claims that it sometimes does not get cooperation from the latter including in matters of budget, and nor respect for its order. The government is also charged with not respecting the election codes of conduct including disrespect shown to the orders of the ECN.

NOTES

1. Dieter Nohlen, *Elections and Electoral Systems* (Delhi: Macmillan India Ltd., 1996), pp. 2-4.
2. G.B. Powell, Jr., *Elections as Instruments of Democracy* (London: Yale University Press, 2000).
3. Nohlen, op. cit., pp. 1-25.
4. David Butler and Austin Ranney (eds.), *Electioneering: A Comparative Study of Continuity and Change* (Oxford: Clarendon Press, 1992), p. 1.
5. N.D. Palmer, *Elections and Political Development: The South Asian Experience* (Durham North Carolina: Duke University Press, 1995), pp. 1-19.
6. Nohlen, op. cit.
7. Ibid., p. 77.
8. Ibid., pp. 34-5.
9. Ibid., p. 78.
10. Ibid., p. 79.
11. Ibid., pp. 78-9.

12. David Robertson, *The Penguin Dictionary of Politics* (London: Penguin Books, 1993), p. 402.
13. Iain Mclean (ed.), *Oxford Concise Dictionary of Politics* (Oxford, New York, 1996), p. 409.
14. Nohlen, op. cit., p. 78.
15. Ibid., p. 78.
16. Robertson, op. cit., p. 402.
17. Ibid., p. 402.
18. Nohlen, op. cit., pp. 78-9.
19. Ibid., p. 84.
20. HMG/N Ministry of Law and Parliamentary Affairs, *The Constitution of the Kingdom of Nepal, 1990,* Kathmandu, 1992.
21. J.F.A. Soza, 'The Election System: The Election Commission: The Poll Arrangements', ICES, *Governance and the Electoral Process in Bangladesh* (Colombo: ICES, 1996), pp. 29-45. See, Dev Raj Dahal, 'Reforms in the Electoral Process of Nepal', in Devendra Raj Panday, Anand Aditya and Dev Raj Dahal, *Camparative Electoral Processes in South Asia* (Kathmandu: Nepal South Asia Centre, 1999, pp. 55-76
22. HMG/N Ministry of Law and Parliamentary Affairs, Law Management Committee, *The Constitution of the Kingdom of Nepal, 1990,* Kathmandu, 1992.
23. Ibid.
24. These acts include Electoral Constituency Delimitation Act, 1990; Member of House of Representatives Election Act, 1990 (and its amendment in 1996); Election Commission Act, 1990 (and its amendment in 1996); Election Offences and Punishment Act, 1990 (and its first amendment in 1996); Local Bodies (Election Process) Act, 1991; and Electoral Rolls Act, 1996 and Electoral Rolls Rules, 1996. ECN, *Electoral Process in Nepal* (Kathmandu, 1998), pp. 10-11.
25. These directives include the Elections for the Members of the House of Representatives Directions, 2055 vs; Electoral Process in Nepal, 1998; Electoral Reforms in Nepal, 2057 (2000) and other information bulletins (including those of election results).
26. HMG/N Ministry of Law and Parliamentary Affairs, *The Constitution of the Kingdom of Nepal, 1990,* Kathmandu, 1992
27. ECN, *Pratinidhi Sabha Sadasya Nirvachan, 2048* (Election for the Members of the HOR Results, 1991), Kathmandu: ECN, 1991.
28. HMG, Ministry of Law and Justice (MLJ), Law Books Management Committee (LBMC), *Pratinidhi Sabha Sadasya Nirvachan Ain, 2047* (Election for the Members of House of Representatives Act, 1990), (Kathmandu, Poush, 2055 vs).
29. According to the new provision two districts were allocated seven seats; one district 6 seats; 6 districts 5 seats; 9 districts four seats; 19 districts

3 seats; 24 districts 2 and 14 districts one each according to which seats in the Himalayan and Hill districts were reduced and districts of Tarai got more seats on the basis of the 1991 population census. In 1991, eleven Himalayan and Hill districts were to elect one MP each whereas in the 1994 redistricting the number of such districts were made 14. Two-member districts in 1991 were 26, which were reduced to 24 in 1994. Similarly 21 districts electing 3 MPs in 1991 were reduced to 19 in 1994.

30. ECN, *House of Representatives, Election 2056: Election Result*, Kathmandu: ECN, 2056.
31. ECN, *Electoral Process in Nepal* (Kathmandu: ECN, 1998), pp. 9-10.
32. Ibid., pp. 10-11
33. ECN, *House of Representatives Election 2056 (1999)*, Kathmandu, 1999, Reform no. 2.
34. ECN, *Electoral Process in Nepal* (Kathmandu, 1998), p. 17.
35. Ishwar Pokharel, 'Nirvachan Vyavasthapan Ka Bibidha Paksha, Tyaska Samasya Ra Sudhar' (Different Aspects of Election Management: Their Problems and Reforms), paper presented in a week-long seminar cum workshop 20-7 December 2000 at Dhulikhel, organized by Nepal Centre for Contemporary Studies (NCCS).
36. ECN, *House of Representatives Election 2056 Results* (Kathmandu, 1999), Challenge no. 4.
37. ECN, *Electoral Process in Nepal*, Kathmandu, 1998, p. 13.
38. Ibid., pp. 15-17
39. Ibid., p. 15.
40. Ibid., p. 17.
41. ECN, *Asthaniya Nikaya Nirvachan Nirdesika 2049* (Local Elections Directions, 1991), Kathmandu, ECN, 2049, pp. 28-33
42. Ibid., pp. 33-7
43. Pokharel, op. cit., p. 14.
44. Ibid., p. 15.
45. ECN, *The Election Code of Conduct, 2053 (1996)*, (Kathmandu: ECN, 1999), pp. 14-16.
46. Ashis Pustak Bhandar, *Aasthaniya Prasashan Ain, 2028* (Local Administration Act, 2028 vs) (including 4 Amendments by ordinance), Kathmandu, 2057 *vs*, p.18.
47. Pokharel, op. cit.
48. ECN, *House of Representatives Election, 2056*, (Kathmandu: ECN, 2056), Reform no. 5.
49. Bishnu Pratap Shah, 'Nirvachan Pranali ra Loktantra ko Sudridhikaran' (Electoral System and the Consolidation of Democracy), paper presented at a seminar on Politics of Consensus and Implementation of Constitution, organized by NCCS in cooperation with Fredrich Ebert Stifftung, 12 November 1998, (Kathmandu). 'Sambaidhanik Nikaya-haruko

Sudridhikaran, Samasya ra Samadhan' (Consolidation of Constitutional Organs: Problems and Solutions), paper presented at a seminar organized by National Democratic Institute (NDI), Kathmandu, 29 November 1998, 'Swachha ra Nispaksha Nirvachan Sudhar ka Prayasharu' (Attempts for Reforms for Free, Fair and Impartial Elections), paper presented in Biratnagar, organized by NCCS, Asadha 28: 1-3.

50. Laxminiya and Mahadev Patti booths in Rautahat-1 were within 1 km distance of Nepal-India border. Bishrampur and Ramauli Bagmati but elections are held for all the nine wards. Thakur Prasad Sharma, 'Pratinidhi Sabha Sadasys Nirvachan Ko Kanuni Ebam Vyabaharik Paksya' (Legal and Practical Aspect of Elections for Members of House of Representatives), paper submitted in a week long seminar cum workshop organized by NCCS on Electoral System and Research Methodology (Dhulikhel, 20-7 December 2000), pp. 1-13.
51. Thakur P. Sharma, op. cit., p. 8
52. Election Commission of Nepal (ECN), *House of Representatives Election 2056,* Kathmandu, 2056, Challenges and Problems, nos. 1 & 2.
53. Thakur P. Sharma, op. cit.
54. Ibid., p. 12.
55. Ishwar Pokharel, op. cit., pp. 18-19.
56. Thakur P. Sharma, op. cit., p. 12.

CHAPTER 3

Election and Governance

Krishna P. Khanal*

Governance in Nepal, today, is in crisis. When asked to recommend suggestions necessary for the consolidation of democracy, 494 (98.8 per cent) out of a sample of 500 respondents stated 'good governance and clean politics' as the most important factors to be considered. This is a reflection of the current state of governance and politics in Nepal from the perspective of the electorate. Elections continue to be held on a regular basis. But their effect on governance seems negligible. The electoral mandate has failed to produce vigour in the body politic. Politics has only been confined to the 'power agenda' and the politicians have failed to relate the 'purpose of power' beyond their narrower and even personal interests.[1] As a result, the institutions of governance have become incapable of fulfilling even their minimum functions and in responding to the emerging issues. The state's authority to exercise coercive power has been undermined. Its capacity to act as a deterrent against those who defy and violate the law and order has been significantly weakened. Its credibility to protect the life, liberty and property of the people is in question. Unless there are serious and sincere efforts to keep the process of governance on track, elections and constitutional provisions of democracy are likely to remain irrelevant to the larger masses. Some attempts are made here to probe into this situation in the context of elections and governance.

Election and Governance: Some Correlations

Democracy is a faith in the ability of ordinary people to govern themselves and shape their destiny. In a democracy government comes to power through a free and popular vote of the adult

*The author would like to acknowledge the cooperation of Bipul Neupane, Mahendra Mainali and Sucheta Pyakurel for collecting field data.

population. Voting is the most important function of the sovereign people in the process of governance. Each vote has equal weight and the decision is generally made on the basis of majority. Election, thus, constitutes a collective expression of the wishes of the people regarding who should govern them and which policies they would accord priority. It is through the electoral participation that the 'government by the people' is realized. Election is therefore considered as an 'instrument of democracy' and competitive elections provide the people an opportunity to have a say in the policy choices and 'an influence over the policy-makers'.[2]

When a democratic change is effected, the new polity has to pass through a transition, a process wherein the democratic norms, values and practices are expected to consolidate and stabilize. The transition is equally important to keep the governance on track. The new polity is likely to miss the opportunity of making the governance relevant with changes in the course of transition and consolidation. The debate and differences among the political forces are normal regarding various issues relating to the nature of the new state. But a minimum consensus among the forces supporting democracy is the basic necessity if the new dispensation is to perform. It requires 'all round loyalty to the democratic process itself, whatever its forms and particulars'.[3] A deep and continuous confrontation and ambivalence about democratic institutions among political parties is not conducive to democratic governance. Accommodation with the new institutions and processes of democracy is an essential condition.

Solely the provisions for the structural outlines and procedure do not characterize the functioning of a democratic political system. Much depends on the behavioural aspect of the political actors at the helms of affairs as well as the expansion of the critical mass of the concerned citizens. This is important because the essence of democratic government lies in being responsive to public wishes. In other words, democratic government needs to be capable of translating public opinion into public policies through established procedures and institutions. The experiments, particularly in the developing countries, have amply demonstrated that despite democratic political structures and provisions the behavioural aspects of the ruling elites are found least responsive to public wishes. This has made democratic consolidation and exercise vulnerable and fragile.

Election produces government based on the consent of the people. It complements three major principles of a democratic polity—representation, legitimacy and consent to govern. It also produces vigour in the polity that helps to sustain the system. Since democracy is the government by the people, election is the basic rule, because the people as a whole cannot be engaged in the government. They elect their representatives, and it is the government by the representatives. As far back as the seventeenth century, the British liberal thinker, John Locke, asserted the principle that government without the consent of the people is a tyranny and is subject to be overthrown. The American war of independence declared 'no taxation without representation'. Therefore, representation is the fundamental norm of the government by the people. Free and fair election based on the universal franchise of the adult population is an accepted basis of representation.

Similarly, election is also the means through which people express their consent to the government's policies and programmes. In modern democracies, election is not simply the selection of people to represent in various organs of the state, it is also the way of ascertaining people's consent to the policies and programmes that the succeeding government would like to take in the next couple of years. Thus, the consent of the ruled is the very basis of liberal democracy. And election constitutes the legitimate means of getting popular consent to the government. Election is considered to be the most explicit way of legitimizing the exercise of authority by the government of the day. An elected government exercises a wide-ranging authority, including the use of physical coercion as provided by law. The political party enjoying the support of the majority is mandated to run the government. The losing parties must accept the outcome and the status of minority parties and wait for the next elections. The minority parties constitute the legitimate opposition and watch the actions of the government.

The electoral process and electoral participation has a central role in a democratic political structure. Periodic elections are one of its regular features. Election is conducted under a set of rules, which may be part of the constitution or that of the substantial legislation. They are normally based on consensus and are followed as the basic rules of the game. It is through the election that an incumbent government's authority to initiate new policies, review old ones and implement them is thus derived form the popular mandate as expressed through the elections. The respective organs as set out in the constitution exercise the executive, legislative and judicial powers of the state.

The term 'governance' has been widely used in recent times, particularly in the development discourse. But it has always been the fundamental concern of the state, i.e. to create an order, a ruling among the populace in a given political society. Its ruling is binding and carries legitimacy to exercise coercive power against those who disobey it. The purpose is to maintain justice and order in the society. Such a notion of governance today may appear conventional, very limited and narrow to cover the role that the private citizens and the public sector require to play in the modern state and development process. The notion of governance has thus a wider meaning, particularly with reference to the distribution of political and economic power. The private citizen has been given prominent place in the management of the state's affairs. Human rights, deregulation, participation, market model, and the like have become new ingredients of state management. The market model of governance has become synonymous with democracy. The role of the state has been redefined as a catalyst and facilitator for private sector development.

The state possesses a wide range of authority, resources and influence, which should be exercised in a responsible way. The government is expected to maintain peace and security in the society, respect freedom of the people, pursue policies and programmes directly aimed at enhancing the well-being of the people, and so on. The rule of law is the basic format of governance. Besides, in democracy the government is accountable to the people through such structures as parliament and is expected to remain responsive to the public opinion. There may be various rules, constitutional and legal provisions and ways to make the government responsible for its action.

The recent concept of governance is donor-driven, and constituted aid conditionality. The World Bank, for the first time, used the terminology 'good governance' in 1989 in its report on

Sub-Saharan Africa. Since then bilateral and multilateral aid agencies and most of the major Western countries have stressed on the relationship of good governance with development.[4] The World Bank appears to have stressed only on the formative aspects. Whether a country is well governed or misgoverned depends on a number of things, viz., the regime-type, the way it exercises authority, its capacity to perform and so on. The governance as used in this study is based on 'competitive democratic politics' and election as major focus. Good governance essentially implies democratic governance in which the form of regime is civilian and democratic. The authority of the state is derived from the people's consent and popular participation, as reflected in the periodic elections based on adult franchise. The authority is exercised in an accountable and transparent way. Equality, freedom and rule of law are the basic norms of order-making and order-maintaining in the society.

Structures of Governance: An Overview

After the advent of democracy for the second time in 1990, Nepal has adopted a parliamentary system of government with the institution of constitutional monarchy. Multiparty democracy, parliamentary system of government, constitutional monarchy and independent judiciary are the basic structures of the state. The sovereign power of the state lies with the people. People are granted and guaranteed the fundamental rights and freedom. These include the right to equality, freedom of opinion and expression and assembly; the right to form unions and associations; the right to reside and move to any part of the country; access to information and free press; rights to property and education; rights against exploitation, preventive detention, exile, etc. The state derives authority and legitimacy from the people. It is a pluralist polity based on free and competitive elections.

Structures of governance may be described into two tiers—the central level and the local level. At the central level it consists of the parliament, the council of ministers often referred to as the cabinet, the bureaucracy and the judiciary. Although the monarchy does not have an independent role, as the constitutional head of the State and as a matter of procedure, the king's procedural role cannot be excluded while talking about the central structures of governance. At the local level there are institutions of local governance like the District Development Committee (DDC), the Municipality and the Village Development Committee (VDC). Besides, the Constitution also provides for such institutions as the Commission for the Investigation of Abuse of Authority (CIAA), the Auditor-General, the Public Service Commission, and the Election Commission. These bodies are responsible for ensuring a representative, accountable and transparent governance system based on the rule of law. The political parties and civil society are not the formal structures of the government. But they play a critical role in the process of governance, particularly as representing public opinion, providing channels of people's participation, and making the government accountable, transparent and responsive to the popular wishes.

Parliament is the principal representative institution of the people, which is not only involved in making legislation but also for scrutinizing the affairs of the government. The majority party in Pratinidhi Sabha, the lower house of parliament, forms the government. The cabinet system of government, of which the prime minister is the leader, holds the executive authority. The ministers are appointed on his recommendation and continue in office at his confidence. They are responsible for the administration of policies under their respective ministries. The specialized units of the civil service carry out the administration of the government.

However, these structures have yet to maintain coherent and consistent bahaviour that would complement the popular wishes as reflected in the periodic elections and contribute to the institutionalization of parliamentary democracy. Yet, the institutional behaviour of the Nepali polity over a period of more than a decade have exposed more incoherence and inconsistencies. Sometimes, even conflicting and competing roles were dominant. It has greatly affected the position of prime minister, as an institution, undermining its authority and capacity with severe implications for governance.

The relationship between the king and the prime minister could not take a proper shape consistent with the spirit of the Constitution and the parliamentary system of government. Normally, the king has abided by the provisions of the

Constitution. But instances are not lacking when the king had either ignored the spirit of the Constitution or wanted to create his own space. In January 1992, King Birendra, in an interview to a weekly, stated that he would like to 'know the people's problems at first hand in their own localities'.[5] Although he had specifically mentioned that he would abide by the spirit and provisions of the Constitution, he was not supposed to make statements and give advice to the political parties through public interviews. He had been meeting the political leaders expressing his concerns over a number of issues including even those related to day-to-day administration. His differences and reservation with the government had surfaced time and again.[6]

Since 1993 the king had used his discretion in the nomination of the members of the National Assembly. As per the constitutional provision, the king was supposed to abide by the recommendation of the prime minister while making such nominations.[7] Similarly, the authority of the prime minister had also been questioned and diluted on such issues as the dissolution of the House of Representatives, giving assent to the bill passed by the parliament. On these issues the king had independently sought opinion of the Supreme Court and pre-empted the normal process.

The use of the military, particularly to contain the Maoist violence, has become a controversial subject. The military in Nepal is traditionally considered to be the prerogative of the king. The Constitution, however, provides that the king shall 'operate and use' the Army on the recommendation of the National Defence Council. Although the council is headed by the prime minister, the government's efforts to mobilize the army in the Maoist strongholds had always been contested by the chief of army staff. There have been instances of the army chief expressing reservations and criticizing the government and political parties for their failure to ensure peace and security pushing the state 'towards dissolution'.[8] Such an attitude and remarks from the armed forces had given ample ground to question whether the army had made an independent assessment or taken the cue from the king. Even when the government took a decision to deploy the army in the Maoist-affected districts, particularly to rescue the police personnel then taken hostage by the Maoist, the army seemed to have played a dual role.

For such a state of affairs, it is not only the king but also the political leaders who are responsible. For the sake of their convenience, political leaders of both the ruling and the opposition camps had time and again sought the king's favour. They had failed to make a distinction between the monarchy as a force to reckon with. As a result, the role and influence of the monarchy in the national affairs has steadily grown with implications for the parliamentary framework of governance.

It is not only in relation to the monarchy, but also that the other institutions have not been able to evolve a coherent relationship. Over the years, the relationship between the government and the parliament, and particularly that between the government and the opposition, was not cordial. The rigidity from both sides had impeded a healthy growth of parliamentary practices. Similarly, the majority party in the parliament had time and again failed to redefine its relations with the prime minister and assure the electorate of a stable and efficient leadership. Particularly the Nepali Congress, which had the majority in Parliament, has been facing such problems from the very beginning.

Executive and Governance

The council of ministers headed by the prime minister holds the executive power of the country. The leadership of the prime minister is very vital to give a drive to governance in the country. The person who heads this institution, is mandated by the people to govern. Therefore, whoever is selected for the leadership of the majority party commands the mandate of the people as reflected in the elections. Moreover, the leadership is not only the product of a technical majority within the ruling party but a very crucial link between the electorate and the party. However, the practice in Nepal has diluted this tradition and is confined more to the arithmetic support from the members of parliament. As a result, unstable leadership and weak governance became a trend in Nepal.

A quick glance at the state of government over the past decade would reveal that the leadership has fast eroded and has been unstable, weak and inefficient. From June 1991, when the first elected government under the premiership of G.P. Koirala was formed, the leadership of the government has changed nine times. Under a hung parliament such changes were obvious. But even during the majority government led by the Nepali Congress (NC), changes took place four times because of intra-party schisms and personal rivalry. Interestingly, such changes were not prompted by issues.

It is relevant here to see how the electorate has evaluated the government and its performance. Table 3.1 will provide some clues to such an evaluation. And the NC, by virtue of being in power for a long time, has had the people's feelings directed against it. The CPN (UML) was in power as a minority government only for nine months.

Most respondents (71.6 per cent) stated that some of these governments were good and some bad. Such response seems to be natural since the respondents were not specifically asked to make a distinction between the governments as such. Although this answer precludes us from finding clues to explanation it gives an idea of how poorly the governments were judged by the electorate. Only 16 (3.2 per cent) out of the sample of 500 respondents stated that they were 'good and effective'. And 16 respondents, i.e. (18.1 per cent), said all of them were 'bad and corrupt'. Cross-tabbing the characteristics of the respondents also do not show much difference in the structure of the response. However, a large number of female (18.9 per cent) and non-party respondents (10.7 per cent) preferred to remain silent on this question.

TABLE 3.1: EVALUATION OF GOVERNMENT AT THE CENTRE AFTER 1990

Variables	Total		Area %		Sex %		Party Affiliation	
	No.	%	Urban	Rural	Female	Male	Member	Non-Member
All good and effective	16	-3.2	4.0	-3.4	2.5	-3.4	2.5	-3.6
All bad and corrupt	83	-16.6	21.8	-15.3	13.4	-17.7	13.5	-18.1
Some good and some bad	358	-71.6	71.3	-71.7	65.6	-73.5	79.8	-67.7
Don't know	43	-8.9	3.0	-10.0	18.9	-5.3	4.3	-10.7
Total (500)			101	-399	122	-378	163	-337

The above assessment of the people may also need to be explained against an overall observation of changes brought about after the restoration of democracy. People's expectations are raised when there is a major departure from one system to another. In Table 3.2 we see how the Nepali people have felt the changes.

TABLE 3.2: CHANGES OBSERVED AFTER RESTORATION OF DEMOCRACY

Variables	Total		Area %		Sex %		Party Affliation	
	No.	%	Rural	Urban	Male	Female	Mem-bers	Non-Mem-bers
Improvement in living standard								
Agree	111	22.2	21.8	23.8	20.4	27.9	20.9	22.8
Partly agree	169	33.8	36.1	24.8	33.6	34.4	38.0	31.8
Disagree	216	43.2	41.1	51.5	45.8	35.2	41.8	44.2
Don't know	4	0.8	1.0	0.0	0.3	2.5	0.0	1.2
Local development								
Agree	87	17.4	17.5	16.8	15.6	23.0	17.8	17.2
Partly agree	296	59.2	58.9	60.4	62.4	49.2	60.1	58.8
Disagree	115	23	23.3	21.8	22.0	26.2	22.1	23.4
Don't know	2	0.4	0.3	1.0	0.0	1.6	0.0	0.6
Increase in employment opportunity								
Agree	45	9.0	9.3	7.9	7.1	14.8	8.6	9.2
Partly agree	177	35.4	35.6	34.7	35.4	35.2	35.0	35.6
Disagree	259	51.8	51.4	53.5	55.8	39.3	55.2	50.1
Don't know	19	3.8	3.8	4.0	1.6	10.7	1.2	5.0
Decrease exploitation and untouchability								
Agree	162	32.4	34.6	23.8	33.3	29.5	28.2	34.4
Partly agree	205	41.0	40.1	44.6	41.0	41.0	42.9	40.1
Disagree	124	24.8	23.8	28.7	24.1	27.0	26.4	24.0
Don't know	9	1.8	1.5	3.0	1.6	2.5	2.5	1.5
Reduction of political and administrative corruption								
Agree	21	4.2	3.5	6.9	3.2	7.4	4.3	4.2
Partly agree	70	14.0	15.0	9.9	13.5	15.6	16.6	12.8
Disagree	358	71.6	70.9	74.3	74.9	61.5	71.8	71.5
Don't know	51	10.2	10.5	8.9	8.5	15.6	7.4	11.6
Total (500)			399	101	378	122	163	337

The composition of response in terms of such factors as area of residence, sex or party affiliation is not different and is almost close to the average per cent. There are only a few areas where the respondents' structures seem to have influenced the response. For instance, regarding the improvement of living standard, the opinion of the rural urban respondents differed by 10 per cent: 51.5 per cent of the urban respondents as against 41.1 per cent rural respondents disagree that there has been any improvement. On whether exploitation and social discrimination such as 'untouchability' has decreased, the urban-rural response varies by about 10 per cent. About 34.6 per cent rural respondents as against 23.8 per cent in the urban area believe that it has decreased. Compared to the urban area such discrimination and exploitation are more rampant in the rural areas. More positive response from the rural respondents indicates that the people have felt some positive changes in this regard. Similarly, 35.2 per cent female as against 45.8 male respondents disagree on the question of improvement of living standards. Likewise, the female respondents differ with their male counterparts on other issues of change. A closer look at the table makes it clear that the female section of the population has a more positive feeling about the changes brought about by democracy.

Parliament and Governance

Parliament, like most legislatures, is a law-making body. In a parliamentary system the government depends on the consent and confidence of parliament. Accountable and limited government constitutes the very fundamental elements of the parliamentary system. Governmental outputs flow from the process of parliament and derive legitimacy.[9] The governance in Nepal, as is usual with the parliamentary principles and practices, is very much influenced by and dependent on the relationship between the government and the political parties in parliament.

Parliament is expected to control the government and ensure its accountability through various means. Although the parliament has a wide-ranging role with respect to governance, there should be clear distinction between the executive authority of the government and the parliamentary scrutiny. The parliament debates on policies, programmes and budget wherein the members may support, criticize or reject it. Those particularly belonging to the opposition parties, seek clarification, criticize and propose amendments to the policies and programmes brought by the government. Failure to get parliamentary approval, particularly in such crucial motions like the annual budget and the policy statement, would mean the government has lost the confidence of parliament. On such instances, the government has either to resign or seek a fresh mandate from the people through elections. On one occasion in July 1994, the NC Government headed by Prime Minister G.P. Koirala failed to get such motion passed in the House of Representatives. The prime minister resigned and recommended mid-term elections.

Often the parliamentary business appears to be more ritualistic and procedural. Because the government commands a majority in the parliament, in most of its business it has no problem getting parliamentary endorsement. The debates on the floors of the parliament are generally based on party lines and the political parties exercise the whip in the voting. But there are many areas where the parliament can exert its influence in the functioning of the government. The Public Accounts Committee and the State Affairs Committee of the House of Representatives have been quite active in probing into the government business so as to make it more accountable and transparent. These committees have consistently drawn the attention of the government regarding irregularities particularly in civil service and financial affairs. The Public Accounts Committee, which is normally headed by a member of the opposition party in parliament, is engaged in investigating the financial deals of the government. The findings of the committee have disclosed many irregularities and deliberate misuse of the revenue in such deals. Besides, separate committees or joint committees may also be formed to deal with issues considered appropriate by parliament.

The relationship between the parliament and government, particularly with the committees, is not good. In fact, the parliamentary committees have had tried to check the government excesses and helped in ensuring accountability and transparency to some extent. However, the role of the committees has often been confusing and motivated by cheap populism and expediency. Their style of functioning has not been free of party politics, often 'reflecting that of the opposition vis-à-vis the government'.[10] There were instances of two committees being simultaneously involved in making inquiries on the same case. Unless there is enough ground, the parliamentary committees should not hold the files of government and ask to withhold the government business. They need to concentrate more on the systemic scrutiny of the government and legislative works than politicking. Moreover, the parliamentary committees have not yet established two-way communications with the government. Most of their reports are not communicated to the government in a systemic and proper format so that the government's response may categorically be sought to the recommendations made by the committee. Even in one of the most controversial cases like the Lauda scam, the PAC never made it clear for what specific reasons the government was involved.

The legislative works do not receive priority. Bills affecting the nation are often passed without debate. Members' interest in the parliamentary business is lacking. Commonality of views on certain bills also does not work. Most of the time, the two houses are preoccupied with political issues frequently causing tension between the treasury and the opposition. When they agree, the legislative agenda becomes a formality.

Recently the king had also sought the advice of the Supreme Court on Citizenship Act (Sixth Amendment) Bill passed by the parliament and sent to him for assent. The bill was first introduced in the House of Representatives, and the State Affairs Committee recommended it to the house with necessary proposal after clause-wise deliberation. The house later unanimously passed it as per the recommendation of the committee. This is the established practice of the legislative process. The bill was stamped as the money bill. But opposition parties changed their position when it was sent to the National Assembly for its consideration. The National Assembly, where the government was in a minority, refused even to deliberate on the bill and suggested improvement. Political parties in the Assembly alleged that the bill provided loopholes for citizenship to foreigners. However, the Lower House asserted its position and the bill with majority votes was sent to the king for assent. All the opposition parties, barring Nepal Sadbhavana Party, boycotted the house in order to mount their opposition to it from the streets.

The king, seeing the controversy, sought the advice of the Supreme Court for determining its constitutional validity. The court opined that section 2 of the bill was contrary to the Constitution.[11] Surprisingly, the king has not yet returned the bill to the house, neither accepting nor rejecting it.

The issue of Citizenship Amendment Bill raises many points in the relationship between the king, government and parliament. As per the constitutional provisions the king does not have the authority to reject any bill sent by parliament for his assent. He may return it to the house for reconsideration. But in the case of the money bill the king is bound to give his assent to it. Indeed, a bad precedent was started from the very beginning to stamp a bill as money bill without giving proper consideration to the criteria set out in the Constitution [Article 68 (3)]. However, the king's action did not escape the criticism that it did not set a good precedent.

Electorate's Expectation from MPs

It will be relevant here to judge the role of the parliament against what the people expected. In the following table the respondents' expectation from the members of parliament (MPs) can be seen.

Conventionally, the role of MPs is to control the government and make the quality of parliament more effective. But the response of the people as stated in Table 3.3 shows that they expect differently. Only 9.2 per cent and 14.8 per cent people in the sampled districts felt that the MPs should confine themselves to making parliament and government effective. Asked to choose three options from the given list, over 84 per cent respondents wanted to see their representatives concentrate on the development of their respective constituencies followed by 56.4 per cent who felt that MPs should recommend for job and others, and 55.4 per cent who felt they should concentrate on social reforms.

Cross-checking the respondents by area of residence, sex, party affiliation, however, suggest some interesting differences. More urban respondents (58.6 per cent) preferred recommendation for job areas than the rural respondents (47.5 per cent). Among the female respondents 63.1 per cent against 52.9 per cent of their male counterparts expected the MPs to devote themselves to social reforms. They also differed with their male counterparts

TABLE 3.3: EXPECTATION FROM MPS

Variables	Total		Area %		Sex %		Party Affliation	
	No.	%	Rural	Urban	Female	Male	Members	Non-Members
Constituency development	421	84.2	85.7	78.2	85.7	79.5	88.3	82.2
Social reforms	227	55.4	56.9	49.5	52.9	63.1	49.1	58.5
Uplift of disadvantaged sections	254	50.8	53.5	50.1	53.7	41.8	50.9	50.7
Make parliament effective	46	9.2	6.3	6.3	11.4	2.5	16.0	5.9
Make government effective	74	14.8	21.8	13.0	16.7	9.0	14.7	14.8
Recommendations for Job, etc.	282	56.4	47.5	58.6	59.3	47.5	55.2	57.0
Others	26	5.2	5.9	5.0	4.8	6.6	8.6	3.6
Nothing	13	2.6	3.0	2.5	1.9	4.9	1.2	3.3
Don't know	5	1.0	1.0	1.0	0.5	2.5	0.0	1.5
Total (500)			399	101	378	122	163	337

on such issues as the uplift of the disadvantaged community, making the parliament effective and give recommendations. Female priority on these issues is significantly lesser than that of the male population. Except on the issue of making parliament effective, the party affiliation of the respondents (16 per cent as against 5.9 per cent non-member favouring positively) did not mark any difference.

People's expectation as illustrated in the above table provides a clue to the popular perception of parliament and the role of MPs. Since the respondents were asked to select three items they expected most from the MP representing their respective constituencies, 84.2 per cent stated their priority for constituency development. Indeed, if we verify this type of response with the pattern of election campaign and commitment of the candidates, it is very natural. During the campaign each candidate tries to impress the voters that her/his number one priority would be the development of the constituency. None of the candidates would emphasize on such items as making the parliament and government effective. As a result, the MPs are compelled to be engaged more in constituency-related issues, including those of a personal nature, than in those related to policy and legislation.

Bureaucracy and Governance

Bureaucracy is the major arm of the government to execute its policies and programmes. It was expected that after the restoration of multiparty democracy, the Nepali bureaucracy would be reformed to meet the challenges of the times. Nepal's bureaucracy had long remained *patrimonial* and parochial rather than competitive and achievement-oriented. It had been based on family ties, loyalty to the ruling elites, favouritism, and social connections. After the restoration of democracy, it was expected that reforms would be initiated in the bureaucracy based on professionalism, political neutrality, efficiency, responsiveness, and clean and quick administrative services. But each government started its work with a reshuffle in the bureaucracy. Frequent reshuffling politicized the bureaucracy along party lines.

The Administrative Reform Commission (ARC) headed by Prime Minister G.P. Koirala in 1991 recommended changes in the organizational structure, simplification of procedure and work, decentralization and delegation of authority, management of public enterprises, reform in civil service, career development, and control of corruption. The ARC had suggested several measures to be undertaken in central ministries, such as reducing the number of ministries by integrating such functional areas that were similar in nature, and streamlining the number of employees by reducing approximately 25 per cent of the existing number.[12] A follow-up unit, comprising a small group of people who had worked in the commission, was constituted to expedite and monitor the implementation process. A new Civil Service Act passed by the parliament, aims at bringing stability in the civil service and enhancing political neutrality and professionalism.

Despite changes made for reform, the administration in general remained shaky, inefficient and least responsive to the public problems. The political connections of civil employees through various employees' organizations and other linkages continued and influenced the functioning of the administration.[13]

Whenever there is a change in the government, it has an immediate impact on the higher echelons of bureaucracy. Secretaries and other top-ranking officers were changed, transferred or kept idle in the reserve pool. Party preferences and priorities were also conspicuous in recruiting and changing the executives and managing boards of the public enterprises. A report of the State Affairs Committee of the House of Representatives reveals that a lot of administrative irregularities continue to plague the civil service in Nepal.[14]

People's Perception of Police and Administration at the Local Level

For the common people, the state and governance means the role and behaviour of the units of administration and police, because they are the primary level with which people have the first contact and concern with the state and the government. The local level administration in Nepal is still controlled by the central government. Posting of personnel in such units like the district administration, education office, revenue office, and police are very much influenced by political consideration.[15] Therefore, the role and performance of the government as a whole, including the leadership may, often, be reflected through these units of administration at the local level. In Table 3.4 people's perception of administration at the local level is shown.

Against the legacies of the authoritarian system and culture prevalent for a long time in the country, the questions asked to the respondents were quite relevant. Regarding such positive roles as cooperation, quick service and control of crime, the people rate the performance of the police and administration at the local level as very low. Only 29.1 per cent respondents found the police and the administrators role cooperative followed by 17.2 per cent to the control of crime and 14.7 per cent to quick service. The table also testifies how corruption and partisan politics have influenced governance in Nepal. The absolute majority (52.4 and 52.0 per cent) of the respondents said that bribery and partiality are instrumental in getting work done from the government at their level. Likewise, 37.8 per cent respondents believed that the administration, including the police, works on the basis of party recommendations. Ever since the restoration

TABLE 3.4: ROLE OF POLICE AND ADMINISTRATION AT THE LOCAL LEVEL

Variables	Total		Area %		Sex %		Party Affiliation	
	No.	%	Urban	Rural	Female	Male	Member	Non-Member
Cooperative	149	29.8	22.8	31.6	34.4	28.3	31.3	29.1
Quick service	71	14.2	14.9	14.0	13.1	14.6	14.7	13.9
Control of crime	82	16.4	17.8	16.0	15.6	16.7	14.7	17.2
On party recommendation	189	37.8	49.5	34.8	22.1	42.9	40.5	36.5
Bribe	262	52.4	55.4	51.6	37.7	57.1	55.8	50.7
Partiality	260	52.0	62.4	49.4	35.2	57.4	60.1	48.1
Chakari	130	26.0	28.7	25.3	24.6	26.5	27.6	25.2
Others	19	3.8	5.0	3.5	5.7	3.2	2.5	4.5
Don't know	43	8.6	2.0	10.3	17.2	5.2	4.3	10.7
Total			101	399	122	378	163	337

of multiparty democracy in the country in 1990, there has been a tradition that the political parties openly instruct the units of administration to give priority to the problems of those whom they recommend. If the administration ignores it, the police and administrative personnel are often threatened with bad consequences.

With regard to the variation of the response in terms of area, sex and party affiliation, this table is also not very different from the previous one. On this question too a large number of female respondents (17.2 per cent) preferred to respond, 'Don't know'. Their response however to such issues as bribery, *chakari* and party recommendation has been softer than that of their male counterparts.

Decentralization and Local Governance

Democracy is for empowering people for self-governance. Decentralization of power to local government aims at bringing people close to the governing process. The concept of local government is 'linked to the delivery of services and goods within certain territorial jurisdiction', which is possible only through decentralization of power and resources from the central state structure to the local units.[16]

The 1990 Constitution specifically mentioned that the responsibility of the state lies in maintaining in a 'condition suitable to enjoyment of the fruits of democracy through wider participation of the people in the governance of the country and by way of decentralization . . .' [Article 25(4)]. The institutions of local government in Nepal have thus found constitutional justification and are accordingly established through parliamentary legislation. Local bodies working basically as development-support agencies are mostly dependent on central grants and assistance.

The Village Development Committee (VDC), Municipality and District Development Committee (DDC) constitute the institutions of local governance. It is a two-layer system with VDCs and Municipalities operating at the bottom and DDCs as intermediary institutions between the central administration and the local government. These bodies are representative units of the people. VDCs and the Municipalities are elected through direct adult franchise and the DDCs by the vote of those elected to VDCs and Municipalities. The local bodies have a tenure of five years. HMG is authorized to suspend or dissolve them after conducting inquiries if they are found engaged in corruption, irregularities or in any other unlawful activities, and fresh election can be held immediately. Likewise, it can also extend their tenure by a maximum period of one year in special circumstances.

The first local election was held in May 1992 through which nearly fifty thousand elected representatives were recruited to the local governing bodies. All of them completed their full tenure in office without interference from the government. Donor agencies were involved in strengthening and capacity building of these units. Federation DDCs, VDCs and Municipalities were formed respectively which strengthened their bargaining capacity vis-à-vis the central government. Attempts have been make to increase financial resources as well as grants through local tax and levies.

In 1999, new Local Self-Government Act and Regulations have been enacted, which have significantly empowered the local bodies for participation in the development activities of their areas as well as local self-governance. It is an important step towards local self-governance. The implementation of decentralization and local self-governance is dependent on a number of factors. Political commitment expressed only through statements for public consumption is not likely to contribute to strengthening decentralization and local governance. Clarity of the concept and sincere dedication at the leadership level is required. A tendency to treat local bodies as the 'outpost' of the central power and 'capture' it by whatever means at hand during the elections persists among the major political parties. It has greatly undermined the spirit of local governance. Centralized party structures and strict polarization of society on party line have also worked as impediments to the effective implementation of the schemes related to decentralization and local governance.

People's Expectations from Local Representatives

There are about four thousands VDCs, 59 Municipalities and 75 DDCs, which constitute the units of local self-governance in Nepal. Every five years, people elect over 200,000 representatives to various units of these bodies. Citizens have direct relations with representatives, particularly at the ward level of the VDC or Municipality. There is provision for five representatives. Therefore, almost all the people of the concerned area know the representatives at this level. How the common people perceive their representatives is shown in Table 3.5.

The respondents have given highest weightage to the local development (92 per cent), followed by social reforms (60.1 per cent), uplift of the disadvantaged communities (42 per cent) and others. The respondents' background such as party affiliation, sex or the area of residence did not affect the choice. However, options like managing local disputes, recommendations for jobs, and making police and administration responsible are some differences owing to such factors as sex and party affiliation. The women respondents compared with male counterparts give lesser weightage to the role of the local body representatives on managing local disputes (22.1 per cent), recommendations for jobs, etc. (23.8 per cent), and making police and administration responsible (11.5 per cent) as against the male response of 33.6 per cent, 32.5 per cent and 23.3 per cent respectively. Party affiliation of respondents has also made some impact on their view: 38.7 per cent of respondents having affiliation with a political party wanted to see local representatives engaged in managing local disputes, while only 27 per cent among the non-member respondents favoured such involvement.

TABLE 3.5: EXPECTATIONS FROM LOCAL BODY REPRESENTATIVES

Variables	Total		Area %		Sex %		Party Affiliation	
	No.	%	Urban	Rural	Female	Male	Member	Non-Member
Local development	460	92.0	91.1	92.2	91.8	92.1	92.0	92.0
Social reforms	306	61.2	64.4	60.4	63.9	60.3	57.7	62.9
Uplift of disadvantaged	210	42.0	39.6	42.6	36.1	43.9	44.2	40.9
Management of local disputes	154	30.8	24.8	32.3	22.1	33.6	38.7	27.0
Recommendation for job, etc.	152	30.4	31.7	30.1	23.8	32.5	28.2	31.5
Making police and administration responsible	102	20.4	33.7	17.0	11.5	23.3	22.7	19.3
Others	6	1.2	3.0	4.8	9.0	2.9	4.3	4.5
Nothing	22	4.4	2.0	1.0	1.6	1.1	0.6	1.5
Don't know	2	0.4	0.0	0.5	1.6	0.0	0.0	0.6
Total (500)			101	399	122	378	163	337

Fulfilment of people's expectation from their central and local representatives can be seen in Table 3.6.

Fulfilment of the people's expectations from the elected bodies, including parliament, is by and large negative. Particularly in relation to Parliament, an absolute majority of the respondents (51.6 per cent) explicitly sated 'no'. Response to the same has been recorded as 34.8 per cent and 26.8 per cent for DDC and VDC/Municipality respectively. This suggests that parliament has yet to make a positive impact on the voters.

The people's response at the VDC/Municipality level is consistent. There is no significant difference in terms of area of residence, sex or party affiliation. However, the table reveals a marked difference on DDC and parliament: 12.9 per cent of DDC respondents said 'yes' against 4.5 per cent rural respondents. Female response to the DDC appears relatively soft compared to the male. One of the most distinct differences in response as seen from the table is that quite a large number of female respondents in DDC and the parliament prefer to say 'don't know'.

TABLE 3.6: FULFILMENT OF EXPECTATIONS FROM ELECTED BODIES

Variables	Response	Total %	Area %		Sex %		Party Affliation	
			Urban	Rural	Female	Male	Member	Non-Member
VDC/Municipality	Yes	20.6	18.8	21.1	17.2	21.7	20.9	20.5
	Partly	51.0	47.5	51.9	51.6	50.8	54.0	49.6
	No	26.8	31.7	25.6	25.4	27.2	25.2	27.6
	Don't know	1.6	2.0	1.5	5.7	0.3	0.0	2.4
DDC	Yes	6.2	12.9	4.5	7.4	5.8	5.5	6
	Partly	41.8	43.6	41.4	30.3	45.5	52.1	36.8
	No	34.8	28.7	36.3	27.9	37.0	36.2	34.1
	Don't know	17.2	14.9	17.8	34.4	11.6	6.1	22.6
Parliament	Yes	5.2	6.9	4.8	5.7	5.0	6.1	4.7
	Partly	29.4	30.7	29.1	19.7	32.5	28.8	29.7
	No	51.6	51.5	51.6	45.9	53.4	57.1	49.0
	Don't know	13.8	10.9	14.5	28.7	9.0	8.0	16.6
Total (500)			101	399	122	378	163	337

Discussions regarding government, parliament, bureaucracy, and local bodies suggest that there is a need to develop coherent policies, consensus and practices on matters relating to the overall processes of governance. Leadership capability of the government as well as opposition party appears to be poorly equipped to deal with various problems confronting the nation. They seem to ignore the fundamental norms of a parliamentary system while being engaged in the power game. There is need to build up consensus among the parties in parliament, particularly between the NC, the UML, and the RPP on crucial issues. Despite several positive aspects of the ongoing democratic exercise, there is a feeling among the people in general that both government and parties have been least relevant to basic issues concerning the people.

Judiciary and Governance

An independent judiciary with powers to ensure freedom of the people and rule of law is a fundamental ingredient of governance in a democracy. The basic and universal function of the judiciary is to resolve the disputes between the citizens and the state. The laws in force, judicial principles, and equity of the judge sitting in the tribunal are the basis to decide on disputes. The most original and primary justification of the state is to deliver justice to the people. It is on this very principle that the concept of the state has been founded and continues to rationalize its existence. The rule of law is the standard norm of democracy, which is possible only when judges are free to adjudicate laws independently of those who exercise the executive and legislative powers of the state. In a democracy the judiciary is regarded as the custodian of justice and protector of the rule of law. It is also entrusted with having to maintain the supremacy of the Constitution.

The role of the judiciary regarding governance has three basic dimensions: (a) protection of human rights, (b) judicial review, and (c) administration of justice. The 1990 Constitution has significantly widened the role and authority of the judiciary in Nepal. Unlike in the past, there exists no authority above the Constitution. The role of the judiciary, particularly the Supreme Court, has implications for the regime as well governance in general.

The decision of the judiciary particularly with regard to the protection of human rights may often cause inconveniences and embarrassments to the government. It is but natural because the judiciary is supposed to protect the people from the excesses of the state. The judiciary has given verdicts against the decision of the government, particularly those related to the dismissal of civil servants and imprisonment of the Maoist activists in custody. However, in these cases, the role of the judiciary is to see whether it has been done with due process of law. But its power to review the constitutionality of the executive's decision often invites political controversy. Some of the judgements, particularly those related to the 'Tanakpur' agreement and dissolution of the House of Representatives, were often criticized as 'judicial activism' vis-à-vis the executive. In the case of the Tanakpur agreement, the Supreme Court defined whether the agreement concluded by His Majesty's government with the Government of India was a treaty attracting the constitutional provision of parliamentary ratification. Against the position held by the government, the court declared that it was a treaty requiring parliamentary endorsement.

Its verdict in August 1995 reinstating the House of Representatives against the dissolution of the house by the king on the recommendation of Prime Minister Man Mohan Adhikari became politically most controversial. This decision had serious political implications for the exercise of Article 53(4) by the prime minister. No recommendation now would be valid if the House's confidence on the prime minister is in question. This is indeed no less than an amendment to the Constitution itself. The Supreme Court's interpretation of the Constitution in the 28 August verdict was based on the spirit and the basic structure of the system rather than the letter of the Constitution. Such an interpretation of the Constitution by the judiciary is consistent with the modern practices of judicial review. However, the conventional attitude is such that the judges sitting in the bench are not expected to guided by their own thinking. They should stick to the Constitution. For them the 28 August verdict reflected political concern *obiter dicta*.[17] Chief Justice Biswa Nath Upadhyaya, in an interview, denied that the majority verdict of the court was based on the law and the Constitution. The court's decision had not taken away the prime minister's power to recommend the dissolution of the house under Article 53(4).[18]

However, the role of the judiciary in the context of governance lies with its universal function of delivering justice. It is reported that every year about 100,000 law suits are being filed with the district courts, about 30,000 with appellate courts and about 27,000 with the Supreme Court. Out of them the district courts dispose of 46 per cent, the appellate courts 56 per cent and the Supreme Court only 25 per cent.[19] This information reveals how slow the Nepali people have been in getting justice from the courts. The courts have many shortcomings in terms of physical and financial resource support, which is often blamed the government. But the public perception of the administration of justice is not better than that of the bureaucracy. Despite the delay, which might be understood for obvious reasons, the judiciary in Nepal is not free from corruption. The use of money from the lower to the higher level to influence the administration of justice is no more a secret. The judiciary is protected from public criticism by the fear of 'contempt of court'. Often this has become a strong protection of judicial irregularities and corruption. The Judicial Council is empowered to initiate action, including the removal from office, against the judge on grounds of misbehaviour and incompetence. However, there has been no case of any action initiated against the judges.

In modern times there have been debates regarding the accountability of the judiciary. Although the contempt of court principle has put constraints on this debate it is argued that no institution can operate without being answerable to society. Judicial independence must match judicial accountability for failure, error and misconduct.[20] The principle of contempt of court should not be a taboo restraining healthy criticism of judiciary as an institution and its shortcomings.

Civil Society and Governance

Governance today attaches much importance to civil society. It is stressed that the participation of citizens through the civil society is considered as a prerequisite of good governance. Civil society, like governance, is a very broad concept. It includes all voluntary and professional organizations, trade unions, sports and cultural groups, social welfare and community organizations, advocacy groups, and the media.[21] Even private sector business groups are included in civil society. Viewed against such a concept, we may regard a wide range of groups working both in the urban and rural areas as constituting the civil society of Nepal. However, for the purposes of our study, we may concentrate only on those organizations, which are relevant to the overall concerns of governance.

The advocacy groups, research and professional organizations, human rights groups, and the media representing the broader community of intelligentsia are particularly concerned with democracy and the quality of governance, often termed as good governance. They are engaged in providing a broad forum for debates, discussions, advocacy, and even for lobbying and representation of cases to the concerned authorities. The international community as represented by the donor agencies joins these groups in the areas of their concerns. The major concerns of the civil society seem to be such issues as democracy, human rights, accountable and responsive government, transparency in financial deals, gender equality, electoral reforms, environmental pollution, functioning of political parties, etc. The media, due to its very nature, is the most forthcoming partner of civil society. The feelings and expressions of civil society are most frequently reflected in the media. The civil society in general and the media in particular put tremendous pressure on the government. Although there might be debate on its effect, no government is in a position to ignore it.

However, civil society in Nepal has to work with many constraints and limitations. It is very much dependent on international donor agencies for funds to carry out its business. A genuine voluntary initiative on the part of citizens' groups is also lacking. Beside, the constituents of civil society are very much politicized along party lines and often cause internal divisions and create factions, and lobbies of political parties. The media is also not free from partisan views. It is often very difficult to make the distinction whether it is disseminating objective information and representing the genuine opinion of the public, or working as the propaganda tool of partisan politics. These tendencies often dilute the very merit of the issues.

Problems of Governance

Enumerating the problems of governance that Nepal has currently been facing may be a long list. Every sector of public activity appears to be in disarray. The policies of the government seem to have lost direction and purpose. Even the normal business of public administration seems to be non-functioning. Politics has become corrupt, stagnant and confined only to a dirty power game. Political leaders have become too weak and too compromising. Moreover, their popularity and image have been fast eroding among the people, particularly the critical masses who influence public opinion. Therefore, when we talk of problems of governance, it is very difficult to know where to start. However, we will deal here with some of the prominent issues of governance that Nepal faces.

Respecting the Mandate

Nepal has been conducting elections to parliament and to the local bodies on a regular basis. Out of the three parliamentary elections held since 1991, the Nepali Congress had won the majority of seats in 1991 and 1999. But its hold on the popular votes had been around 37 per cent only. The 1994 elections produced a fractured mandate. None of the parties got a working majority in the house. The UML emerged as the largest party though it had polled less popular votes than the Nepali congress. Parliamentary elections have always been multi-cornered contests among the parties. The margin between the winner and the runner up has become increasingly closer in each election. In the 1991 elections, 79 candidates were elected with 50 per cent plus votes. In 1994 and 1999 this figure went down to 21 and 16 respectively. Similarly direct contest between the two principal candidates has decreased and multi-polar contests between three or more candidates have been on the increase. In the 1991 elections there was a direct contest between the two main candidates in more than 109 constituencies. This figure was drastically reduced to 48 in 1994, and relatively raised to 70 in the 1999 elections. The number of candidates winning with less than 30 per cent of votes is also increasing with each election. In the 1991 elections the number of such candidates was 11, which went up 17 and 21 in the 1994 and 1999 elections respectively. Moreover, the NC had always had the advantage due to the division of the left votes. This division was instrumental in the NC's getting a majority in the House of Representatives both in the 1991 and 1999 elctions.

Against this background the electoral victory of any party or candidate appears more technical than a sound popular support. In the context of the first-past-the-post system and the multi-polar contests among the parties, this is but natural. However, it has given ground to questions about the mandate with implications for governance. A typical characteristic of the 'adversary democracy', it had created a sharp divide between winners and losers, government and opposition, producing a negative effect on governance. It is always alleged that the elections are rigged and therefore do not reflect the genuine choices of the electorate. There is no doubt that many electoral malpractices persist, which need to be rectified. But in the given condition, the post-election behaviour of the political parties has adversely affected the spirit of the electoral mandate with serious implications for governance.

Many problems of the electoral process lie in the behavioural realm. For the political parties and candidates, electoral victory is the number one priority. They compromise every thing for it. Secondly, the financial and other physical support to the party has also become one of the most influential factors in the nomination of party candidates. There are other unwanted nexuses and linkages that work in determining party candidates. Even the prime minister (and president of the NC), G.P. Koirala, who was responsible for nominating his party's candidates, has admitted that smugglers have entered parliament by 'spending huge amounts of money and they want to earn money by ill-means, for which they need to become minister and the prime minister'.[22] The background of the candidates, thus, plays a very important role in keeping the election campaign clean and fair. Parties' commitment and sincerity of leaders have thus become crucial.

Respect for the mandate of the people along with the reforms is the essence of representative democracy. While keeping the momentum for reforms and improvements in the electoral system, there is also a need to develop the healthy tradition of respecting the mandate as expressed through the elections. The majority party should not be obstructed in governing the country as per the rules of parliament. The loser parties must wait for another election. Political parties contesting elections do not have the authority to distort or alter the role and status given by the people in the elections. Elections should work more as the instrument of strength in the governance process rather than as an impediment.

Instability of Government

It is often argued that compared to the presidential system, the parliamentary system is relatively unstable by its very nature. The government is created by the parliament and has to constantly rely on parliamentary support and confidence for its continuity. The government in this system is the product of the majority in the parliament and the moment it is short of majority it is certain to fall. The parliamentary system relies on such primary rules that first, the party in power should be ensured that its policies are enacted provided it follows the rules and procedures of parliament. Secondly, parties compete with each other to have control over the government not over the society.[23] The failure of political parties to reconcile to such principles create problems in Nepal.

Leadership and stability are two aspects much related to governance. Three reasons are worth noting in this respect: weak and uncommitted leadership, lacks of clarity of thought and corrupt power politics. The NC, which had called for the movement and provided leadership to it, had never thought of the post-movement scenario for transition and consolidation. Nor did the UML, which had emerged as the second-most important player in the politics of the country, make itself free from the hangover of the conventional Marxist-Leninist political ideology. The RPP, the third largest player in the Parliament had yet to earn credibility in the post-change politics. As a result, despite the comfortable majority in the parliament, the leadership of the government was frequently challenged within the party. The majority government of the NC in 1991 could not survive a full tenure. Failure to manage the relationship between the government and the party executive and to resolve the conflicts ultimately led to the fall of the NC government in 1994.[24]

The issue of stability became more acute in the second parliament following the mid-term polls in November 1994. This time the House of Representatives lacked a majority. The UML, which had emerged as the largest party in the house, instead of trying to have coalition with other parties to ensure the stability government, opted for a minority government of its own. When it was challenged by a vote of no-confidence in the house, it recommended the dissolution of the HOR and a mid-term poll within a period of six months. This move was foiled by the Supreme Court and the UML government was voted out by the parliament. The equation of the political parties in the house was such that no two political parties other than the NC, UML and RPP could make a majority in the house. The coalition between the NC and the UML was most unlikely since they were the major rivals for power. Therefore the coalition with RPP was vital for a party, i.e. the UML or the NC seeking to form the government. Besides, minor parties like the NSP, NWPP or even the individual MPs had become decisive factors in determining the fate of the government. This brought chronic instability in the government. From November 1994 to January 1999 before the dissolution of the HOR, Nepal had five prime ministers, heading seven different types of governments.

In this game of coalition making and breaking all the parties in the parliament faced a serious challenge of division and split. The UML, the largest party in the parliament, split. So did the RPP. The NC, by default became the largest party in the house. Now the NC had the advantage that each splinter group was eager to be partner in the government. Splinter groups were created to join for power. However, the split in the RPP became less relevant to bargaining politics. Thus, the NC was able to form its minority government. But for it too, it was equally risky to continue in power without including the other party in the government. After a few months, the NC inducted the breakaway group of the UML, called as the CPN (ML), into the government. But the two parties could not agree on the prime minister's preference to go for early polls. As a result, the ministers belonging to the ML resigned en bloc. However, the prime minister was able to reach at an understanding with the UML and the RPP on holding elections.

Proliferation of Corruption

Corruption is a major challenge to democracy in Nepal. All spheres of the state—judiciary, bureaucracy and other agencies of government—are full of corruption. It persists in various forms such as bribes, kickbacks, commissions and any other 'deviation from the formal rules of conduct' governing the actions of a person holding public authority with a motive to acquire' wealth, power or status'.[25] Corrupt practices and behaviour in bureaucratic and judicial institutions have been most common since quite a long time. But political corruption has become the most serious challenge, questioning the very credibility of democracy. Contrary to the belief that transition from an authoritarian regime to the democratic system would reduce corruption, the flow of illegitimate money 'up and down' the political network has been solidified.

Nepal is not an exception to such tendencies. Out of the sampled 500 respondents, 66.2 per cent people considered corruption as one of the major problems facing the country in the post-1990 period. Aside from the continuing problem of bureaucratic and judicial corruption, the nexus between politicians and business houses and other commission agents is evident. As a consequence, no political leader, whatever his past standing and respect has been able to save his prestige. Much interested in exercising their influence on the affairs of the government, they encourage corruption at all levels.

Corruption at the political level is both formal and informal. Many undue practices and incentives inducing politicians, especially the MPs to corruption and corrupt behaviour have been formalized in such ways as duty exemption to vehicle import, a perk in the name of constituency development and maintaining secretariat, and unchecked payment for so-called medical expenses. Unlimited grants of money have been made available to politicians and their relatives through the home ministry on the pretext of medical treatment. It had been alleged that the concerned minister or political party takes big amounts from the persons who are given political appointments or contracts especially in public enterprises. Political leaders' lifestyle has visibly become lavish beyond their legitimate income. Erosion of values in public life is faster and widespread which has created a negative impact on the people's psyche regarding the ongoing political experiment.

Party expenses in election campaigns in particular have increased for which political parties depend on donations offered by business groups. Party expenses are usually met with the money offered by the business groups who want favours in such deals as import facilities, commission through increase in the price of certain commodities, awarding of major development contract, etc. State-owned public enterprises are easy tools of the government for such purposes. Scandals involving an individual minister or even the prime minister have become a routine affair.

As the Minister of Agriculture, Shailaja Acharya said in 1992 that the commission network had been active in the HMG including her own ministry. She admitted before the House of Representatives in July 1992 that there had been corruption in the procurement of fertilizers and demanded an inquiry by the House. During the interim government, Jhal Nath Khanal of the CPN (UML), too admitted the existence of corruption in the Agricultural Input Corporation which had been solely engaged in deciding the procurement of fertilizers in Nepal.

Each government as a matter of principle and policy has

pledged to fight corruption. The ministers are asked to declare their assets soon after joining their ministries. A Special Police Department for anti-corruption drive is in existence but it seldom works. Ironically, the government received representatives of the Berlin-based Transparency International and asked suggestions for corruption control measures.[26] Yet, corruption has continued to thrive and each succeeding government seems to be involved in one scams or the other.

The Public Accounts Committee (PAC) of the House of Representatives monitors the government's financial policies and transactions. Besides, the Constitution has also created the Commission for Investigation of Abuse of Authority (CIAA), which is responsible for investigating abuse of authority by political and bureaucratic officials or by anybody holding public office. The PAC has conducted inquiries on several issues mostly related to scandals involving financial irregularities. In this process, it has also summoned the prime minister, ministers and other high-ranking officials. However, the work of the PAC has, in most cases been confined to seeking clarification from the concerned persons rather than issuing rulings to those found guilty. Its inquiries of Royal Nepal Airlines Corporation (RNAC), and other cases have remained inconclusive.

The CIAA has an extensive mandate to make inquiries into the abuse of authority by officials including the prime minister. It usually makes investigation based on the complaints received by it. In recent years its popularity has grown because of its initiation of legal procedures in the court involving the prime minister, ministers and secretaries. As a result, Padma Sundar Lawai, the Minister of Agriculture, had to resign in December 1996 in a case related to fertilizer import.[28] More recently, in a case involving the RNAC jet aircraft lease, it had demanded Rs. 50 million as a bail each from the ex-executive chairman and the board member. The concerned minister was also asked to submit his passport and not to leave Kathmandu valley without permission. Besides, it had also sought clarification from Prime Minister G.P. Koirala and made him alert. The opposition parties' charge against the prime minister's alleged involvement in the deal had gained ground. This created a great deal of political and moral pressure on the prime minister to step down.

Each financial deal of the government is generally tainted with corruption charges. Whether it is chemical fertilizer import, purchasing or taking on lease an aircraft, making contracts for development projects ranging from road maintenance to major hydropower plant, stories of commission and other forms of deals play a role. People in the higher echelons of decision making, either in politics or bureaucracy, are believed to have amassed wealth. Their ostentatious lifestyle is taken as evidence. How can the politicians spend millions of rupees to contest elections. Without substantial money, no parliamentary election can be contested. Although each leader of a major parties often raises the issue of corruption, each however knows that he/she cannot manage to get elected without substantial funds.

Law and Order

Protection of life and liberty is the minimum action expected by the people from any government. In post-1990 Nepal, maintaining law and order has become a challenging job. Now the Maoist violence has increased the threats to the life of citizens. The nexus between criminals and the police and administration is growing. People have difficulties in getting a response from the police and administration in time. Political cover-up of a crime has received prominence in the name of party cadre and organization. Taking advantage of the political nexus, criminals have been able to escape from judicial prosecution.

Political parties have frequently defied the law for political interests. Frequent use of *bandh* and strikes—*Nepal Bandha* (nationwide or partial shut down), *Mashal Julush* (torch procession), etc.—have been a routine affair affecting the life of people as well as harming national economic activities.

A survey conducted in 1996 revealed that over 80 per cent people felt that such agitational politics had created 'threat, insecurity and terror'. Over 87 per cent people were against it and suggested that the protest programme should be 'symbolic and dignified'.[28] Civil society and the media have time and again warned of the negative impact of such programmes on the health of the nation and appealed to refrain from it. The government's efficiency and capability is limited in preventing such frequent strikes. Though the people are disgusted with them, political parties which opt for such measures often take pride in organizing such bandhs. It seems that such extreme measures can hardly be popular contrary to the claim of success by the organizers.

The Maoist Problem

Starting with minor attacks on police posts and killings of the NC activists in the remote corners of the country in February 1996, Maoist violence today has become a major threat to the very existence of the political system. The Communist Party of Nepal (Maoist) was formed in February 1995 out of the breakaway group of the Communist Party (Unity Centre) with the decision of launching 'an armed people's war against the reactionary forces'. A year later it declared a 'people's war' with the objective of establishing 'a new people's republican state by overthrowing the reactionary state power through force'. The Maosists also declared that this alone was the 'path toward the liberation of the people'.[29]

The Maoist 'people's war' has not only survived over the period but has also grown both in space and influence. The present polity seems to have almost failed to contain them, both administratively and politically. Politically there exist differences of opinion among the political parties about the nature of this problem and strategies for a solution. The government also is not very consistent about this problem. Sometimes it considered the problem to be a terrorist one and wanted to deal it through administrative and legal measures. Sometimes, it has shown willingness to enter into a dialogue with them for resolving the problem through negotiation. Even within the ruling party the opinion differed between those in the government and others. The Maoists were able to take advantage of these differences and inconsistencies prevailing in the country.

Ever since this problem cropped up in February 1996 each succeeding government has made attempts to resolve the problems in its own way. For the first time, the RPP-UML coalition under Prime Minister Lokendra Bahadur Chand tried to probe into the nature of this problem instituting a commission headed by an UML MP, Prem Singh Dhami. The report of the Dhami Commission had, indeed, made an in-depth inquiry into the nature, organizational network, national and international linkage and the striking potential of the CPN(Maoist) and its 'people's war'. However, the government could not make any dent in the resolution of the problem. Its attempt to initiate a legislation to curb the violent and terrorist activities was strongly resisted by the opposition parties. The NC government under Prime Minister K.P. Bhattarai constituted a high-level committee under the convenorship of ex-Prime Minister Sher Bahadur Deuba to recommend measures for resolving the problems. The Deuba Committee, in addition to consultation with various political parties, established contacts with the CPN (Maoist) and made efforts to initiate a dialogue with them. The Deuba Committee, which had become a scapegoat due to intense fighting within the party, could not make any progress. Its report termed the Maoist insurgency as activities with 'political objectives' and urged the government to hold talks while strengthening the security apparatus.

The civil society groups also started showing serious concern over the growing problems of violence, and voluntarily initiated their efforts for negotiation. Padma Ratna Tuladhar, an ex-MP who had contacts with the Maoist leadership was able for the first time to bring the government and the Maoist togeter for an informal talk. The Deputy Prime Minister Ram Chandra Poudel held talks with a representative of the CPN (Maoist). However, even after meeting some of the preconditions that the Maoist had put forth, the government could not efficiently handle the affair and the Maoist backtracked from the talks. They suspected the government's commitment to the talks.

This has become more acute since the beginning of 2001. The Maoist had formed people's committees in the villages as well as at the district level, a parallel unit of local government, in their stronghold districts. In other areas they have been openly conducting rallies and mass meetings with sporadic events of attacks and killings. The government had been forced to withdraw from these areas and was very delicately confined to the district headquarters. The police posts had been attacked and blasted with loss of several lives. The police was found ill-trained and ill-equipped to deal with the guerilla techniques of the Maoist cadres. The government's attempt to make a separate legislation to deal with the problems had been foiled by the opposition. The creation of a separate paramilitary force or the use of the Royal Nepal Army also became controversial in political circles.

Now the government has established a separate armed police force through ordinance to this effect. The opposition parties have criticized it and demand its withdrawal. It will take time for this force to be fully equipped to deal with such an armed revolt. Deploying the military against the Maoist insurgency is left as the only available coercive means. However, this has raised several questions regarding the relationship between the government and the monarchy. The Constitution provides that the king will mobilize the army on the recommendation of National Defense Council headed by the prime minister. The government has introduced an 'Integrated Internal Security and Development Plan' in order to deal with this problem. However, top-ranking officers of the army, particularly the Chief of the Army Staff himself, had repeatedly put conditions on such deployment. He had demanded the 'lasting and continuous political commitment of all the political parties and the entire citizenry' if the army was to be involved in the internal security and development plan.[30] However, the government has finally been able to convince the king and the army to initiate the implementation of the Plan in the affected districts. But successive developments have shown that it was more a camouflage of the palace that in fact did not endorse the government's plan. Presumably, sensing the role of the palace and the army, Prime Minister G.P. Koirala resigned in August 2001.

In the given situation, the Maoist insurgency problem appears to be intractable due to lack of coordinated effort on the part of the state agencies. The king, who actually controls the military, appears reluctant to use the army. Unless there is full-fledged commitment and cooperation from the king, the army factor remains as elusive as ever before.

The government has also adopted a strategy for talks and negotiations to deal with this problem. For this purpose too, it needs to deal with strength. The wrangling between the government and the army will only help the Maoists to grow. It has already grown nationwide assuming characteristics of both a mass movement and a guerilla war. They have been able to establish contacts and build alliances with other forces as well. It is now a parallel state. The political forces who claim to have a popular base among the masses and who identify themselves with an open, free and plural polity have not been forthcoming with political offensives to face this challenge.

Conclusion

Foregoing discussions on the problems related to governance in Nepal make it clear that there is a need to address these issues seriously and with a long-term perspective. It is felt that the restoration of the process of 'transferring power' to the people is incomplete. There is need to review the eleven years' experiment for reorienting the polity suitably to match the spirit of the present Constitution and democratic governance. Much of today's crises of governance are related to the behaviour of political parties. The Constitution provides some key principles for regulating political parties. A comprehensive law to this effect can help to improve the functioning of political parties in the context of transparency and accountability. Political parties have yet to develop coherent policies, minimum consensus on matters affecting the nation and parliamentary democracy. Political parties also need to build their institutional and leadership capabilities to meet the changing aspirations of the people. There is also a need to build up consensus among the major political parties on broader issues of governance such as parliamentary accountability, the depoliticization of the bureaucracy and state-owned enterprises, major development agenda, providing clean and efficient administration, and major foreign policy issues particularly related to India such as security, water resources, and the like.

Despite several positive aspects of the ongoing democratic exercise, there is a feeling among the people that political parties have not been able to properly address the basic issues concerning governance and efficient administration for the country. As a result, violence in the name of 'people's war' aimed at overthrowing the existing state and establishing a 'Maoist' republican system has expanded its influence and presence. Although such violent politics is not likely to survive in an open political environment of today's Nepal, it has caused severe strains and has had destabilizing effect on the parliamentary politics.

Democracy has scope for self-correction. Political leaders too have realized that they need to reform the behaviour of political parties. However, they are still shy of making a decisive breakthrough. Public pressure for reforms is also growing. Although weak and divided on partisan political line, civil society is also asserting its role for improving the behaviour of political parties and members of parliament on its visible impact has been seen in certain policy measures.

NOTES

1. V.A. Pai Panadiker (ed.), *Problems of Governance in South Asia* (Delhi: Konark Publishers, 2000), p. xiii.
2. G. Bingham Powell, Jr., *Elections as Instruments of Democracy: Majoritarian and Proportional Visions* (New Haven: Yale Press, 2000).
3. Adrian Leftwich, 'Governance, Democracy and Development in Third World', *Third World Quarterly*, vol. 14, no. 3, 1993, pp. 605-24.
4. There have been extensive debates on the theme of good governance followed by a wide range of literatures. See, the World Bank, *Sub-Saharam Africa: From Crisis to Sustainable Growth* (1989), ibid., *Governance and Development* (1992). UNDP, *Public Sector Management, Governance an Sustainable Human Development* (1995). *IDS Bulletin* (Sussex), 24(1), 1993 and 26(3), 1995; Adrian Leftwich, op. cit. (1993) and Adrian Leftwich, 'Governance, the State and the Politics of Development', *Development and Change*, vol. 25, 1994, pp. 363-86.
5. *The Independent*, Kathmandu, 8 January 1992.
6. There are instances of the King making suggestions to the government on several issues such as political anomalies, economic decline, natural calamities, etc. 'Warning letters' were reportedly served twice to Prime Minister G.P. Koirala. See *Ravibaar* (Weekly), 6 September 1998. Likewise, the parliament had also received 'direction' containing notes on the issues such as legislating the party affairs, managing the elections and resolving the Maoist problem. *Himal Khabarpatrika* (Fortnightly), 14-2, March 2000, pp. 29-33.
7. Article 35(2) of the Constitution states, 'Except as otherwise expressly provided as to be exercised by His Majesty or at His discretion or on the recommendation of any institution or official, the powers of His Majesty under this Constitution shall be exercised upon the recommendation and advice, and with the consent of the Council of Ministers. Such recommendations, advice and consent shall be submitted through the prime minister. *The Constitution of the Kingdom of Nepal 2047 (1990)* (Kathmandu: Law Books Management Board, Ministry of Law, Justice and Parliamentary Affairs, HMG/Nepal, 1992).
8. The Chief of the Army Staff, Mr. Dharmapal Bar Singh Thapa reportedly made such comments in his farewell speech before the armed personnel. *The Ghatna ra Bichar*, 26 May 1999. Mr. Prajwal Shamsher Rana, who succeeded Mr. Thapa, had repeatedly stated that an all party consensus is needed if the army is to be deployed in the Maoist area. See *The Kantipur*, 21 April 2001.

9. David Judge, *The Parliamentary State* (London: Sage, 1993), p. 2.
10. Krishna P. Khanal, *Sansad ra Sarkarko Sambandha: Uttardayi Sarkarko Pratyabhutika Sandarvama Samitiharuko Bhumika* (Relationship between Parliament and Government: The Role of Committee in the Context of Providing Accountable Government). A paper presented at a seminar on the Role and Effectiveness of the Parliamentary Committees, organized by the State Affairs Committee of the House of Representatives in Kathmandu on 3 May 2000.
11. *The Gorkhapatra,* 26 April 2001.
12. *The Report of the Administration Reform Commission, 1992* (Kathmandu, 1992).
13. Interviews with the CDOs and Police Officers in sampled districts (15-30 January 2001).
14. *Reports of the State Affairs Committee* (House of Representatives), 1998.
15. In the interview, one of the CDOs of the sampled district stated that the administrative officials, including the police, were usually treated by the political leadership as their 'agents' (*Pokhara*), 15-30 January 2001.
16. Tulsi Narayan Shrestha, *Concept of Local Government and Decentralization,* (Kathmandu: Ratna Pustak Bhandar, 1996), p. 13.
17. Shiva Sigdel, *Nyayik Punarabalokan ra Sambidhanko Prastabana* (Judicial Review and the Preamble to the Constitution); Anup Raj Sharma (ed.), *Sambidhan sambndhi lekhharoko sangalo,* vol. 24 (Kathmandu: Nepal Law Society), 1996, pp. 25-35.
18. *The Rastra Pukar,* 6 September 1995.
19. The Chief Justice himself told this in a conference of the judges at Kathmandu, *The Rising Nepal,* 3 August 1999.
20. Mizanur Rahman, 'Governance and Judiciary', a paper presented at an International Seminar on Good Governance, Dhaka, 4-6 August 1998.
21. Local Government Division (Government of Bangladesh) and UNDP, International Seminar on Good Governance: A Concept Paper (Dhaka: 4-6 August 1998), p. 21.
22. *The Kathmandu Post,* 12 August 2000.
23. Allan Ware, *Citizens, Parties and the State: A Reappraisal* (Cambridge: Polity Press, 1987), pp. 185-90.
24. A group of MPs belonging to the NC, who were opposed to Prime Minister G.P. Koirala, abstained from the voting in the House of Representatives in a crucial government motion related to its policies. As a result, the government was defeated. Prime Minister Koirala immediately resigned and recommended the dissolution of the house two and half years before the expiry of its tenure and mid-term elections were held in November 1994.
25. J.S. Nye, 'Corruption and Political Development: A Cost-Benefit Analysis', *American Political Science Review,* vol. XI, no. 2, 1967.
26. *Rising Nepal,* 26 March 1996.

27. *The Gorkahpatra,* 7 December 1996. However, the Lalitpur Appellate Court dismissed the charges of corruption in the procurement of fertilizer filed by the CIAA against Minister Lawati and others related to the case. See, *The Gorkhapatra,* 11 July 1997.
28. Krishna P. Khanal et al., *Nepal People, Polity and Governance. A Survey Analysis of People's Response to the Democratic Experiment (1991-1995),* (Kathmandu: Centre for Consolidation of Democracy, 1996), pp. 158-9.
29. *The Janadesh,* 20 February 1996.
30. *The Kantipur,* 21 April 2001.

CHAPTER 4

Political Parties and Elections

Krishna Hachhethu*

'Do you take this man (or woman) to be your lawfully wedded husband (or wife)'? 'I do'. This analogy, borrowed from the Christian marriage ceremony, with its twin notions of legitimacy and obligation, can apply in politics when we see the election as a mutual trust and contract between the voters and their representatives, between people and political parties, and between society and government. In a competitive system, election is considered as the only legitimate means through which contesting parties achieve power and authority to run the government. Acquisition of legitimacy to be in power is accompanied by obligation and responsibility, which is generally phrased 'respect for popular mandate' and 'representative democracy'. To respect and represent the popular mandate means that political parties are responsible to the interest of people and society. If a party fails to balance between legitimacy and responsibility, the people are likely to choose an alternative party in the next election.

Elections provide a channel of communication between the mass of society and political parties. For citizens, exercise of their voting rights may mean many things, i.e. political participation, dialogue with political actors, articulation of individual and collective interest, negotiation/bargaining with the political elite, choice of an individual candidate and/or choice of party's policy and programme, and involvement in the process of government formation. The periodic election links the people's power with political parties' interest. Electoral interest of political parties obviously seeks maximum number of votes and seats with which they obtain social consent and political legitimacy to be in power and position. It involves multiple processes, i.e. candidate select-

*I acknowledge the cooperation of Gehandra Malla, Ganesh Datta Bhatta and Mrs. Sarita Giri for collecting field data.

ion, political socialization in line with a party's image, ideology and policy, mobilization of party workers, campaigning and setting of election agendas and issues that are thought to have popular appeal.

A system of linking people's expectations with parties' policies in governance has recently been introduced in Nepal after the restoration of multi-party democracy followed by the enactment of a new Constitution in 1990. The Constitution ensures the stability of newly established democratic regime stating categorically that constitutional monarchy, multi-party parliamentary system, citizen's fundamental rights and popular sovereignty are unamendable.[1] Popular sovereignty in the political sense is ensured by the people's inalienable right to choose their representatives to the local and central government. It has adopted the first-past-the-post-system in elections for the 205-member of the House of Representatives (HOR), the Lower House of the bicameral parliament. A party which obtains majority seats in the HOR through general elections forms the government. In case none of the contending parties obtains the required majority of 103 seats, a provision of coalition government of two or more parliamentary parties or minority government of the largest party is prescribed as an alternative system of government formation. To be precise, the Constitution properly safeguards the system of popular elections as the only legitimate means of making the state's power and authority responsible to the people.

The formation of government through elections contributes to the consolidation of democracy. Nepal has undergone certain democratic experiences during the last one decade with the successful completion of three general elections and two local elections. The last three general elections, held in 1991, 1994 and 1999 have created a dominant two party system which is generally considered as an ideal situation for political stability and institutionalization of democracy. The 1992 and 1997 local elections were also remarkable for people's participation in competitive politics at the grass-roots level. Such electoral practices have multiple positive impacts, e.g. increase of political awareness, people's participation in competitive politics, penetration of contesting parties in society at the grassroots level, assimilation of previously non-conformist forces into the mainstream politics, legitimization of multi-party parliamentary democracy, etc. Above all, these elections significantly stressed the principle of people's right to choose and reject the government.

This paper focuses on party-people relations in the electoral landscape of Nepali democracy. The paper is organized into four parts. The first part briefly touches upon the introduction of Nepali political parties with their ideological identity, and the party system brought out by the last three general elections and two local elections held after the restoration of democracy in 1990. The second part focuses on the internal dynamics of the party's electoral management. This covers a multiple process, i.e. candidate selection, resolution of internal disputes and dissents, mobilization of party workers, designing of campaign strategy and electoral alliance with other party(ies). The third part highlights the external dynamics of a party's vote mobilization strategy which involves the role of actors and factors, i.e. leadership image, candidate's popularity, transmission of the party's ideology, image and policy in society, election agendas, issues and programmes. Finally, an assessment is made on parties' post-election performances in the light of people's expectations and parties' promises made during elections.

Political Parties and Party System in Nepal

Nepali political parties originated in the 1930s-40s as opposition to the oligarchic Rana regime (1846-1951). The Praja Parishad, formed in 1935, is the pioneer party but it could not survive the Rana repression. The Nepali Congress party (NC)[2] and the Communist Party of Nepal (CPN) were founded in 1947 and 1949 respectively in exile in India. The NC was instrumental in launching the armed movement against the Rana regime in 1950-51 and became successful in ending it.

With the overthrow of the century-long Rana regime, Nepal entered the phase of multi-party system for the first time in the history of the country. The NC was the most dominant party but it had long been kept out from power until it scored two-thirds majority in the 1959 general elections and formed its government under the prime ministership of B.P. Koirala. Before this election, King Tribhuvan and his successor Mahendra favoured a number of small personality-based parties picking them up sto be in the government to counter the NC's dominating position. But only a few small parties, i.e. Samyukta Prajatantra Party, Praja Parishad (Acharya) and Praja Parisad (Mishra) achieved nominal seats in the parliament. Instead, the Gorkha Parishad, formed by the former Rana rulers and their clients, succeeded in becoming the major opposition party. But the oppositional politics outside the parliament, before and after the 1959 elections, was dominated by the CPN, which had only 4 seats in the House of Representatives.

The era of the party system (1951-60) was dominated by both intra-party and inter-party conflicts on the one hand, and the power struggle between the parties and the monarchy on the other. But this era was terminated by a coup in December 1960, staged by King Mahendra who, then, introduced the partyless panchayat system.

During the authoritarian panchayat regime (1960-90), political parties were forced to recast their roles to work as outlawed organizations. Out of the eleven political parties registered for the 1959 elections only two, the NC and some splinter groups of the CPN, could survive to conduct anti-regime activities. The NC and some Communist groups had constantly shown their presence in the society through anti-establishment struggles, some times peacefully and at other times violently, thus presenting themselves as extra systemic opposition, as Baral has stated.[3] The NC's struggles were constantly directed to achieve multiparty democracy. But the Communists were divided and fragmented.[4] Only few moderate left parties adjusted to broad democratic movements considering the multi-party system as more 'progressive' than the partyless panchayat. But the extremists, like the CPN (Marxist-Leninst or ML), which later changed its name to CPN (Unified Marxist-Leninist or UML) in January 1991 following a merger with the CPN (Marxist), concentrated on organization building rather than participation in the democratic movement. Its boycott of the 1980 referendum, held to choose either a multiparty or a partyless system, manifested its antipathy to liberal democracy. But it later changed its line in favour of a broad democratic movement, which led to the formation of the United Left Front (ULF consisting of seven Communist Parties), and an agreement with the NC for a joint struggle against the partyless panchayat regime. The 1990 *Jana Andolan* succeeded in restoring the multiparty system.

From the time of inception of political parties, party politics has become part of Nepali society in one way or the other depending upon the parties' changing roles and positions in different contexts and times, e.g. as revolutionaries (1935-51), as legal entities (1951-60), as illegal movement organizations (1960-90) and as parliamentary groups (1990). So, Nepalis have long been familiar with political parties and the party system. Their understanding/perception of a political party is very significant in determining the future course of the party system in Nepal.

People at large appeared faithful in the party system when they were given positive as well as negative images of the party (see Table 4.1). Most respondents across age, sex, class, education occupation, religious and caste/ethnic groups understood a political party, in preferential order, as 'agency of interest articulation', 'ideologicsal community', 'indispensable for democracy' and 'agent of development'. Some took it otherwise. The negative image of a party, i.e. as 'merely a means of getting

TABLE 4.1: PEOPLE'S UNDERSTANDING AND PERCEPTION OF POLITICAL PARTY

(Total number of respondents: 500 % based on multiple responses)

Political Parties as	Total		Sex %		Area %		Party Affiliation %	
	No.	%	Male	Female	Rural	Urban	Member	Non-Member
Ideology community	228	45.6	50.3	31.1	42.6	57.4	53.4	41.8
Agency of interest articulation	272	54.4	58.7	41.0	53.4	58.4	68.1	47.8
Indispensable for democracy	217	43.4	48.4	27.9	40.9	53.5	55.8	37.4
Agent of development	191	38.2	40.5	31.1	38.6	36.6	43.6	35.6
Merely a means of getting power	130	26.0	26.5	24.6	25.8	26.7	19.6	29.1
Instrument of elite's self-interest	104	20.8	20.1	23.0	21.6	17.8	13.5	24.3
Others	05	01.0	01.1	0.8	00.5	03.0	01.2	00.9
Don't know	49	09.8	05.6	23.0	10.8	05.9	03.1	13.1

power' and 'instrument for elite's self interest' scored 26 and 21 per cent respectively in public opinion surveys about the political party. The cross tabulation of data from different variables shows that the negative images of the party appeared a little more than average in the understanding of youngsters, women, the just literate, agricultural occupation group, Newar, Terai's low caste and Dalit communities, and non-party members. Moreover, the majority of respondents belonging to the Buddhist community, hill ethnic groups, business community, and rich class took the party in a negative light, either as 'merely a means of getting power' or/and 'instrument for elite's self interest'. But in totality, the positive dimension prevails in people's perception of a political party.

People's positive remarks on the political party are contrary to their evaluation of party leaders. A number of opinion surveys reveal that the people blamed the party(ies) leaders for a constant erosion of democratic norms and values in a decade-long experience of the multiparty system in Nepal.[5] Though leaders and parties are not mutually exclusive, the people at large distinguish them in different ways: faith in the party system but disenchantment with the party leaders. Such a paradoxical situation can be noted in the result of the 1999 elections to the third parliament. Among the 205 members of the HOR of the second tenure of parliament (1994-9), 79 per cent was wiped out in the 1999 parliamentary elections. And none of the independent candidates succeeded in gaining even a single seat in parliament.[6] There are many reasons to explain such a puzzle—faith in the party system but disenchantment with the party leaders.

Nepali political parties originated in the background of the struggle against the oligarchic Rana regime. The party's image as a change agent in political realm that was built through the anti-Rana movement expanded to the social and economic spheres as well as in the post-Rana period. During the first experiment of multiparty democracy (1951-60), Nepal made an attempt to break away from its past and look forward to political freedom, economic development, social justice, spread of education and communication.[7] Political parties led a campaign to abolish the land-based feudal social and economic system. The CPN, while introducing Marxist ideology in Nepali politics but through participation in liberal democratic process, sought a radical and revolutionary transformation in Nepali society.[8] The dominant party at that time was the NC, which adopted the ideology of democratic socialism. The NC government (1959-60) under Prime Minister B.P. Koirala took a number of progressive social and economic policy measures directed against the land-based feudal exploitation system. It is, therefore, observed,

> Nepal presents a unique case of party formation. Unlike the genesis of political parties in the West as product of democratic process and also unlike the case of other south Asian countries where political parties appeared as a consequence of the modernization process, political parties in Nepal originated to accomplish democracy and modernization.[9]

This explains why political parties in Nepal have been acknowledged as agents of change in the social, economic and political structures of the country.

The whole context changed after the dismantling of multiparty democracy by a royal coup in 1960. During the period of the partyless panchayat regime, the parties' image as change agents was retained, but mainly in the political sphere. Since party activities were legally prohibited, political parties concentrated more on building public opinion against the authoritarian panchayat system rather than in mass mobilization through public policy platforms. The credentials of these parties were boosted further because the NC and the ULF being the catalysts of the 1990 *Jana Andolan* (mass movement), which overthrew the three decade long partyless authoritarian panchayat system and restored multiparty democracy. They are also key actors in making the present constitution with which sovereignty is transferred from the king to the citizens for the first time in the history of Nepal.

The other reason behind people's positive remarks to the party system is that the political party has been perceived as an ideological community. Ideology is one of the dominating factors in determining voting behaviour of Nepali citizens at least in the early phase of democracy. Looking back to the principal doctrine enunciated by each party at the time of their formation, the major parties at present can be categorized into three ideological blocks: the NC symbolizes multiparty system; the UML professed one-party Communist system; and the Rashtriya Prajatantra Party (RPP) is popularly considered as a party of former *panchas* with their political background of being ardent advocates of the partyless system.

The NC, with its ideological trademark of 'democratic socialism', has constantly professed constitutional monarchy and parliamentary democracy. It has been considered as a liberal and centrist party. The UML, though its dominating partner the ML originated from the extremist plank with its ideology of *Naulo Janabad* (New People's Democracy as propounded by Mao in China), modified its ideology to fit itself in the changed context after the restoration of democracy. The UML's journey towards liberalization reached its climax in 1993 when the party's Fifth Congress passed a resolution of *Janatako Bahudaliya Janabad* (People's Multi-party Democracy). However, it has retained its credential as a moderate left and progressive party. In the right of the political spectrum is the RPP, a party of old *panchas* that was formed soon after the restoration of democracy in 1990. The political background of its leaders/workers is closely associated with the dismantled panchayat regime, which professed the principle of absolute monarchy and a partyless system. The RPP, however, accepts constitutional monarchy and parliamentary democracy today.

There are many small semi-underground Communist Parties—e.g. Mashal (its electoral front: National People's Front), Unity Centre (its electoral front: United People's Front), Nepal Workers and Peasant Party (NWPP)—which stand against the fundamental principles of a multi-party democracy. They have, however, participated in the parliamentary process with a view to wrecking the system. Moreover, the Nepal Communist Party (Maoist) is violently opposing the present political structure since February 1996.

On the whole, Nepali political parties can be broadly divided into four categories in so far as their commitment to multi-party democracy and representation in parliament is concerned: (1) conformist and parliamentarian (NC, UML, RPP and ML), (2) conformist and parliamentarian but regional (Nepal Sadbhabana Party (NSP), (3) non-conformist but parliamentarian (NWPP, Mashal, and Unity Centre) and (4) non-conformist with extra-parliamentary opposition (Maoist).

The line of ideological divergence among political parties is constantly getting thin over time. There is a broad consensus among the major ideological forces of the country—RPP (conservative), NC (liberal democrat) and UML (leftist)—on the fundamentals of the Constitution, i.e. human rights, popular sovereignty, constitutional monarchy and multi-party democracy. The assimilation of political parties in the constitutional framework also reveals the fact that they have transformed themselves from ideology oriented movement organizations of the pre-1990 situation to power seeking parties after the restoration of democracy. The NC no longer remains a political forum of social democrats, it rather appears as a 'broad political platform'. This applies to the UML and RPP as well. Change of parties' goal from ideological persuasion to quest for power is the dominating phenomenon in the present party politics of the country, which has both a positive and negative impact on the party system. Because of the integration of political parties by the Constitution and the power factors, the ideological factor no longer becomes an obstacle in managing inter-party relations. This was evident during the formation of a number of coalition governments between Right and Left, between Right and Centre, and between Centre and Left during the hung parliament in 1994-9. This shows a contradiction between people's perception of the party as an ideological community and the decline of ideology in realpolitik.

Despite the erosion of ideology, political parties have remained as omnipotent institutions in linking the state and society in the post *Jana Andolan* period. Though the restoration of democracy brought in its wake a mushrooming growth in non-governmental and other social organizations, hardly any of these organizations are independent from political the parties. In the absence of meaningful civil society, political parties have become central in determining state-society relations. The state has long been perceived as the provider of basic needs to the people and the parties are seen as engines of social change and economic development. Ideologies of both the NC and the UML demanded an active state. Yet, the overall activities of the political parties are hardly suited to their own ideologies, but they, time and again, particularly during elections, tend to rejuvenate the image of Nepal as an omnipotent state—provider of basic necessities to the people and political parties as a dispenser of state resources.

Political parties as omnipotent institutions are very much alive in the minds of Nepali voters, manifested in the result of the last three general elections and the two local elections (see Table 4.2).

In the 1991 general elections, the NC gained a mandate with

TABLE 4.2: PARTIES' POSITION IN GENERAL AND LOCAL ELECTIONS

Parties	General Elections			Local Elections (% of seat)					
	1991	1994	1999	1992			1997		
	(Seat in HOR % of popular votes)			VDCs	Mun-icipa-lities	DDCs	VDCs	Mun-icipa-lities	DDCs
NC	110	83	112	50.24	50.84	64.80	29.47	28.92	14.32
	37.75	33.38	36.14						
UML	69	88	70	26.05	22.33	17.94	50.10	55.98	68.05
	27.98	30.85	30.74						
ML	Did not exist		0	Appear as a separate party only since March 1998.					
			06.38						
RPP	04	20	11	9.73	10.32	7.63	12.22	8.15	9.94
	11.94	17.93	13.46						
NSP	06	03	05	2.94	3.38	1.96	1.21	1.59	1.42
	4.10	3.49	3.13						
NPF	-	-	05	5.09	1.50	3.54	-	-	-
			1.36						
NWPP	02	04	01	Included in the section of independent and other parties					
	1.25	.98	.54						
UPF	09	0	01						
	4.35	1.32	083						
CPN (Democratic)	02	0	0						
	2.43	.38	.05						
Independents	03	07	0	5.93	11.63	4.10	4.93	5.36	6.27
	4.17	6.18	2.83						
Other parties	0	0	0						
	6.04	5.49	4.54						
Total	205	205	205	99.98	99.99	100	100	100	100
	100	100	100						

Note: VDC = Village Development Committee, DDC = District Development Committee.

Source: Election Commission, *House of Representative Members, 2048 (1991): Final Results; House of Representative Members, 2051(1994): Election Results; a House of Representative Members, 2056 (1999): Election Results;* Pancha Narayan Maharjan, 'Local Elections in Nepal, 1997' (CNAS Professional Paper), Kathmandu: CNAS, 1998.

37.75 per cent popular votes and 110 seats out of 205 in the HOR to govern the country. The UML emerged as the largest opposition party with a sizeable strength, 27.98 per cent popular votes and 69 seats in the HOR. The political equation changed following the 1994 mid-term elections that produced a hung parliament. The NC's strength declined to 83 seats in the HOR and 33.38 of the popular votes. The UML, as the largest party in the HOR with its 88 seats and 30.85 per cent popular votes, formed its minority government. The NC leaders/workers felt that their party was defeated in the mid-term elections because of internal divisions and conflicts in the party. The same logic could apply to the results of the 1999 general elections. The UML tracked back to being the major opposition party from its earlier expectation to be in power, mainly because of a split in the party in March 1998.[10] The NC restored its first position in the 1999 general elections winning a comfortable majority of 112 seats in the HOR. The result of the post-1990 elections showed that the question of integration and disintegration made a big difference in parties' positions in elections.

Besides, the results of the last three general elections established a correlation between the government (non-)performance and election results. The simple logic suggests that the party in the government could renew its position if it has had performance legitimacy. Charles W. Anderson, therefore, said, 'The primary task of the voter is to evaluate the quality of government received in the last period. The decision is between the ins and the outs. If generally satisfied, the voter elects to retain the incumbents. If not, the choice is to throw the rascals out'.[11] Change of parties' position after each election suggests that elections also mean exercise of the people's right to reject the party in government. This logic sounds more valid, which was also proven by the result of the 1997 local election. The NC captured local governments after the 1992 local elections but its strength was reduced to around 30 per cent in the 1997. The UML's position changed from opposition to the ruling one in the local government of many areas. In the 1997 local elections, the UML won 50.10 per cent seats of the VDCs, along with 55.98 per cent of Municipalities and 68.05 per cent of DDCs seats. It showed that any party in power could influence the local elections in its favour.

The glaring fact of the emergence of a dominant two party system in Nepal is evident if we see Table 4.2. The exception was the second tenure of parliament (1994-9) in which the RPP acted as a balancing force between two major parties, the NC and the UML, which Baral calls a 'two and quarter party systems'.[12] Otherwise the first and the third parliamentary elections and the local elections of 1992 and 1997 created a dominant-two party system. The NC and the UML appear as alternatives to one another for the competitive politics of the country.

Now, a system of two-party dominance appears as a trend in the party system of South Asian countries. But unlike its bases of social cleavages in India,[13] the Nepali character of the two dominant party system emerged on different grounds. Except for the NSP championing the cause of Madhise community (people of Terai region), none of the political parties associate themselves with a particular caste, class and community. This shows that political parties in Nepal are not byproducts of social cleavages and economic problems. Rather, they evolved with broad political mission or ideology. The support bases of the NC, the UML and the other parties cross social, cultural, religious and caste/ethnic divisions of the people. Though the Constitution recognizes the pluralistic nature of Nepali society consisting of diverse cultural and linguistic groups, it takes enough care to separate politics from caste, ethnicity, language and religion. Article 112(3) of the Constitution categorically prohibits the formation of political parties on the basis of religion, community, caste, tribe and region. In this spirit, the election code of conduct states that '. . . voters shall not be encouraged to vote on the basis of caste/ethnicity, religion, tribe, and language'.[14]

The NC's and the UML's domination in Nepali politics is likely to continue in the future. Some factors contribute to stabilize a two dominant party system in Nepal. One, the majoritarian electoral system that Nepal has adopted is obviously against the minority parties, i.e. despite the ML score of 6.38 per cent popular vote in the 1999 general elections, it does not have a single representation in the HOR. Two, the Constitution itself discourages the existence of smaller parties by its provision of rejecting the national party status to those who fail to gain 3 per cent popular votes in the general elections. Three, Nepali adult citizens, by and large, appear as stable party voters. The margin of difference in popular votes received by the NC in the last three elections was only 4.37 per cent, minimum 33.38 per cent in 1994 when it was unpopular and maximum 37.38 per cent when its popularity was at the peak in 1991. The UML's popular votes in the last three general elections were around 28-31 per cent.

Internal Dynamics of Parties' Electoral Management

Elections provide a fair ground to wage a struggle for power among contending parties. Intra-party competition for candidacy precedes the elections among the parties. A party which manages internal competition effectively will certainly be in a better position in an election battle with other parties. The internal exercises for the preparation of competitive elections start with the selection of candidates. Parties' decision of candidate selection intertwines with their objective of the maximization of popular votes and seats to the elected bodies. This obviously indicates that the political parties generally select those candidates who are perceived to be capable enough to pull more votes. Candidate selection is also a task of sending parties' representatives to local and central governments. A candidate's personal ability of holding the post is also taken into consideration. Candidate selection is a complex process and a number of factors, i.e. social background, political socialization, political attitude, social and political environment, party history and time of association, personality, continuity, popularity, lobby, support of party workers, backing of factional group, proximity to party high commands, etc., interplay in the eventual outcome of selection of persons as party candidates for elections.

The question of candidate selection relates to a number of other issues, i.e. respect for a public opinion vis-à-vis a candidate's popularity and ability, consultation with party workers on account of the need for electoral mobilization of party's volunteers and possible dissent by other aspirants of candidacy. Election time is always a high time for intensifying intra-party conflicts and crisis. Among many aspirants, only a few will be lucky to get a chance. Managing dissidence is, therefore a very significant task to maximize the prospect of victory. The other important challenge is to motivate party activists for election campaigning and vote mobilization. Besides, a party can score some more seats through forging alliance with other parties.

Candidate Selection: Two important things related to the nomination of candidates are formal/informal procedures of decision making and fixing the criteria for party's candidacy. The NC and many other political parties have set up their own Parliamentary Board to look after the business of candidate selection. The Parliamentary Board of each party is constituted by a small number of hard core central leaders having formal authority to take decisions on candidate selection for the general and the local elections.[15] The UML's constitution does not specifically provide such a permanent structure though it constituted an Election Board in 1991 and 1994 general elections to take a decision on party's candidates which was done by the party Standing Committee in the 1999 general election. This small structural difference however does not contradict the uniform pattern-centralization-adopted by all competing parties for candidate selection. Despite uniformity among the political parties in following the procedure of candidate selection, there are some divergences due to each party's unique organizational character and behaviour.

The NC is basically a personality-based centralized party. The party had long operated under the authority of its troika, Ganesh Man Singh, Krishna Prasad Bhattarai and Girija Prasad Koirala. Its formal structures, the District Committee (DC) and the Central Committee (CC), had played just a supplementary role for the troika's decision. This pattern remained unchanged despite the exit of G.M. Singh from the party on the eve of the 1994 mid-term elections. But coming to the 1999 general elections a slight change was introduced on account of the decline of the party high command's authority and the emergence of mini power centres inside the party. Next to Koirala and Bhattarai, some other second rank leaders, Sher Bahadur Deuba, Ram Chandra Poudel and Khum Bahadur Khadka in their capacity as members of the Parliamentary Board, appeared influential in taking decisions regarding ticket distribution for the elections. Unlike the past when decisions were made in consultation with only two or three top leaders, the NC Parliamentary Board played a decisive role in selecting candidates for the 1999 general elections.

Unlike the NC, the UML—an organization based party—is not under the exclusive control and command of one or more leaders. It has long followed a system of collective leadership and collective decision-making process. At the same time, the UML has adopted the oligarchic and centralized system. The centralized authority structure in the UML is acknowledged by its prescribed manner of vertical relationship, 'Each party member is under the committee, each lower unit is under its immediate higher unit, and all members and organizations are under the authority of the Central Committee.'[16] This is well reflected in the decision-making process for candidate selection and in which the party Standing Committee, constituted of around 12 top leaders, has final authority in this regard. This pattern has more or less been followed by other Communist Parties such as the UPF and the UNF.

The RPP has adopted a system of collective discussion among the party central leaders in taking decisions for candidate selection. Many other parties have also followed this pattern except the NWPP and NSP. The decision of one top leader prevailed more in these parties.

Centralization is, therefore, a rule of all parties for candidate selection. But in practice, the parties' apex bodies have not exercised all their powers arbitrarily. Particularly in the process of candidate nominations, central leaders consult local leaders for better electoral prospects, as can be noted from Table 4.3.

Of the total 500 respondents, 163 were party members. Around two-thirds of the party members said they had been fully or partly consulted by the central leaders before taking the final decision of candidate selection. This general finding is applicable to all political parties. In response to a question on consultation, the

TABLE 4.3: CONSULTATION WITH PARTY LOCAL LEADERS/WORKERS IN CANDIDATE SELECTION

Total no. of respondents 163

Variables	Total		NC	UML	RPP	Others
	No.	%	%	%	%	%
Agree	87	53.4	50.8	54.2	61.8	45
Partly agree	36	22.1	26.2	22.9	17.6	15
Disagree	31	19.0	14.8	18.8	17.6	35
Don't know	9	5.5	8.2	4.2	2.9	5

respondents belonging to the NC, the UML and the RPP affirmed it (51, 54 and 62 per cent respectively). Those who partly shared this opinion were 26, 23, and 28 per cent respondents of the NC, the UML and the RPP respectively. Only a very few party members (NC's 15 per cent, UML's 19 per cent and the RPP's 18 per cent) disagreed. The general finding confirms that nomination of candidates was made by the party centre in consultation with the party local leaders.[17] The question that arises here is: how are parties' local leaders/workers involved in the candidate selection process?

In the first general elections held after the restoration of democracy, the NC granted the authority to its DC to recommend three possible candidates from each parliamentary constituency. Besides, the party sent its central representative in each of the 75 districts to collect the opinion of party local leaders/workers about the prospective candidates and then submitted the report to the Parliamentary Board. These procedures had been followed as precedents in subsequent general elections held in 1994 and 1999. Besides, the NC, being in power in all the last three general elections, had additional advantage of receiving information from the local administration. It had been practiced that on the eve of elections, the district administration submitted a report to the government with its evaluation on the position of contending parties and prospective candidates. But many felt that the party centre relied more on the opinions of its local organizational leaders than the report of the local administration.[18] It was believed that the NC high command largely respected the recommendations made by the party DC while taking the final decision for candidate selection. But the party organizations at the local level in many districts later failed to be strict on their responsibility to recommend only 3 prospective candidates for one constituency. Instead, the party DC sent the list of many aspirants from one constituency, which further enlarged the scope for manipulation by the centre.

Like the NC, the UML, the RPP and many other parties allowed the DC of their respective parties to recommend three prospective candidates from one constituency. And each party deputed a team of central representatives in each district seeking opinion of local leader/workers. By way of consulting with the party local organization, the party rank and file got involved in candidate selection process in different ways. Their role would not only be limited in providing their personal opinion to the concerned authority. Particularly in the selection of the party candidates for significant posts at different levels, ranging from VDC chairman to member of parliament (MP), most party's local units at different levels and leaders of different ranks had shown their favour to particular aspirant in written form.

The space for the party local leaders/workers' involvement in the decision-making process of candidate selection is much wider in local election than in the general elections. The NC, the UML, the RPP and many other parties delegated the authority to their own party, DC, in taking decisions of candidate selection for local elections, except for the top posts in Municipalities and DDC. In both the 1992 and 1997 local elections, most parties followed a standard format—recommendation of 3 names for one post by the party lower units (Village/Town Committee, Area Committee, Constituency Committee) and final selection by the party district organization. However, the selection of party leaders for elected bodies, VDCs, Municipalities and DDC, was also done with a top-down approach. The NC usually set up a selection committee—consisting of a small coterie of local leaders including MPs—which took the final decision in the nomination of a party's candidates for VDCs and Municipalities. The UML also formed an election board constituting a small number of secretariat members of the party DC, which actually selected all candidates for the 1992 and the 1997 local elections.

Though candidate selection is an internal affairs of political parties in which organizational leaders and workers are involved in different ways, public opinion is supposed to be respected while doing so. The more the respect of the public opinion the more votes a party receives. But none of Nepal's political parties has adopted a scientific mechanism to collect the voters' opinion on a party's prospective candidates. Besides the office bearers of the party organizations at local level, parties also have to rely on information supplied by their own activists, mostly those involved in the party ancillary and affiliated organizations. The accuracy and impartiality of such information has always been questionable and so it would have least impact on the decision-making process, but the local situation and sentiment cannot be completely overlooked. This implies that the contending parties largely respect the public opinion in the nomination of their own party candidates despite the lack of a scientific mechanism to undertake this task.

Nearly two-thirds of the total 500 respondents fully or partly responded affirmatively to the question whether political parties respected their opinion in candidate selection. Most respondents of different age, occupation, cast/ethnic groups, rural and urban dwellers, and male and females shared this opinion. But majority of the respondents belonging to the poor, illiterate, Dalit, Buddhists and Muslims expressed that their opinions were not considered in candidate selections. This shows the negligence of the unprivileged strata of society by political parties in taking decisions of candidate nomination. Besides, around one-forth of total 500 respondents disagreed with the view that political parties respect public opinion in candidate selection. But in totality, the positive dimension prevails in relations between public opinion and candidate selection.

The correlations between public opinion and candidate selection are linked with the choice of appropriate persons for parties' candidacies. While justifying the NC's nomination of candidates for the 1991 parliamentary election, party President, Krishna Prasad Bhattarai said, 'The party had nominated its candidates on the basis of three criteria: their record of struggle and sacrifices, their prospect of victory, and their capacity to play an effective role in the parliament.'[19] These factors were included in the form, which the NC distributed to all aspirants for MP ticket in the 1994 and the 1999 general elections. The primacy of continuity, personality and popularity factors was, therefore, distinct.[20] But many felt changes later in giving weight to particular qualities. Factors like wealth, family and kinship ties, proximity

TABLE 4.4: RESPECT FOR PUBLIC OPINION IN CANDIDATE SELECTION

Total no. of respondents 500

Variables	Total		Area %		Sex %		Party Affiliation %	
	No.	%	Rural	Urban	Male	Female	Member	Non-member
Agree	218	43.6	44.1	41.6	44.4	41.0	50.9	40.1
Partly agree	108	21.6	19.5	29.7	23.5	15.6	18.4	23.1
Disagree	128	25.6	25.6	25.7	27.8	18.9	28.8	24.0
Don't know	46	9.2	10.8	3.0	4.2	24.6	1.8	12.8

to high command leader, etc., played a more important role than the factors of continuity, honesty, dedication and commitment.[21]

The NC developed some positive and negative criteria for the simplification of the selection process. The NC granted MP tickets to all CC members and incumbent ministers, except those who had voluntarily stayed away from the contest. The party allocated 5 per cent of 205 candidates to the former panchas who joined the NC in all the last three general elections. For others, the overriding consideration in the choice of the MP candidates was their prospect of victory in the elections. The NC's central representatives who were assigned to recommend candidates from the deputed districts for the 1994 and the 1999 parliamentary elections normally recommended those persons with good prospects rather than those suggested by the local leaders and workers.

So far as negative criteria were concerned, the NC denied a ticket to the Upper House MPs, and its representatives holding top posts in Municipalities (mayor and deputy mayor) and DDCs (chairman and vice-chairman) in the 1994 mid term elections. It was followed in the 1999 general elections in addition to two more negative consideration: misuse of diplomatic passport and violation of party discipline during the 1994 mid term election.

The office secretary of the UML, Bhim Acharya, said that his party developed some criteria to be eligible for the candidacy of parliamentary election. Accordingly, a person must be of high morals, disciplined, capable, popular and committed to a party's interest and principles.[22] Similar opinion was expressed by most of the UMLs local leaders of the sampled districts.[23] Besides, preference was also given to the minority communities in those constituencies where they constitute the majority group. The party CC members were exempted from all criteria, except those who voluntarily stayed away from the contest. The UML also developed certain negative criteria. The party denied tickets to its members of the Upper House, mayor and deputy mayor of Municipalities and chairman and vice-chairman of DDCs. Furthermore, it disqualified most of its 22 ex-MPs for the 1994 election who violated party discipline by defying the party whip in the elections of the Upper House held in June 1993 in which a dissident candidate Jagat Bogati won. In the 1999 general elections, the party threw out those members of the second tenure of parliament who were involved in the diplomatic passport scandal.

The smaller parties including the RPP bothered least about the positive and negative criteria for candidate selection due to the lack of serious internal competition for candidacy. Many of them even failed to give their own party candidates from most areas out of a total of 205 parliamentary constituencies. Some parties like NWPP gave candidacy from many districts irrespective of the personal quality and ability of candidates, just for accumulation of more votes, if possible 3 per cent in total voting turn-out which is necessary to get recognized as a national party. Never the less in areas of high internal competition for candidacy and better prospects of victory, the minor parties also considered factors like continuity and contribution to the party, personal ability and popularity.

People's assessment of political parties and the criteria they set for candidate selection are significant. Because, it is the people who decide the faith of candidate contesting the elections. The voters view on the criteria of candidate selection is shown in Table 4.5A and 4.5B.

TABLE 4.5(A): BASIS OF CANDIDATE SELECTION FOR THE 1997 LOCAL ELECTION

Total no. of respondents: 500
% based on multiple response

Variables	Total		Area %		Sex %		Party Affiliation %	
	No.	%	Rural	Urban	Male	Female	Member	Non-member
Continuity/ seniority	236	47.2	46.6	49.5	49.2	41.0	54.6	43.6
Caste/ ethnicity	159	31.8	32.8	27.7	35.7	19.7	31.9	31.8
Popularity	328	65.6	67.4	58.4	69.8	52.5	76.1	60.5
Rich	101	20.2	19.0	24.8	20.9	18.0	15.3	22.6
Favourate of dist. leader	153	30.6	28.6	38.6	34.4	18.9	30.7	30.6
Favourate of central leader	63	12.6	10.8	19.8	14.0	08.2	15.3	11.3
Opportunist	38	07.6	07.3	08.9	09.0	03.3	08.0	07.4
Others	03	00.6	00.5	01.0	00.8	00.0	00.6	00.6
Don't know	51	10.2	10.8	07.9	05.8	23.8	04.9	12.8

TABLE: 4.5(B): BASIS OF CANDIDATE SELECTION FOR 1999 GENERAL ELECTION

Total no. of respondents: 500
% based on multiple response

Variables	Total		Area %		Sex %		Party Affiliation %	
	No	%	Rural	Urban	Male	Female	Member	Non-member
Continuity	281	56.2	55.6	58.4	58.5	49.2	67.5	50.7
Caste/ ethnicity	102	20.4	20.8	18.8	22.8	13.1	20.9	20.2
Popularity	309	61.8	62.7	58.4	64.0	54.9	71.2	57.3
Rich	135	27.0	26.3	29.7	29.4	19.7	24.5	28.2
Favourate of central leader	199	39.8	36.8	51.5	45.0	23.8	40.5	39.5
Opportunist	46	09.2	08.8	10.8	10.6	04.9	09.8	8.9
Others	06	01.2	00.8	03.0	01.1	01.6	03.1	00.3
Don't know	58	11.6	13.0	05.9	08.2	22.1	04.9	14.8

While responding to the question, (What criterion did you find parties consider in selection of candidates for the 1997 local election and 1999 general elections in your own constituency?) 'popularity' and 'continuity' were indicated as the most important factors in preferential order. The third important factor was, 'favour of central leaders' for general elections but caste/ethnic consideration for the local elections. A local leader of NC said, 'In local elections, all parties tried to get candidate from numerically majority caste/ethnic and class groups at that particular VDC.'[24] Major political parties appeared sensitive to the need of maintaining a certain level of caste/ethnic balance. This was manifested in the selection of candidates for significant posts (i.e. DDC's chairman and vice-chairman) in the sampled districts in the 1992 and the 1997 local elections. In the 1991, 1994 and 1999 general elections also, the NC the UML and the RPP had largely maintained caste/ethnic balance among major communities of the sampled districts, e.g. hill ethnic Rai/Limbu community and hill caste groups in Dhankuta, Hindu and Muslim and migrant hill caste and plain caste in Rautahat, hill caste Gurung and Brahmin/Chhetri in Baitadi districts.

A small variation appeared among different groups of respondents in identifying the third important factor. Majority respondents belonging to the Buddhists and the hill ethnic groups found caste/ethnicity as the third important criteria even in selection of candidates for the general elections. In contrast, the urban dwellers and the rich class gave low weight to the caste/ ethnic factor. The rich considered money power as the third important factor. The significance of favour of central leaders reflects a fact that centralization prevailed in candidate selection for general elections. But this factor appeared least important in local elections; instead 'favour of local leaders' counted more. This reveals decentralization in candidate selection for the local elections.

Resolution of Internal Dispute: Elections often create or intensify internal conflicts since candidate selection is the choice of few among many aspirants. If dissidence is not well managed, the aspirant candidates who fail to get a ticket, and their followers may become opponents or non-cooperative against the party's official candidates in the elections. This could have a serious impact on a party's position in elections as was witnessed by the defeat of the NC in the 1994 mid-term elections.

Despite several hundreds Congress members' claim of candidacy, the NC faced least trouble in the 1991 general elections. At that time the party's troika leadership was cohesive and its authority and design candidate selection was not seriously challenged. The level of tolerance among the party rank and file was also high. But a completely reverse picture was presented during the 1994 midterm elections with several party members contesting elections as rebel candidates. The party largely failed to manage internal conflicts that were rooted in the emergence of two distinct factional groups, one led by Girija Prasad Koirala and the other by Ganesh Man Singh and Krishna Prasad Bhattarai.

The factional conflict in the NC was a prelude to the power struggle within the troika that was intensified by subsequent events, i.e. cabinet reshuffle in December 1991 by the then Prime Minister G.P. Koirala without proper consultation with Singh and Bhattarai, internal sabotage against party president, K.P. Bhattarai's candidacy for the February 1994 by-election, absence of the NC's 35 members of the HOR during voting on the government's annual policy and programme leading to collapse of the Koirala government, and Koirala's retaliation by dissolving the HOR and calling for a mid term poll. The internal crisis culminated in Singh's exit from the party and in the formation of a separate political platform, *Jana Jagaran Abhiyan*, which openly called for a revolt against the NC official candidates belonging to the Koirala group.

In order to minimize the impact of internal revolt, the NC gave the candidacy to almost all incumbent MPs. It also warned of taking disciplinary action against rebels to the extent of expulsion from the party. But these decisions could not become effective. One of the main reasons was Bhattarai's absence as a candidate in the elections. As the NC failed to manage its internal problems, the party was defeated in the 1994 mid term polls. Alen Ware's view can be cited here to explain the defeat of the NC, 'When internal conflict becomes too intense a party becomes much less credible as a governing party and its electoral prospect can be reduced.'[25]

This situation, however, changed in the 1999 general elections. Yet, the dissidence resurfaced in the NC. A number of party leaders, including 33 MPs of the second tenure of parliament and presidents of the party DC of several districts who were excluded from the list of party candidates, vehemently opposed the decision of the Parliamentary Board. As their demands were not met, dissidents filed their nominations as rebel candidates from 53 constituencies[26] though many of them withdrew later. The problem was however managed by reviewing the decision already made by the Parliamentary Board and changing the list of candidates in 22 constituencies. G.P. Koirala as the prime minister and the party president led the course of internal conflict management. Koirala's announcement that Bhattarai would be the prime minister after the 1999 polls and his decision to keep her daughter Sujata Koirala out of the fray significantly reduced internal dissension of the party.

The UML's decision of candidate selection and dissent management had been conditioned by many factors. For the 1991 parliamentary elections—the first general elections held after the restoration of democracy—the UML proposed an electoral alliance among the partners of the 1990 mass movement, particularly with the NC. But the NC refused to make even an understanding for mutual cooperation in some constituencies from which the top leaders of both parties contested. The UML then turned to seeking alliance with all the left forces, which was materialized at a limited level with the UPF only. The electoral alliance among the left forces could be very significant. In the 1991 general elections, 'The Left's percentage of the total vote was only 1.25 per cent behind that of Congress and, if the leftist candidates standing against each other in 14 constituencies had not let Congress win by default, both sides would have had 96 seats each. . . .'[27] With due consideration to this fact, the UML tried to have a broad alliance among the left parties in subsequent general elections held in 1994 and 1999, but all the time it had to satisfy itself with limited achievement. In the last two general elections held in 1994 and 1999, the UML left out around 10 of the total 205 constituencies from the contest for the candidates of other left parties, particularly for those of the UPF and UNF. For the 1992 local election of the DDC, the UML made the RPP one of its alliance partners. But in the 1997 local election to the DDC, the RPP and the NSP largely swung to the NC in forging alliance in many areas despite the coalition government of the RPP, the UML and the NSP at the centre at that time.

The problems from inside the party were more challenging for the UML. In the 1991 general elections, one section of party belonging to the former Marxist group revolted against the party's decision of candidate selection. The conflict between the former ML and the Marxist groups surfaced due to the disregarding of an earlier agreement, reached in January 1991 for equal sharing of power and position. The Marxists felt a sense of deprivation in the nomination of party's candidates. Most of these who received party tickets were given difficult constituencies. For the ML, the unification signified merely acquiring the trade mark of the Marxist party (which inherited the identity of the original CPN, founded in 1949) and some of its well known leaders. The UML, therefore, took disciplinary action against a number of former Marxists for their *antarghat* in the 1991 general elections that suited the former ML's deliberate plan of displacing them from the party. Ultimately the party dissidents belonging to the Marxist group founded a new party, the CPN (September).

In the 1994 mid-term elections the internal problems in the UML arose from another factional group led by C.P. Mainali. As a dissident faction, the Mainali group had long existed in the party since 1982. The internal conflicts were waged on ideological lines during the party's Fifth National Congress 1993 in which the programme of *Bahudaliya Janabad* proposed by Madan Bhandari was passed by the overwhelming majority of 77.62 per cent votes against 14.49 per cent votes for the Mainali group's proposal of *Pariskrit Naulo Janabad.*[28] The defying of the party whip by 22 members of the HOR loyal to C.P. Mainali in elections to the members of the Upper House in 1993 sparked of trouble since the party decided to disqualify the violators of party discipline from the candidacy to the 1994 mid term elections. As a precautionary measure, the UML set a new formula that party candidates were required to submit their resignations from the HOR prior to filing their nomination papers.[29] C.P. Mainali demanded at least 15 per cent seats for his factional group in proportion to the strength of the minority group shown in the party's Fifth National Congress, but the party's dominant section rejected this. Party General Secretary Madhav Nepal's decision not to contest the election strengthened his bargaining capacity vis-à-vis the minority faction. Eventually the minority faction was compelled to satisfy itself with getting a few candidates in the elections. The situation completely changed in the 1999 elections. Because of the split of the party in March 1998 by dissident group, which formed the ML as the new party, the UML appeared as the most cohesive party. The UML's leaders and workers' common sentiment to take revenge against the splinter groups led to the neutralization of the factors leading to internal problems and dissidence.

Parties' Vote Mobilization Strategy

Elections provide an opportunity for mutual and active interactions between the people and parties and between the candidates and voters. Though elections are a reciprocal process of meeting people's expectations and parties/candidates' promises at one juncture, election agendas are always set unilaterally by political parties. The people most often appear as receptive or reject the policy and programme presented by parties. The contending parties generally try their best to put forward such policies, programmes and plans, which would have high appeal to the masses. The transmission of parties' ideology, identity and election agendas to the larger mass of the people is another vital part of elections, for which the contending parties/

candidates rely on mass media, party workers and other means. Parties' election campaigning can roughly be divided into two broad levels: national level and local/constituency level. Campaigning at the national level is generally conducted through mass media, parties' election manifestos and public speeches and addresses by the' national leaders of the parties in mass meetings. Parties' candidates and activists mostly carry out the local level campaigning.

National Level Campaign: The NC had tried its best to steer the competitive elections, 1991 general elections in particular, on ideological line. Its political identity is closely associated with the achievement of the 1990 *Jana Andolan*: restoration of multi-party democracy. So, it propagated 'Congress means multi-party system' and 'multiparty democracy means Congress'. Because of its long struggle for the parliamentary system and constitutional monarchy since its inception, the NC has long been considered as the main protagonist of democracy in Nepal. The party was, therefore, ideologically in an advantageous position vis-à-vis the UML's non-conformist stand on the parliamentary system in the initial phase of democracy. As it was suggested by one of its propagandas during the 1991 elections: vote for RPP is a vote for partyless system, vote for communist is a vote for one-party dictatorship, and vote for NC is a vote for democracy.[30]

Guided by its interest in vote maximization the NC naturally made high promises at election times. But on the other hand, the party being the protagonist of parliamentary democracy appeared as a symbol of status quo in the post-movement period. It resisted social demands for rapid and radical changes. The NC's psychology of 'would be ruling party' also impacted in adopting 'peace, stability, democracy and development' as its pet slogans in the last three general elections and the two local elections.

The UML, because of its history and Communist trade mark, had always been ideologically awkward and in a defensive position in the elections held under the parliamentary system. But in retrospect, its radical and revolutionary image associated with a Communist identity proved as an asset to catch the people's sentiment and the national psyche for revolutionary change that appeared in the early phase of democracy.

The national psyche for more change shaped the people's

political judgement. Merely a change of political regime from partyless panchayat to multi-party democracy did not satisfy the people. The popular feeling of inadequacy of change surfaced time and again in different ways. The advent of democracy in Nepal has in its wake raised the voices of different group of people who had hitherto emained silent. The demands of the minority and the disadvantaged sections of the society did sharply appear soon after the restoration of democracy. People of all segments of society asserted the demands for better and quick benefits which were denied during the panchayat.[31]

Against the NC that strove to stabilize and normalize the situation against the revolution of people's rising expectations, the UML instigated for the radicalization of social demands. The UML had tried to combine the class interest of the poor and ethnic interests of the minorities while radicalizing the interest of the people and society. The UML's general principle of uplift of the downtrodden had been moulded with the party's strategy of expanding its support bases along ethnic lines by pumping sectarian sentiments into minority groups. The UML, thus, established its image 'as a party of new ideas'[32] espousing rapid and radical change and also projecting its image as a champion of the poor and the disadvantaged sections of society. The UML, therefore, adopted a populist slogan: 'bread for the hungry, jobs for unemployed, land for landless, and shelter for the homeless' in the last general and all the local elections.

Unlike the UML's presentation as a moderate left, other Communist Parties, i.e. UPF, NPF and NWPP had fought the elections with their non-conformist stand against the monarchy and parliamentary system. Their election campaigns also included anti-India and anti-West postures.[33] The RPP had always projected itself before the voters as being close to the institution of monarchy in addition to being nationalist. The NSP had contested the elections in one single banner: uplift the Terai community against exploitation and discrimination by the hill high caste groups. The NSP appeared as a distinct regional party different from others. Its election manifestos, presented to the last two local elections and three general elections, had similar contents, e.g. to turn Nepal into a federal state, recognition of Hindi as a national language, reservation for Terai people in administration, police, army and other state organizations.[34]

But divergence of ideological/political identity and the postures of contending parties has hardly been reflected in their policy agendas presented before the voters, particularly in the case of the three major parties, the NC, the UML and the RPP. These parties gave emphasis to infrastructure building, rural development, land reform, agro-based and labour intensive cottage industries, social security, uplift of the minority and disadvantaged sections of society in all elections.[35] One study concluded that 'The two big parties (NC and UML) convey the same message on development, but in different languages.'[36] However, some changes were distinct in subsequent elections insofar as a policy shift was concerned.

Policy shift could be observed in the case of the UML in the 1994 general elections. Two factors influenced the party. One, the UML's tactical and qualified support to multi-party democracy which had been transformed into its commitment to the fundamental principles of liberal democracy following the party's Fifth National Congress in 1993 that had passed the resolution of *Janatako Bahudaliya Janabad.* Two, owing to the magnitude of *ghat-antarghat* in the NC on the eve of the 1994 mid term election, the UML seemed confident enough to gain power and and hence its slogan, 'Next government is the UML government'. The changed context demanded that the UML make some policy shift in some areas. As was expected, the UML's utterances about republican goals and its demands for restructuring the administration embodied in its previous manifesto were now omitted.

The 1999 general elections also witnessed some changes in the election agendas with some issues getting priority of the parties. The background of a hung parliament and change of government eight times between 1994 and 1999, indicating political instability in the country, worked in favour of such changes. This period was marked by the introduction of a number of aberrations, i.e. political corruption, horse-trading, manipulation of constitutional loopholes, perennial factional infighting and break-ups of political parties, etc., in Nepali politics. As the people were fed up with such politics, parties' opinions were divided according to their strength. The minority parties, the RPP in particular, stood for the continuation of a coalition system, blaming others for erosion of individual aspects of the political elite. The RPP was the greatest beneficiary of a political instability. Return of a majority government had, however, become the common agenda for both the major contesting parties, the NC and the UML, all of whom considerd it as a panacea for all problems facing the country. Another notable issue before the 1999 elections was the ongoing Maoist violent activities, pervasive corruption and unemployment. Such major issues were naturally reflected in the parties' election policies and programmes. Table 4.6 shows how the people saw the parties' agendas for the 1999 elections.

The table reveals that political parties raised the problems faced by the average Nepali and their needs in their campaigns. The opinion of all 500 respondents shows that the problems of 'security, control of corruption and price rise' (which were put in one basket in the questionnaire) scored 76 per cent in a list of parties' election agendas. This reflected the state of pervasive corruption and sky-rocketing price rise. Moreover, it also showed the deteriorating situation of law and order in the country after the Maoist started their violent activities in February 1996. The

TABLE 4.6: PARTIES' MAIN AGENDAS FOR 1999 ELECTIONS

Total no. of respondents: 500
% based on multiple response

Variables	Total		Area %		Sex %		Party Affiliation %	
	No.	%	Rural	Urban	Male	Female	Member	Non-member
Political stability	106	21.2	19.3	28.7	24.6	10.7	30.1	16.9
Infrastructure building	357	71.4	73.4	63.4	72.8	67.2	72.4	70.9
Nationality	46	9.2	6.5	19.8	10.6	4.9	14.7	6.5
Land reform	22	4.4	5.3	1.0	5.6	.8	7.4	3.0
Employment	236	47.2	48.1	43.6	51.1	35.2	47.2	47.2
Security, control of price and corruption	380	76.0	74.9	80.2	79.6	64.8	78.5	74.8
Uplift of dis-advantaged	172	34.4	32.1	43.6	32.5	40.2	36.8	33.2
Others	09	1.8	2.3	.0	1.3	3.3	.6	2.4
Don't know	26	5.2	6.0	2.0	3.4	10.7	1.2	7.1

number of deaths, including police, Maoists and general people, reached around 1,500 before the 1999 general elections. The Maoist war also forced the local people to migrate to other places thus creating the problem of displacement.

The respondents also found that political parties gave almost same weight to infrastructure building when they went before the people for votes. The variable of infrastructure building scored 71 per cent in party' priorities among election issues. Employment figured as the third major agenda, followed by uplift of the disadvantaged (34 per cent), political stability (21 per cent), nationality (9 per cent), and land reform (4 per cent). The cross tabulation of data by sex, class, occupation and religion reveals a small difference in identifying the third major agenda of political parties for the 1999 elections. Majority among women, housewives, rich and Buddhist respondents found that parties gave priority to the uplift of disadvantaged sections of society than to problems of unemployment. This explains the entry of caste, ethnicity, language, religion and other issues of exclusion in electoral politics. Some local leaders across parties felt the increase of ethnic and communal feeling among the social groups and its impact on voting behaviour.[37] Candidates across parties indirectly promoted communal sentiments to collect popular votes from the dominant cluster of minority communities. The question of nationalism and land reform were in the shadow in parties' election campaign in 1999. This explains why the radical communist parties, the ML and the rightist parties, the RPP (Chand group) in particular, which tried to build public opinion against India and the West, failed to cash in on such campaigns.

Local Level Campaign: The local problems and needs prevailed more than national and international issues in the parties' election campaign. A study team of Dang district observed, 'Election manifesto of parties do not have much meaning for the purpose of the election campaign. Even educated people do not take much interest in manifestos. So political parties, besides significant local concerns and issues, use popular and catchy slogans to appeal to the people. Development, security, nationalism, employment are some examples of such slogans.' Parties' strategic issues that were used for vote maximization also indicated the significance of local campaigning as can be seen from Table 4.7.

TABLE 4.7: ISSUES FOR VOTE MAXIMIZATION

Total no. of respondents: 500
% based on multiple response

Variables	Total		Area %		Sex %		Party Affiliation %	
	No.	%	Rural	Urban	Male	Female	Member	Non-member
Party' ideology and policy	217	43.4	42.6	46.5	48.7	27.0	54.6	58.0
Image of leadership	121	24.2	23.3	27.7	25.9	18.9	29.4	21.7
Candidate's personality	183	36.6	34.1	46.5	38.6	30.3	46.6	31.8
Assurance of development	416	83.2	83.0	84.2	83.9	81.1	81.6	84.0
Distribution of development material	192	38.4	39.3	34.7	42.1	27.0	36.2	39.5
Others	34	6.8	6.5	7.9	5.8	9.8	6.1	7.1
Don't know	32	6.4	6.5	5.9	4.5	12.3	1.8	8.6

In response to the question 'what are the major strategic issues parties generally used for vote maximization' almost all of the 500 respondents identified 'assurance for development' as the most important factor. The issue scored the highest mark of 83.2 per cent suggesting that the question of development is far more significant than other agendas in election strategies and peoples' voting behaviours. Even in the 1991 general elections—held in the background of the successful 1990 mass movement, when the ideological factor predominated in vote mobilization strategy—the question of development remained one of the major concerns of the people. A foreign observer cited what one NC candidate for the 1991 elections observed, 'We want to teach them (voters) about political rights and freedom, but they want to talk about schools, roads, drinking water and electricity.'[38] The localization of the election campaign in the 1994 mid term election too was expressed as follows, 'People were more interested in problems of drinking water, canals, roads, food, schools and range of other issues affecting their villages. . . .'[39] The local leaders of the sampled districts also identified the development as the key issue of election campaign. One can therefore conclude that the issue of infrastructure development heavily dominates elections in Nepal. Most candidates, irrespective of their party affiliation, sought the people's mandate on the basis of their promises to provide services like drinking water, schools, health post, transportation, communication, etc.

'Parties' ideology and policy' came as the second important issue for vote mobilization, with 43 per cent of the total 500 respondents expressing this view. But the opinion of the respondents differed in giving priority to particular issues. For the majority of female respondents, housewives and businessmen, the question of ideology and policy come only after the 'candidate's personality' in the order of priority order. The strategy of 'distribution of development material' by parties ranked the second in importance for the majority of rich and poor classes, agriculture, labour and service occupation groups, illiterate and literate persons, Newar, Dalit and Terai community, and for non-party members. This clearly indicated the decline of the role of ideology in elections despite it remaining the second most important factor. The convergence of most political parties under the constitutional framework and erosion of ideology in realpolitik explains why the ideological factor has increasingly become less relevant for vote mobilization strategy.

Distribution of development materials by contending parties/ ranked third in party' strategies of vote maximization. The practice of distribution of money and material for construction or other purposes in the name of development is increasingly becoming a trend to woo voters. Despite the fact that the election code of conduct forbids the use/abuse of state resources and power from the day of announcement of election, the party(ies) in power hardly followed it. The NC had always been in an advantageous position since it was in power in the last three general elections. Two of them (1991 and 1999 elections) were, however, conducted by a coalition government of three forces/ parties. The excessive manipulation of state power and resources was more acute in the local elections. So the party in power, the NC in 1992 and the UML in 1997, had won the local elections.

Candidates personality and image of party leadership came as the last in preferential order of parties' strategies of vote mobilization. This clearly shows the decline in popularity of role of leadership in the latest elections. Otherwise the image of parties' national leader was highly saleable in the early phase of democracy. In the early phase of the post-*Jana Andolan*, the NC organization building strategy was the highlight of its troika leaders' image as the *nayak* (hero) of the country. G.M. Singh's (commander of mass movement) refusal to become prime minister, Bhattarai's simple lifestyle with *chhata* (umbrella), one *surahi* (an earthen water pot), and one *tinko bakas* (a tin trunk), were invariably mentioned by the NC leaders, workers and sympathizers. But soon such an image of leaders declined when they started exercising power and influence. Many leaders were projected a as selfish and power hungry politicians, contrary to the people's perception as men of principle.

The UML lacked charismatic leaders except Madan Bhandari. His popularity reached its peak due to his victory over the interim PM K.P. Bhattari in the 1991 parliamentary election but Bhandari died in May 1993 in an accident. The position of the RPP leaders is mostly determined by their status in the dismantled Panchayat system. So the RPP lacks a crowd-puller personality.

Table 4.8 reveals that the modern means of election campaigning through the print and electronic media had been least used in Nepali elections. Instead, 'door to door campaigning' 'mass meeting/rally', 'workers mobilization' and 'pamphlet distribution' came in preferential order among several means adopted by political parties/candidates. An observation of 500 respondents might have been influenced by the situation of the latest 1999 general elections, which was distinct from previous elections in many respects. It was observed that election *mahol* was noticed least on the street in comparison to the past elections. Voters were silent before the polling day which was unusual and unprecedented in comparison to their active participation and involvement in the previous elections. Party candidates and campaigners, instead of 'wasting' time for rally, mass meeting and other demonstrative activities, adopted the most practical way of meeting the voters at their doorsteps.

The door to door campaign strategy had been used heavily in the 1999 election in comparison to the previous elections. The direct contact between the candidates and voters has its own positive dimension in bringing the potential ruler and ruled closer. But, it has been widely felt that a tendency of seeking a price for the vote in monetary terms or in the hope of getting job is

TABLE 4.8: PARTY/CANDIDATE—VOTERS COMMUNICATION

Total no. of respondents: 500
% based on multiple response

Variables	Total		Area %		Sex %		Party Affiliation %	
	No.	%	Rural	Urban	Male	Female	Member	Non-member
Door to door campaign	418	83.6	82.2	89.1	85.7	77.0	89.0	81.0
Mass meeting/ rally	348	69.6	69.7	69.3	70.4	67.2	73.0	68.0
Pamphlet distribution	223	44.6	44.9	43.6	44.2	45.9	38.7	47.5
Newspapers	11	2.2	2.0	3.0	1.3	4.9	1.8	2.4
Radio/ Television	5	1.0	.3	4.0	.8	1.6	.6	1.2
Village elite	96	19.2	21.3	10.9	21.2	13.1	16.6	20.5
Workers mobilization	304	60.8	60.4	62.4	63.2	53.3	62.6	59.9
Others	5	1.0	.8	2.0	1.3	.0	3.1	.0
Don't know	5	1.0	1.0	1.0	.3	3.3	1.2	.9

increasing. A previous study also found that individual interest rather than collective interest of society prevailed more in party-people relations during and after elections.[40] Leaders and workers across parties openly realized that elections have become increasingly expensive.

One of the reasons for elections becoming more expensive lies in the decline of voluntasrism in political parties. The party candidates generally try to activate party workers by granting them collective incentives (ideology, policy and leadership) and selective incentive (power, status, money, job and other opportunities). In the early phase of democracy party sympathizers, particularly those of the NC and the UML, were involved actively and spontaneously in election campaigns. But over time, parties have been losing their capacity of mobilization by means of granting collective incentives. The NC workers appeared relatively least active in the 1999 general election compared to their mobility in previous elections. This was also a hard reality of the UML, the RPP and the NSP. This trend was a consequence of decline of a ideology, value and morality in politics. During the hung parliament, politics had turned into a cruel game of government making and unmaking in which all kinds of manipulations had been used. Parties are increasingly becoming instrument for self-aggrandizement.

Parties in post-Election Times

Elections can be seen from two perspectives. First, as a process of getting people's mandate to rule over the country and, second, use of state power and resources for the benefit of the larger sections of people and society. For the post-election time, the moot question is whether the parties and people's elected representatives fulfil the promise made during elections, and whether the agendas they presented before the voters are translated into the government policy. Though the people at large have become critical of parties' role in post-election time, some appreciation was shown for parties' initiative in bringing about social reform and economic development in all the five sampled districts.

The restoration of the multiparty system is equated in both conceptual and operational terms with the citizen's freedom to speak without fear. This has given a sense of empowerment in both subjective and objective ways that reflects the rise of social movements among the disadvantaged sections of society. Social reforms against untouchability, women's movement against exploitation, ethnic upsurge against deprivation, political awareness and consciousness could be seen in all the five sampled districts. Credit has been given to multi-party democracy rather than to any particular political party in creating people's awareness, confidence, and assertiveness. Another common thing that was observed in all five sampled districts was development in the sector of infrastructure building, e.g. education, road construction, school building, health, electrification, communication and telecommunication.

But making an assessment of parties' performance in post-election time in totality, the voters seemed to be very disappointed with political parties and their representatives. The advent of democracy has in its wake brought into focus a number of pervasive socio-economic problems in different forms, i.e. gender issues, minority problems, grievances of the disadvantaged groups, unemployment, corruption, etc. But political parties appear largely not sincere in addressing such emerging social and economic problems and in providing realistic and pragmatic policy incentives. The first tenure of parliament (1991-4), featured by a bitter confrontation between the NC government and the Left-dominated opposition and internal conflicts in the ruling party, ended without any significant achievement. Politics deteriorated to the lowest ebb in the second parliament (1994-9) featured by a hung parliament and coalition government. The third parliament appears indifferent to resolving a number of problems facing the country. Political parties within parliament have failed to present a common agenda of parliamentary parties to counter the Maoist threat.

People's anger and frustration against the non-performance of political parties and their representatives in the local and central government was manifested distinctly during the field study. In Table 4.9, one can see how people see the performance of party representatives' in elected bodies.

In response to a question about the fulfilment of promises by the parties/candidate after they are elected, only 2.2 per cent fully agreed. Those who partly agreed were 22.6 per cent. But 72.4 per cent of the total 500 respondents completely disagreed with the statement that parties/candidates fulfill their promise after they are elected. Even the respondents belonging to party members shared this general feeling by an overwhelming count of 71.8 per cent. This shows a vast gap between the people and the parties in Nepal.

TABLE 4.9: POST-ELECTION PERFORMANCE

Total no. of respondents 500

Variables	Total		Area %		Sex %		Party Affiliation %	
	No	%	Rural	Urban	Male	Female	Member	Non-member
Agree	11	2.2	2.0	3.0	2.4	1.6	1.8	2.4
Partly agree	113	22.6	23.3	19.8	23.3	20.5	25.2	21.4
Disagree	362	72.4	71.7	75.2	72.8	71.3	71.8	72.7
Don't know	14	2.8	3.0	2.0	1.6	6.6	1.2	3.6

People's complaints against parties and elected representatives comprise a long list accumulated from the sampled districts. Accordingly, most party(ies) leaders, once they are elected, hardly looked back and visited their constituencies; nor did they care and hear people's grievances. They were only involved in party politics by an means.

Once the elections are over, the distance between the people and the party increases. A number of opinion surveys show that 'poverty, price rise and unemployment' are the most important problems of the country.[41] But these problems were put as 'miscellaneous' in parties agendas and priority lists. The gap between the people and the party has been further widened by the ways political parties perform patronage distribution function. Instead of maintaining direct contact with the masses, party leaders rely on a small group of activists, many of them local leaders who pursue personal interests. Only these people, not the masses, are getting benefits from the patronage of the party leaders.

Conclusion

Of the twin electoral functions of political parties—acquisition of legitimacy and respect for people's interest—the latter has been neglected in Nepal. A decade-long democratic experience, during which general elections were held thrice and local elections twice, shows that political parties represented only votes, not the interest of the people. This has a negative impact on parties' image as change agents. Parties' credential as change agents remains only in theory, in formal documents (i.e. election manifestos and agendas), and in promises and assurances to the voters. Parties' potentials to bring about change in social, economic and political spheres have not well been transformed into reality. What is wrong?

The candidate selection process, though centralized, is not seriously objectionable so long as parties' respect public opinion and consult their own local leaders in the 'decision' making process. But the exclusion of marginalized sections of society, i.e. women, Dalit, poor, illiterate shows the candidate selection process as an elitist affair. The process, therefore, needs reformation for broader participation and decentralization for the future. The consideration of continuity and popularity factors while choosing persons for candidacy is admirable. But, at the same time, the entry of money power, family and kinship ties, proximity to party high command and other ascriptive factors in nomination of party candidates certainly impede a party's ability to work in post-election times.

The last general and local elections have shown that parties contested and campaigned during elections on general and vague agendas: development, political stability and social security. Lack of specific policy agendas to attract voters seem to show an immaturity in political parties. Abuse of state power and resources by the ruling party(ies) is another form of manipulation of elections. Moreover, the decline of parties' ability to motivate their own workers and mobilize voters through collective incentive has allowed the role of money and muscle power in elections.

Party-people relations have become more problematic in post-election times. Since Nepali politics is perennially bogged down in intra-party and inter-party conflicts, people's problems and needs have always been sidelined. Conceivably, political parties in general have become too selfish to take up the burning issues concerning ordinary voters. Consequently, political parties appear largely not to be sincere in addressing emerging social and economic problems, and to give realistic and pragmatic policy incentives.

To rectify such a situation, some concrete measures should be taken to improve the overall relations within and among the parties. While doing so, one should keep in mind that the smooth functioning of multiparty democracy requires effective leadership, responsible government, constructive opposition, healthy competition, primacy of policy and programme, good governance, etc. Moreover, crisis management within the party is a prerequisite for healthy development of the party system. So, parties may regain their ability to work as true linkage institutions between the people's interest and the government's policy.

NOTES

1. *The Constitution of the Kingdom of Nepal,* 1990.
2. The party adopted its name as Nepali Congress party in 1950 after the merger of Nepali Rashtriya Congress (1947) and Nepali Prajatantra Congress (1948).

3. See Lok Raj Baral, *Oppositional Politics in Nepal,* New Delhi: Abhinav Publications, 1977. For understanding panchayat system and various forms and types of opposition at that time, see Rishikesh Shaha, *Nepali Politics: Retrospect and Prospect,* New Delhi: Oxford University Press, 1978; *Essays in the Practice of Government in Nepal,* New Delhi: Manohar, 1982; Lok Raj Baral, *Nepal's Politics of Referendum: A Case Study of Groups, Personalities and Trends,* New Delhi: Vikas Publishing House, 1983.
4. See Bhim Rawal, *Nepal ma Samyabadi Andolan: Udbhav, Vikas ra Bartaman Abastha* (Communist Movement in Nepal: Origin, Evolution and Recent Development), Kathmandu: Samana Prakashan, 1988; C.P. Mainali, *Bartaman Prajatantrik Andolan ko Sandharva ma* (On the Present Context of Democratic Movement), Kathmandu: Subhakamana Prakashan, 1990.
5. Lok Raj Baral, Krishna Hachhethu and Hari Sharma, *Leadership in Nepal,* New Delhi: Adroit Publishers, 2001, pp. 56-71; Sudhindra Sharma and Pawan Kumar Sen, *1999 General Election Opinion Poll: How Voters Assess Politics, Parties and Politicians,* Kathmandu: Himal Association, 1999, p.16; Krishna Hachhethu, 'Reading the Opinion Poll', in Himal Association, *Political Opinion Survey Nepal 2001,* Kathmandu: Himal Association, 2001, pp. 3-10.
6. Krishna Khanal and Krishna Hachhethu, *Amnirbachan 2056: Sansad ra Sarkar ka Chunautiharu* (General Elections 1999: Challenges to the Parliament and the Government), Kathmandu: Centre for Nepal and Asian Studies (CNAS), 1999, p. 28.
7. For details about party politics in 1951-60 see Anirudha Gupta, *Politics in Nepal : A Study of Post-Rana Political Development and Party Politics,* Bombay: Allied Publishers, 1964; Bhuwan Lal Joshi and Leo E. Rose, *Democratic Innovations in Nepal: A Case Study of Political Acculturation,* Berkeley: University of California Press, 1966.
8. For early period of Communist movement in Nepal, see K.C. Surendra, *Nepal ma Communist Andolanko Itihas* (History of Communist Movement in Nepal), Kathmandu: Vidyarthi Pustak Bhandar, 1999.
9. Krishna Hachhethu, *Party Building in Nepal: Organization, Leadership and People, The Nepali Congress Party and The Communist Party of Nepal, Unified Marxist-Leninist,* Kathmandu: Mandala Book Point, 2002, p. 70.
10. The split of the UML in March 1998 had directly affected its position as 43 seats were lost by the party. Were the votes polled by the candidates of the breakaway group, the ML, to add to the candidates of the UML, the party would gain a comfortable majority of 112 seats instead of the present 69 seats in the HOR. See Khanal and Hachhethu, op. cit., p. 25.
11. Charles W. Anderson, *Statecraft: An Introduction to Political Choice and Judgement,* New York: John Wiley & Sons, 1977, p. 155.
12. Lok Raj Baral, 'The 1994 Nepal Elections: Emerging Trends in Party Politics', *Asian Survey,* vol. 35, no. 5, May 1995, p. 440.

13. For social cleavage based two dominant party system in India, see Pradeep K. Chibber, *Democracy Without Association: Transformation of the Party System and Social Cleavages in India,* New Delhi: Vistar Publications, 1999; Subrata K. Mitra, 'Indigenisation, Locally Embedded Values and Parties as Instruments for State-Society Relations: An Agenda for Research', paper presented to international workshop on Political Parties in South Asia, in Nottingham, UK, 29 March-1 April 2001.
14. Election Commission, *The Election Code of Conduct, 2053 (1996),* Kathmandu: Election Commission, 1999 (1st edn).
15. *The Constitution of Nepali Congress 1960 (Amended in 1995); The Constitution of Rashtriya Prajatantra Party 1990.*
16. *Text of Organizational Report Passed by Eight, National Congress of UML, 1993,* p. 7.
17. Ram Kumar Dahal, 'Electoral Campaign: Candidate Selection Process of Political Parties,' in Political Science Association of Nepal (POLSAN), *Political Parties and the Parliamentary Process in Nepal: A Study of the Transitional Phase,* Kathmandu: POLSAN, 1992, pp. 104-13.
18. Interview with Sambhu Koirala (Chief District Officer [CDO] in Dhankuta), Gupta Bahadur Shrestha (District Superintendent of Police [DSP] in Dhankuta), Mahendra Kumar Pokhrel (DSP, Rautahat), Ram Bahadur Gurung (DSP in Dang), Narayan Gopal Malegu (CDO in Dang), Ram Krishna Bhurtel (CDO in Baitadi) on 15-30 January 2001.
19. *Saptahik Bimarsa,* 29 March 1991.
20. Dahal, op. cit., pp. 104-13.
21. Interview with NC local leaders of sampled districts: Ramesh Amatya (Dhankuta), Majdul Huk (Rautahat), Sukra Raj (Kaski), Dipak Regmi (Dang) and Narendra Singh Thapa (Baitadi) on 15-30 January 2001.
22. Interview with Bhim Acharya, 20 February 2001.
23. Interview with UML local leaders of sampled districts: Tika Ram Chemjong (Dhankuta), Ram Chandra Patel (Rautahat), Som Nath Pyasi (Kaski), Devi Pokhrel (Dang) and Maya Bhatta (Baitadi) on 15-30 January 2001.
24. Interview with Ramesh Amatya (NC, Dhankuta) on 15-30 January 2001.
25. Alane Ware, *Citizens, Parties and the State,* Cambridge: Polity Press, 1987, p. 158.
26. Ram Kumar Dahal, 'Candidate Selection in the 1999 Parliamentary Elections', *NCCS Occasional Paper I,* Kathmandu: Nepal Centre for Contemporary Studies, December 2000, p. 16.
27. John Whelpton, 'The General Elections of May 1991', in Michael Huut, ed., *Nepal in Nineties,* New Delhi: Oxford University Press, p. 71.
28. 'A Glimpse of Communist Party of Nepal (UML) Fifth National Congress', *New Era* (published by Foreign Affairs Department of UML), April 1993, pp. 4-10.

29. Institute for Integrated Development Studies (IIDS), *The Third Parliamentary Election: A Study of the Evolving Democratic Process in Nepal,* Kathmandu: IIDS, 1994, p. 25.
30. IIDS, *The Second Parliamentary Election: A Study of Emerging Democratic Process in Nepal,* Kathmandu: IIDS, 1993, p. 36.
31. Martin Hoftun, William Raeper and John Whelpton, *People, Politics and Ideology: Democracy and Social Change in Nepal,* Kathmandu: Mandala Book Point, 1999, pp. 115-86.
32. Loe Borre, Sushil Raj Panday and Chitra Krishna Tiwari, *Nepalese Political Behaviour,* New Delhi: Sterling, 1994, p. 52.
33. See *Election Manifesto of United People's Front 1991, 1994, 1999; Election Manifesto of Nepal Workers and Peasants Party 1991, 1994, 1999; Election Manifesto of National People's Front 1999.*
34. See *Election Manifesto of Nepal Sadbhabana Party 1991, 1994, 1999.*
35. See *Election Manifesto of Nepali Congress 1991, 1994, 1999; Election Manifesto of Nepal Communist Party, Unified Marxist-Leninist 1991, 1994, 1999; Election Manifesto of Rashtriya Prajatantra Party 1991, 1994, 1999.*
36. IIDS, op. cit., p. 24.
37. Interview with Ramesh Amatya (NC, Dhankuta), Sarad Shrestha (Independent, Dhankuta), Khajanchi Saha (CPN, United Rautahat), Majdul Huk (NC, Rautahat), and Tek Nath Gautam (Independent, Dang) on 15-30 January 2001.
38. Fred Gaige and John Scholz, 'The 1991 Parliamentary Elections in Nepal: Political Freedom and Stability', *Asian Survey,* vol. 31, no.11, November 1991, p. 1047.
39. Baral, op. cit., p. 434.
40. Baral, Hachhethu and Sharma, op. cit., pp. 110-14.
41. Nepal Opinion Survey Centre (NOSC), *Political Opinion Survey of Kathmandu Valley 1993,* Kathmandu: NOSC, 1993; SEARCH, *The Three District Political Opinion Survey,* Kathmandu: SEARCH, 1994; Krishna Khanal et al., *Nepal: People, Polity and Governance: A Survey Analysis of People's Response to the Democratic Experiment 1991-1995,* Kathmandu: Centre for Consolidation of Democracy, 1996.

CHAPTER 5

Social Structure and Voting Behaviour

Dhruba Kumar*

THE NEPALI STATE AND SOCIETY: AN OVERVIEW

Nepal is predominantly an agrarian community where 90 per cent of the people live in its politically demarcated 4,000 village development committees constituting the lowest rung of electoral units in the country's electoral system. Social relationships in Nepal are therefore firmly rooted in the bonds formed at the village level. The villages where the *Thalus/Mukhias* (chiefs) or the *Hune Khane* (economically prosperous) people command both respect and obedience in general from the rest of the inhabitants mostly shine in politics.

The social construct in Nepal, carved in accordance with the Hindu ethos based on *Manusmriti*, has always been thoroughly discriminatory in organizing society. Throughout its history prior to and beginning with the Shah dynasty (1769), the state's policy in governance has been the policy of exclusion as was evidenced in the *Dibya Upadesh* of the first Shah king of present-day Nepal, Prithvi Narayan Shah, which in fact remains the directive principles of state policy in constituting the Nepali State. The social segregation stipulated in the divine instructions of Prithvi Narayan Shah was later codified into a national legal code by the first Rana prime minister, Jang Bahadur Rana, in 1854 through the adoption of a *Muluki Ain* (civil code) classifying the human species living in the territory of Nepal into different categories on the basis of the caste system by officially institutionalizing the process of social injustice.

Through the codification of the caste system Nepali society was made hierarchical, not pyramidal, where the minority at the

*The author acknowledges the cooperation of Shikha Prasai, Mrigendra Karki and Rishi Ram Pangeni for collecting field data.

top asserted the rights to dominate the majority at the bottom by broadly dividing society into high castes, touchables, touchable but enslavable, and untouchables as the outcaste. Thus caste has become an institution protected and promoted by the state by nurturing customized laws in accordance with the Hindu *Dharma.* Religion and rituals prohibit the inclusion of those considered impure, lowly and untouchables, into the social sphere. Caste therefore has in itself become an exclusionary social institution forcing those considered low caste and outcaste to live a life on the margins and struggle to survive on the crumbs. Ultimately the caste system has become a process of social exclusion through which participation is restricted and claims to social opportunities denied.[1] Though the New *Muluki Ain* promulgated by the late King Mahendra in 1963 has legally ended the overt social discrimination embedded in the1854 *Muluki Ain,* it did nothing to eliminate the caste system which in fact is the originator of social segregation.

As the law of the land has created the social divide, it is but natural for the high caste people to form coalitions with the rulers of the country at the centre and the periphery to coexist and govern with the consent of the central authority as their subordinates. Thus the beneficiaries of the political system are high caste people who are protected by the law of the land and privy to the state purse through different means. Continuation of this factor has led to the emergence of local elites based on caste, ethnicity, law and the possession of wealth principally derived from their coalition with the ruling class. As the country was ruled by the 'land-military complex' throughout its past history between 1769 and 1951, the socio-political as well as the economic situation was akin to the virtual enslavement of the common people to both de facto and de jure rulers. As Adhikari has noted: 'For the common illiterate mass, however, there was nothing to choose between absolute rule by the Shah dynasty or by the Rana family. Under either system the people in general were considered no more than *Raitis* and *Prajas* (tenants and subjects), who had duties to perform but no rights to enjoy.'[2]

Till recently, Nepal was a closed society where politics was the profession of the courtiers and participation was more selective than elective. The rulers had no social obligation other than to control and punish the offenders of the law of the land.

Prohibition was rigidly maintained even in the apolitical sphere of public life like education until 1951. There were very few schools and access was given to a few people besides some Sanskrit schools open for the Brahmins to pursue traditional learning. The first public school that was established for the select people in AD 1854 in Kathmandu later became famous as the Darbar High School.

People aspiring to join professions other than traditional agricultural occupations had to undergo several spells of *chakari* system seeking favours from the rulers or the powerful to join government jobs. The system of sycophancy was so entrenched in Nepali society that with every change of ruler or the power elite the group of people either shifted their loyalty or were purged from their positions to be replaced by another group of persons loyal to the incumbent. This has led to the emergence of *apno-manchhe* (one's own men) system, which according to Bista, led to the creation of one's own defined group in the society. As he says:

> Most of the time Nepali individuals remain indifferent to and unaffected by events that concern the people outside of one's own group. [Thus] the distinction between the in-group of 'us' and the rest of the outsiders as 'they' manifests in every walk of social, sultural and economic life. Everything inside the circle of 'us' is predictable and manipulable, and outside the circle is unpredictable. So there is a constant need to maintain the line of that circle.'

Bista further says:

> There is no security without the existence of this circle. The persistence of ethnic or regional identity in addition to the social and ritual hierarchy is a manifestation of a need to have one's own circle defined clearly and maintained permanently. By inference then the ethnic or regional or caste identity would collapse only when new circle of classes, professions or new residential areas with permanent migration are created.[3]

Traditionally, political power in Nepal was thus enjoyed by three dominant high caste people constituting primarily Brahmins, Chhetries and Newars as the latter were accommodated to the Royal Court by virtue of their being the architects of Nepal's statecraft during the Malla period that ended with Prithvi Narayan Shah's conquest of the Kathmandu valley in 1769. Since then, as one study noticed, 'There is an astonishing continuity in the predominance of the high caste and specific ethnic groups in administration since the formation of the Nepali state more than two centuries and a quarter ago, which appear to have occupied 98 per cent of top civil service posts in 1854 [the date of codification of *Muluki Ain*]. More than a century later, in 1969, this percentage came down only marginally, to 93 per cent.'[4] Available data for 1998 suggest that the composition of civil service had hardly changed, as the three traditional elite caste groups occupy some 88 per cent of the secretary level, 92.3 per cent of additional secretary, 89 per cent of deputy secretary, 95 per cent of section officer level positions in the bureaucracy.[5]

As Hinduism becomes the source of legitimization of the Nepali State and *Hukumi Shashan* (rule by pre-emptory command) the law, it was but natural for the political power of the country to rest on the choicest few of the monarch or the person ruling on his behalf in the course of centralization of the governing authority. In the course of territorial expansion between 1769 and 1816, Nepal was struggling to attain the features of an unitary state. The segmentary nature of the state was prominent as its territorial sovereignty over the conquered land was yet to be recognized and scentralized control established. Relations between the centre and periphery were moreover maintained by forging a vertical coalition of interests competing for power, position and wealth through the manipulation of local authority as the central authority declined in the far-flung areas of the conquered territory.

Consequently the formation of the power elite in the country constitutes a phenomenon based on the traditional forces entrenched in society in the course of the territorial integration of the Nepali State. Though the rulers under the Shah dynasty had conquered the outlying territories, they had not abolished the *Raja* and *Rajauta* system of the vanquished land till 1960s. Instead, the vanquished *Rajas* of the *Baishes* (22) and *Chaubishes* (24) petty-states of Nepal and their hangers-on were appropriately awarded for their compliance and loyalty to the central authority in Kathmandu. Except for the vanquished Malla rulers of the Kathmandu valley, the vassals therefore became the nobility under the Shah dynasty. Till date the tradition for the king of Nepal declaring four of his choicest vassals as *Rajas* has continued. This system retains its influence not only in the formation of local authority but in the process of the creation of both political and power elites after the dawn of a short-lived democracy in Nepal in 1951. The social networking established by the high caste people and the members of the abolished petty-states' royal family remained influential enough to determine and shape the political course of the areas they inhabited either by becoming members or local leaders of political parties or Royal nominees, etc., during the panchayat regime in the country between 1960 and 1990. The nexus between the ex-Royals and their loyal has woven a strong social fabric, which remains a dominant political ethos in the country. One of the reasons behind the persistence of such a situation in the country is the preponderance of the patronage flowing from the central authority which has continued to influence the local political dispensations as well as the electoral processes under democratic Nepal post-1990.

The political choice under democracy, while selecting a leader during the ticket distribution for electoral candidacy, has increasingly been based on the candidates loyalty to the central leader, his money and muscle power rather than his popular base while aspiring for the candidacy. Political parties, by necessity and choice, virtually work for regrouping the same traditional forces' same support to be used as a ladder to climb to power that brings prestige and wealth. As a result, the electoral process has become virtually stagnant, the electoral recruitment process highly personalized, and the representational pattern confined mostly to the top echelon, of society much to be desired in leaving the question of power sharing with the backward communities and social inclusion. Social inclusion, as a measure, can be achieved by broadening the participation providing constrain free opportunities to the citizenry irrespective of class, caste, and ethnic background.

However, the composition of the influential organs of political parties, parliamentary representation as well as the cabinet suggests otherwise. All the major political parties are top-heavy with the high caste groups; representation in the parliament features the same thus leading to the formation of successive cabinets constituted by the high caste people. Consequently, the policies emanating from these democratic institutions are favourably disposed towards catering to the interests of the same group dominating these organs. Thus 'procedural democracy' has also fundamentally continued to preserve the traditional social norms that do not work towards broadening the scope of participation as stipulated in the Directive Principles and Policies of the State in the 1990 Constitution.

> The social objective of the State shall be to establish and develop, on the foundation of justice and morality, a healthy social life, by eliminating all types of economic and social inequalities and by establishing harmony amongst the various castes, tribes, religions, languages, races and communities.
>
> It shall be the chief responsibility of the State to maintain conditions suitable to the enjoyment of the fruits of democracy through wider participation of the people in the governance of the country and by way of decentralization, and to promote general welfare by making provisions for the protection and promotion of human rights, by making tranquility and order in the society.[6]

This incites a fundamental question: what does the electoral process under democracy actually mean and what the Nepali citizens as eligible voters think of election and the vote? Have the voters understood the value of vote and therefore how have they voted. What are the preferences for the choice of their representatives? Does personality, ethnicity, kinship or caste affect the voters' orientation and choice of the candidate to represent them? How have they inculcated the worth of the person they have voted for to represent their thinking and voice to the state's legislature and how do they relate their objective of electing a responsible representative to the state legislature to attain and address their cause? Is the candidate from a constituency of his/her choice or is he/she imposed from above by the party's high command?

Election is a process of empowerment of the people under democracy. Vote enfranchises a person and makes him/her a citizen whose decision counts. Vote also symbolizes choice of a representative. Moreover the representative is dependent on the people of his/her constituency. In the final analysis, vote entrusts the collective will of the people in choosing a particular candidate to make their sovereign representation.

The primary objective of this paper is therefore to understand the voting behaviour of the Nepali people against the background of the three national elections as well as the two local elections held under democracy in the post-1990 period. Party politics have provided them a choice to choose the leaders of their political preference. But as the results of the three elections have shown, the Nepali electorate has confined its choice to the three prominent parties as their preferred representatives to the parliament. Ethnically, all the three political parties are high caste dominated parties. Several ethnic groups raising their voices against social discrimination and misrepresentation have vehemently opposed their policies. Still these parties have managed to come at the top through elections. Seen against the background of the ethnic clamour for their rightful representation in the political mainstream, elections in Nepal have proven to be the misrepresentation of the popular will. Therefore, elections held democratically are also manipulative. So what makes the election click and why have the people vote?

The paper therefore endeavours to answer the questions raised on the basis of the results of the three elections and the electoral processes in Nepal. Secondly, the paper also tries to provide a general perspective on the Nepali electorate considering the social perception and attitudes of voters, their expectations, needs and priorities. Thirdly, the paper deals with the political orientation and political choice of the voters. Finally, the paper concludes with an observation of the pattern and trend set particularly by the empirical finding of the survey research.

THE ELECTORATE

According to the Constitution (1990), 'Any citizen of Nepal who has completed the age of eighteen years shall be entitled to vote in one electoral constituency in a manner specified by law.'[7] Thus, when democratic Nepal prepared for the first general election in the post-1990 period, the number of eligible voters was recorded at slightly over 10.1 million out of the total population of 18.4 million. The total vote cast in the 1991 election was 72,91,084 which was 65.15 per cent of the total voters and around 40 per cent of the total population. The voters then elected 205 representatives to the parliament (the lower house) under the multiparty polity, which, when divided on the basis of representation of the total population, comes to a number of people per one representative or the member of parliament (MP). One MP's representation in terms of votes cast is 35,566 on an average and in terms of eligible voters is 54,594 on an average. If one were to indulge in member game, the 1991 election to the parliament shows the representation made by an MP was above 35,000 voters, but in reality in some constituencies the votes actually received by a candidate during the election was far below that number. There are constituencies (districts) in Nepal like Manang, Mustang and Dolpa, to name but three, where the total eligible voters were 6,358, 11,312 and 16,528 respectively. Similarly, the votes cast in these constituencies were 3,793, 7,535 and 14,181 out of which the valid votes were 3,681, 7,226, and 13,720. The candidate in Manang who won the election by receiving just 3,060 votes represented more than 35,000 eligible voters in parliament. The same candidate represented nearly 90,000 people on the national average if non-voting minors were also included. The MP who receives only a portion of the votes actually cast in the election is empowered by nearly 90,000 people on average to decide their fate. This is the consequence of the electorate system that makes at least on representative from each of the 75 districts in Nepal compulsory. With demographic change, and population growth on an average of 2.4 per cent per annum the number of voters also increased in the subsequent elections. In 1994, the total number of voters were 1,23,27,329 with 61.86 per cent (76,25,348) votes were cast. Comparably, there were 1,35,18,839 voters in 1999 and the votes cast were 65.79 per cent (88,94,566). For the average electorate in Nepal the election of an MP to the House of Representatives is actually a misrepresentation.

The three general elections indicate a certain consistency in voting by the people. Over 60 per cent of the votes cast by the people can be considered as the peoples' enthusiasm for participation as well as for their collective interests in strengthening the democratic process. The increase in the number of eligible voters, however, has not led to any substantial change in the percentage of votes cast. A marginal dip in the percentage occurred in the 1994 mid term elections because that election was fought agendaless by the political parties. Otherwise, even with the frustrating experience of the democratic process people voted en-masse in the 1999 elections, continuing their belief in the democratic process.

Compared with the world standard the proportion of eligible

Nepalis who cast their vote is low. In most democracies the percentage is as high as 90 per cent and above and as low as 70 per cent. But Nepal compares well with India—the largest democracy in the world and its neighbour—where 50 to 60 per cent is the standard voting proportion in general. Although, the system of representation as generally practiced in the democratic world today is a system of misrepresentation in which the numbers game is played with majority and minority votes, the electoral system adopted on the basis of first-past-the-post makes the 'winner takes all' as an imperative. Representation therefore is majoritarianism. The electoral system in Nepal is an adaptation of the British parliamentary system with a single representative election from all the constituencies to the House of Representatives. Constitutionally, elections are held as a routine affair within five years of the previous elections as a right given to the electorate to choose their representatives. But democracies do not necessarily follow this pattern. Elections are also held in between the stipulated period of five years if the government does not work, if the government fails to muster popular support in the parliament, if the government is voted out of the parliament through vote of no-confidence, and if the popular government desires so to further restore the popular mandate for another term. Nepal had three elections within ten years. Comparably, India had three national elections between 1996 and 1999.

The electoral politics thrives on the political parties' support base built primarily on their ideological foundation and popular mobilization. In a multi-party democratic system, political parties are the genuine instruments linking government with society. Vote, in this context, becomes the decisive factor representing the popular will to put a certain political party to power to govern for a fixed period of time. The voters' preference therefore is critical in making choice of the political party to make their representation in the government. Voters' choice cannot be considered straightforward; the choice is made out of the influence of several complicating factors ranging from societal, economic, religious, and ethnic as well as ideological. The candidate representing a political party in his/her constituency also makes voters conscious and sensitive of the situation in the respective constituency leading the voters to determine who and what should be their choice.

The three national elections in Nepal have already demonstrated the choices of the voters. The voters had differentiated between political parties while making their choice and they had chosen different representatives from different political parties from their constituencies. If one were to make the unit analysis of the voting behaviour of the three national elections, one may find that there is no unilinear representation of candidates of a particular political party from a particular constituency in general. This shows that the voters had alternated between and among different political parties while electing their representatives. Thus, the voters in general lacked a fixed view of either political parties or their programme or the person representing the policies. Such a situation arises just because of the performances of the representatives that the voters had sent to the national legislature in the previous two elections. Generally, the voters expect their representatives to be loyal and responsible to their constituencies' needs. When the delegation of authority to representatives by the voters does not work or becomes unresponsive to the constituency's needs, it would be natural for the voters to turn away from their previous choice. Such vote fluctuation is observed in the electoral process in Nepal as evidenced by the field surveys undertaken for this study. Voters' choice of a representative is made on different preferences, constituting the political party, policy and performance of the party in government, personality of the candidate, as well as primordial relationships, the latter being particularly responsible in the choice of the candidate at the local level elections than in the context of the national elections. But, election studies particularly focusing on the electorate in general have found the following types of voters everywhere on the basis of which a typology of voters is constructed (see Table 5.1).

In the electoral history of the country, Nepal had its first general elections based on universal suffrage in 1959. Nine political parties had contested the elections of which four parties emerged with 93 per cent of the total parliamentary seats. The Nepali Congress party won with only 37.2 per cent of the total popular votes and suceeded in capturing more than 72 per cent of the parliamentary seats.[8] Two elections were held on the basis of adult franchise in 1981 and 1986 during the panchayat regime. Panchayat election system had passed through several stages—

TABLE 5.1: TYPOLOGY OF VOTERS

Cultural Type	Behavioural Type	Attitudinal Type	Rational Type
Parochial voters	Stable or loyal voters	Party voters	True issue voters
Subject voters	Party changers	Candidate voters	Material interests
Participant voters	Marginal voters	Issue voters	Performance
	Apathetic voters		Oriented
	New voters		

Source: Based on Ole Borre, 'Election Survey and Voter Types', paper presented at a seminar on Electoral Process in Nepal: Review and Prospects, organized by Political Science Association of Nepal (POLSAN), Kathmandu, 3 August 1990.

indirect to controlled to direct elections based on adult franchise after 1981. Yet such elections educated the voters to make their choice.

Restoration of multiparty democracy in 1990 changed the context in which the electorate gained their fundamental rights of making the government of their choice through political competition, so far denied to them after 1960. One of the crucial aspects of the political change in Nepal is that the voters have their experiences with the politician irrespective of their being members of political parties or the socially influential. The voters have also observed the shifting loyalties of politicians from one political dispensation to another and the rush of the erstwhile *panchas* to join and regroup under different political parties. They are also aware of the sociology of different political parties under democracy. The voters in Nepal, though living in a traditionally orthodox society, being illiterate, poor, and ignorant and inexperienced, have, in fact, shown a surprising degree of social awareness and political sense while choosing candidates. The stimuli provided to the voters by democracy is that there vote represents the collective will of the people to form a government and making their vote again as a decisive factor in pulling down the government whenever they wish so. The three national elections held so far are an indication of the voters' perception of the performance of political parties in treasury and opposition benches. The changing dynamics of the voters' choice to seat and unseat a certain political party in the government by exercising their political rights seems to have given a sense of empowerment to the people. Unfortunately it is limited to the ballot box.

As a study conducted in 2001 suggests, individuals with vested interests may have different considerations in their political choice during elections. For the people the choice was largely determined by the two prominent factors: the impact of the *Jana Andolan* 1990 and the preference of ideology.[9] As the *Jana Andolan* was led by the Nepali Congress with the crucial support provided by the United Left Front of the Communist Parties, the people in general tend to treat the Nepali Congress and the CPN (ML) as political parties with high esteem. But if one were to note the popular votes received by these two competing political parties, the Nepali Congress has to satisfy itself with a similar proportion of the popular votes it received in the 1959 elections (37.2 per cent) whereas the Communist Party of Nepal that had won just 4 seats and received 7.2 per cent of popular votes in 1959 has made its strong presence in post-1990, enabling the CPN (UML) even to form a minority government after the 1994 mid term poll. Following these two parties is the conglomeration of the erstwhile *panchas* in the shape of the Rashtriya Prajatantra Party (RPP) that came into being with the advent of democracy in Nepal. Several other parties are in competitive politics. Many of them however have miserably failed to show their presence in the national parliament. Election results of local bodies held twice in 1992 and 1997 have shown it clearly. Political parties, which have been able to come to parliament, have also retained their presence in local bodies too. According to the results of these elections one can easily say that the political parties that have prominently gained their seats in the national parliament have been predominant in the formation of the local bodies too. Thus both the NC and the CPN (UML) and a few other political parties have fared well in the local elections.

Interestingly, the local elections had U-turns in the peoples' verdict in giving opposite results. The election results also indicate two specific aspects of national politics, which should be taken into perspective while assessing the impact of the voters' choice and the electoral outcomes. First, the shift of verdict in the local bodies election from the NC to the CPN (UML) between 1992 and 1997 clearly shows that the political party in power at the centre best influences the election results. Second, the commitment of the national electorate is also unstable. Otherwise, the votes would not have swung drastically from the earlier 50 per cent to NC in 1992 to the later 50 per cent to the UML in 1997 at the local level. Factors influencing such shifting trend could be many but the influence and intervention of the central authority had been distinct in such a turnabout in voting. Our field studies and interviews substantiate this too.

Another facet of the electoral politics in Nepal is basically societal which is also becoming politically sensitive enveloping ethnic, caste, and economic dimensions. Ethnicization of politics is one of the crucial agendas of research in the contemporary milieu. More so when ethno-politics becomes a driving force in organizing political societies and demands for equitable power sharing and social inclusion are being raised. Nepal is also not an exception to the worldwide trend of ethnic determination of politics through regrouping of the people on religious, linguistic and cultural terms. As the Constitution of Nepal (1990) has invoked the reality of the State as being multi-ethnic, multi-lingual and multi-religous, the fundamental urge of the people has become their sovereign right to represent the reality. But the very Constitution that has accepted the ethno-religious diversity categorically prohibits the people forming political parties on a religious, community, caste or tribal basis and contest elections on that line. Article 112(3) of the Constitution firmly rejects the recognition of any political organization or party formed on the basis of religion, community, caste, tribe or region from contesting election. Following the spirit of the Constitution, the Election Commission in its Code of Conduct clearly states that the 'voters shall not be encouraged to vote on the basis of caste, ethnicity, religion, tribe and language'.[10] The legal restrictions imposed by the Constitution as well as the Electoral Laws of the country on the voting behaviour of the people thus are incongruent to the human rights and freedom of the voters to determine their choice. As shown in Table 5.2, the politics of representation to the national legislature are still biased in favour of the traditionally influential entrenched caste and ethnic groups despite the undercurrents of ethno-politics.

On the whole, the data in the table is representative of the high caste Hill groups with the predominance of Brahmin, Chhetri and Newar in the national polity. Among these three caste groups, the data for the post-1990 election results suggest that the Brahmins have been more successful in winning the

TABLE 5.2: CASTE/ETHNIC COMPOSITION OF LEGISLATURES

(*in percentage*)

	Democratic Phase	Panchayat Phase			Post-1990 Democracy		
Ethnic	1959	1964-79	1981	1986	1991	1994	1999
Brahmin	27.5	23.5	14.81	21.24	36.6	44.39	46.34
Chhetri	31.2	35.5	34.82	38.68	18.53	18.53	17.07
Newar	03.7	13.0	08.15	06.60	06.8	06.34	06.34
Hill tribes	15.6	14.9	21.48	17.51	16.6	11.70	12.19
Terai caste groups	22.0	11.4	18.10	13.86	21.01	18.53	17.07
Others		01.0	02.6	02.19	00.5	00.48	00.97
Total	100	100	100	100	100	100	100

Sources: Harka Gurung, 'Representing an Ethnic Mosaic', *Himal*, May/June 1992, *Report on the Study and Research on the Local Elections in Nepal, 1992*, Kathmandu, 1992; and Election Commission, *Results of House of Representatives*, 1991, 1994 and 1999.

elections to the House of Representatives than the Chhetris whose representation in the parliament is more or less stable and those of the Newars' representation being constant. Their representation altogether constitutes 61.93 per cent in 1991, 69.26 per cent in 1994 and 69.75 per cent in the 1999 parliament. The impressive show of the continuing dominance of the three caste groups in the competitive and representative politics under democracy makes the claim of the ethno-politics unimpressive perhaps because of the unfavourable constitutional dispensation against ethno-politics. Although the principle of one man one vote recognizes the equality of citizens irrespective of their caste, sex, religion, and race it basically overlooks the embedded inequalities characterizing the social structure of the country where gender inequality is pervasive and caste classifies as well as qualifies a person's leadership. This is reflected in the composition of the central committee members of the three prominent political parties which can be seen in Table 5.3.

Castewise the Brahmins retain the prominent position by occupying more than 50 per cent of the central committee memberships of the three national political parties. Following this the Chhetris have an overwhelming majority in the parties' central committees. The Hill Brahmins and Chhetris combined make 29 per cent of the total population of the country, according

TABLE 5.3: CASTE AND ETHNIC COMPOSITION OF THE THREE PROMINENT POLITICAL PARTIES' CENTRAL COMMITTEE

Variables	NC		CPN (UML)		RPP		Total	
Hill Caste Group	No.	%	No.	%	No.	%	No.	%
Brahmin	18	58.1	25	71.4	5	17.2	48	50.5
Chhetri	6	19.4	6	17.0	8	27.5	19	20.0
Newar	1	3.2	2	5.7	2	6.9	5	5.3
Hill Ethnic Groups	3	9.7	1	2.85	8	27.9	13	13.7
Terai Caste/Tribals	3	9.7	1	2.85	6	20.7	10	10.5
Others	-	-	-	-	-	-	-	-
Total	31	100	35	100	29	100	95	100

Source: Lok Raj Baral, Krishna Hachhethu and Hari Sharma, *Leadership in Nepal*, New Delhi: Adroit Publishers, 2001.

to the 1991 population census. But they constitute more than 70 per cent in the highest leadership structure of the three prominent political parties, which is also reflected in their representation in the national legislature in the 1990s. For the general critics, Nepal is therefore constitutionally framed to deny the rights to represent the nationalities that are numerically in a majority but treated as national minorities. This situation determines the policies of the State and their implementations oriented towards catering to the interests of the governing caste groups. Such policies are reflected in the recruitment pattern of the national bureaucracy, corporate bodies, highest echelons of the university, police, army and even in agencies with governmental liability. Thus it is but natural for the governments in Nepal to ignore the plight of the socially disadvantaged groups because their voices rarely reach the corridors of decision making.

The voters are ultimately given candidates imposed from above to make their choice. They have therefore no choice either to elect or reject the person they had elected previously as their representatives. In the 1994 elections, the voters rejected the Nepali Congress party in government. Their experience with different coalition governments following the failure of the UML minority government after 1994 again led them to catapult the NC into power in 1999. The 1999 elections were interesting for another reason. Of the total 205 members of the parliament,

79 per cent elected members are newcomers. Thus they constituted a new breed numbering 132 of 205, constituting 64.39 per cent of the total.[11] Another element of the 1999 election concerning the voting behaviour and the voters' choice was that they had consciously discarded political parties with radical slogans and those parties like the RPP (Chand) and CPN (ML) splintered from their parent organizations. The third significance of the 1999 elections was that the average vote cast in some districts held by the Maoist was recorded at 44 per cent. Despite the peoples' dissatisfaction with the performances of successive governments after 1991 election, the voters had expressed their trust in democracy with their overwhelming participation. Also another significant aspect displaying the voters' choice in the Maoist infested areas is that the voters had defied the Maoist influence by electing the wives of the victims of the insurgents to the parliament.[12]

This overview of the national election and the voters' choice suggests several general conclusions. First, the voting behaviour of the electorate has expressed a certain degree of maturity while determining their choice. Through their overwhelming participation in the electoral process, particularly in the 1999 elections, they have rejected the political radicalism of the Maoist variant as an alternative to the democratic practice. Second, their desire for political stability and a functional government is reflected in their choice to elect the NC as a centrist party, with a comfortable majority to prevent the national polity from falling into the trap of either left or right extremism. Third, the voters' extreme dissatisfaction with the political tantrums observed during the coalition period following the 1994 elections was expressed by the election of fresh representatives to the parliament by rejecting those considered undesirable. Fourth, the parochial, ethnic, or even caste bias in electing the candidates of their choice did not lure the electorate; rather they are apparently guided by their decision to elect the most pluralist party, the NC, to power. Fifth, the 1999 elections show the continuing commitment of the voters to the democratic order despite the fragility of the process. And finally, communalization is not the course taken by the Nepali democratic system in the course of political development.

EVIDENCE FROM THE SURVEY

Against the background of the national scene in general this section focuses on analysing the findings of the five districts where research was conducted on the spot by administrating questionnaires to the voters and their responses enumerated. Before proceeding to the data analysis some specific characteristics of the interviewees follows: Of the 500 respondents 61 (12.2 per cent) are illiterate and 121 (24.2 per cent) are with higher education. Occupationwise, 204 (40.8 per cent) are agriculturists or farmers and 17 (3.2 per cent) are artisan workers; 340 (68 per cent) are from low-middle class groups with 107 (21.4 per cent) are poor in comparison to 12 (2.4 per cent) from rich social strata.[13]

Of the 500 respondents, 163 (32.6 per cent) belong to different political parties; of which 61 (37.4 per cent) are the members of the NC; 48 (29.4 per cent) are the cadres of the CPN (UML); 34 (20.9 per cent) are RPP members; 9 (5.5 per cent) are the members of the NSP; 7 (4.3 per cent) belong to the CPN (ML); 2 (1.2 per cent) each are the members of the Rashtriya Janamukti Morcha (National Liberation Front) and other political parties. According to the overall composite index of economic development the surveyed districts feature from worst to best. The ICIMOD study has pointed out Baitadi and Rautahat amongst the worst districts whereas Dhankuta and Kaski districts are amongst the best and Dang falling in between. In the case of poverty and deprivation, Rautahat is ranked number 4 and Baitadi at number 18 on the national average. The situation is also adequately reflected in the gender politics in the representation of women in the VDCs, DDCs, and Municipalities as per cent of the total members elected. Kaski ranked the best with 3.44 per cent, followed by Dhankuta 0.24 per cent, Dang 0.21 per cent, Baitadi 0.13 per cent and Rautahat 0.9 per cent of women elected.[14]

Perhaps this situation reflects the lower participation of women in the national average. During the election to the local bodies in 1997, of the 716 members elected to the DDCs from the 56 districts the share of women was only 5 (0.7 per cent). Of the total 112 positions for the chairperson and vice-chairperson in those 56 districts where elections were held in 1997, only one woman was elected as the vice-chairperson. Women's representation at various levels of VDCs is less than 1 per cent, which is also the case in four of the five districts surveyed. The reason for this being the case is not only that the women are less favoured by the voters as their representatives but also that they are socially embedded to domestic environs than outdoor activities. According to Dahal, this is especially so in the high caste Hindu society where women are more socially backward and economically exploited than in other ethnic/caste group. As women's relatively positive participation in politics in Kaski in comparison to other districts shows, Dahal's finding carries some sense when he asserts that the women in the Hill/Mountain ethnic groups have the liberal social structure which permits them to participate in public domain in comparison to the high-caste Hindu traditional life. Dahal further says that the Nepali culture is strictly hierarchical where the status of women is lower than that of men. Social behaviour thus is essentially a product of cultural conditioning. Politics have increasingly attracted status-motivated persons who have effectively undermined other persons having low or no social status.[15]

The respondents in the surveyed districts are also adequately aware of the situation where illiteracy, poverty and virtual dependence of women on their husbands or family members prevents them from entering public life (see Table 5.4). Thus, when asked about women's participation in the VDCs/Municipalities' candidacies in the local election, 323 (64.6 per cent) respondents said that their participation is few; 81 (16.2 per cent) said it was negligible against 63 (12.6 per cent) who said it was adequate. This social conditioning of the lower participation of women was also reflected in the course of participation in politics from the *Janajati* and untouchable groups of the people. Only 1.8 per cent of the respondents said that the untouchables' representation in the VDCs/Municipalities was adequate. In the same vein, just 0.8 per cent said that the untouchables' representation in the DDCs was adequate. On the tribal/ethnic representation in the VDCs/Municipalities, 35.6 per cent of the respondents said it was adequate against only 7.8 per cent who said it was negligible. However, the respondents suggesting the adequate tribal/ethnic representation in the DDCs declined to 14.6 per cent. The data in general show that political participation, in essence, is still the preserve of the high caste, rich and influential people in the village, Municipalities as well as the district level on the basis of

TABLE 5.4: REPRESENTATION OF TRIBAL, UNTOUCHABLE & WOMEN IN LOCAL ELECTIONS

		Total		Ethnicity							
				Hill High Caste	Hill Tribal	Newar	Terai High Caste	Terai Other Caste	Terai Tribal	Other	Dalit
		No.	%	%	%	%	%	%	%	%	%
Tribal-Ethnic	Adequate	178	35.6	21.9	68.7	27.8	10.0	8.8	41.2	16.7	26.1
Representation in	Few	151	30.2	15.9	21.6	38.9	70.0	64.9	42.6	50.0	17.4
VDC/Municipality	Negligible	39	7.8	7.3	3.0	11.1	10.0	14.0	7.4	33.3	10.9
	No	104	20.8	53.0	.7	11.1	.0	3.5	2.9	.0	37.0
	Don't know	28	5.6	2.0	6.0	11.1	10.0	8.8	5.9	.0	8.7
Tribal-Ethnic	Adequate	73	14.6	9.3	32.8	27.8	5.0	.0	1.5	16.7	15.2
Representation in	Few	118	23.6	11.3	15.7	22.2	65.0	56.1	32.4	50.0	13.0
DDC	Negligible	53	10.6	9.3	3.0	16.7	15.0	15.8	19.1	16.7	13.0
	No	114	22.8	53.6	3.0	11.1	.0	10.5	4.4	.0	39.1
	Don't know	142	28.4	16.6	45.5	22.2	15.0	17.5	42.6	16.7	19.6
Untouchable	Adequate	9	1.8	1.3	2.2	5.6	10.0	1.8	.0	.0	.0
Representation in	Few	178	35.6	48.3	24.6	27.8	50.0	50.9	14.7	50.0	32.6
VDC/Municipality	Negligible	198	39.6	38.4	44.8	27.8	25.0	26.3	44.1	16.7	52.2
	No	61	12.2	7.9	14.2	22.2	5.0	10.5	19.1	16.7	10.9
	Don't know	54	10.8	4.0	14.2	16.7	10.0	10.5	22.1	16.7	4.3
Untouchable	Adequate	4	.8	.0	1.5	5.6	5.0	.0	.0	.0	.0
Representation in	Few	79	15.8	16.6	11.2	11.1	50.0	36.8	1.5	33.3	6.5
DDC	Negligible	134	26.8	29.8	23.9	22.2	25.0	22.8	19.1	33.3	43.5
	No	109	21.8	29.8	13.4	27.8	5.0	21.1	20.6	.0	30.4

(*contd.*)

TABLE 5.4 (*Contd.*)

		No.	%	%	%	%	%	%	%	%	%
	Don't know	174	34.8	23.8	50.0	33.3	15.0	19.3	58.8	33.3	19.6
Women	Adequate	63	12.6	7.3	20.9	16.7	.0	8.8	19.1	.0	6.5
Representation in	Few	323	64.6	77.5	51.5	61.1	55.0	64.9	66.2	66.7	63.0
VDC/Municipality	Negligible	81	16.2	11.9	16.4	22.2	40.0	15.8	10.3	33.3	23.9
	No	5	1.0	2.0	1.5	.0	.0	.0	.0	.0	.0
	Don't know	28	5.6	1.3	9.7	.0	5.0	10.5	4.4	.0	6.5
Women	Adequate	13	6.7	16.7	.0	.0	.0	.0	.0	2.8	.0
Representation in	Few	325	23.1	22.2	20.0	31.6	20.6	16.7	23.9	26.4	16.7
DDC	Negligible	430	12.7	27.8	15.0	7.0	23.5	33.3	28.3	25.0	33.3
	No	33	6.7	16.7	35.0	36.8	4.4	33.3	13.0	11.2	33.3
	Don't know	199	50.7	16.7	30.0	24.6	51.5	16.7	34.8	34.6	16.7
Total		100	100	100	100	100	100	100	100	100	100

Source: Field Survey, January 2001.

which the national political parties' central committees assess the context in selecting their electoral candidate to field in the constituencies to compete in national elections.

The elections to the local bodies are in themselves evidence for discouraging socially downtrodden people from seeking local leadership. Because at the village level or Municipality level elections in particular, people from the untouchables class are hardly favoured by the local electorate to represent them. Elections at these levels are observed to have been skewed in favour of the persons belonging to the voters' own community, that is, from their own ethnic groups or kith and kin relations than others. Such tendencies are reflected in the district level elections too where the voters tend to be ethnically conscious rather than that of their affiliation either to a certain party or the programme. The respondents in the surveyed districts said such a tendency declines when the question of national elections comes to the fore: the voters conform either to party line or search of able or honest candidate. Ethnicity does not seem to be sensitive criteria for the voters in the national elections. Moreover the voters seem to have been motivated by different factors like party affiliation, ideological orientation, performance of the candidate during the election campaigns, proximity of the candidates to the voters and their commitment to the constituencies along with the resourcefulness of the candidate to attract the voters.

In Table 5.5 below the trend of popular participation at the national election in the surveyed districts is shown.

Of the five districts surveyed, only in Rautahat popular participation declined in 1999 while in the other four districts, the percentage of popular participation increased, even at the

TABLE 5.5: PERCENTAGE OF POPULAR PARTICIPATION IN THREE GENERAL ELECTIONS

Elections	Dhankuta	Rautahat	Kaski	Dang	Baitadi	National
1991	70.71	70.44	65.93	67.97	48.08	65.15
1994	63.60	71.05	58.83	61.52	42.13	61.86
1999	71.61	67.62	66.10	67.84	49.12	65.79

Source: House of Representatives, Election Results: 1991, 1994 and 1999, Kathmandu: Election Commission, various documents.

nominal level at some, tallying with the national average. However, situated in the Far Western Nepal, Baitadi had lagged behind with below 50 per cent participation in all national elections in comparison to other surveyed districts. This does not, however, mean to suggest that the high voters' percentage in other districts in comparison to Baitadi is an indication of the high political awareness among the voters. Nor does the low participation of voters in Baitadi district signify their apprehensions and alienation either towards the candidates or political parties or even the electoral process. Environmental factors sometimes determine low voter turnout.

As a matter of fact, a large proportion of Nepali voters do not actually have the proper understanding of the political system except *Bahudal Ayo* (the multi-party politics has arrived) and the choice is given to cast vote for a person/candidate of their liking and reject the person they dislike. Similarly, most voters in Nepal have seen *the four stars* and *Hammer and Sickle flags* belonging to the two oldest political parties—the Nepali Congress and the Communist Party of Nepal. As most of the voters over the period have grown along with these political parties' oppositional activities during the panchayat period, they are easily drawn to them. The election symbols of these two political parties—the Tree and the Sun—are amongst the most easily identifiable. Despite this a majority of voters are non-committal to any political party. Family and community considerations might also motivate them to vote. Yet their votes carry weight in seating and unseating political parties in government.

This survey has tried to determine the voters' view on elections on the basis of five questions framed comprising the socio-political context. Though these questions are not comprehensive, they facilitate a certain understanding on how the voters view elections in a democracy.

In Table 5.6 election are presented in a positive light as per the voters' concern. In both rural and urban areas of the districts surveyed 210 (42 per cent) voters agreed with query that they had voted on the basis of the party, with 37 per cent of the voters interviewed disagreeing with the contention that elections contribute to raising communal feelings as party candidates manipulate peoples' sentiment for their interests in winning elections. However, 29 per cent of the voters agreed and

TABLE 5.6: VOTERS' VIEW ON ELECTIONS

		Rural		Urban		Total	
		No	%	No	%	No	%
Voting on the basis of party principle	Agree	175	43.9	35	34.7	210	42.0
	Partly Agree	116	29.1	39	38.6	155	31.0
	Disagree	88	22.1	25	24.8	113	22.7
	Don't know	20	5.0	2	2.0	22	4.4
Raising communal feelings by party candidate	Agree	109	27.3	36	35.6	145	29.0
	Partly Agree	100	25.1	28	27.7	128	25.6
	Disagree	152	38.1	33	32.7	185	37.0
	Don't know	38	9.5	4	4.0	42	8.4
Voters will be affected by communal slogans in future	Agree	89	22.3	28	27.7	117	23.4
	Partly Agree	105	26.3	30	29.7	135	27.0
	Disagree	135	33.8	39	38.6	174	34.8
	Don't know	70	17.5	4	4.0	74	14.8
Increase representation of ethnic/tribal groups in future	Agree	134	33.6	39	38.6	173	34.6
	Partly Agree	110	27.6	31	30.7	141	28.2
	Disagree	69	17.3	22	21.8	91	18.2
	Don't know	86	21.6	9	8.9	95	19.0

(contd.)

TABLE 5.6 *(contd.)*

		Rural		Urban		Total	
		No	%	No	%	No	%
Issues concerning women, untouchables and marginalized people will be election agenda in future	Agree	164	41.1	44	43.6	208	41.6
	Partly Agree	108	27.1	23	22.8	131	26.2
	Disagree	67	16.8	24	23.8	91	18.2
	Don't know	60	15.0	10	9.9	70	14.0
	Total	399	100	101	100	500	100

Source: Field Survey 2001.

25.6 per cent partly agreed on this. There were 23.4 per cent of the respondents who feared that ethno-politics is on the rise and the voters will be affected by communalism in the future while 27 per cent partly agreed. Regarding the issues concerning women, untouchables and marginalized people, 41.6 per cent agreed that voices would be raised in the future for their social and political space in society. Those who partly agreed on the issue are 26.2 per cent, that is, over 67 per cent of respondents are concerned about the issue.

During the course of interview, the voters' common skepticism on the electoral process was also observed. Though this chapter does not deal with the electoral process, voters' perception on the process should be recorded to determine their voting behaviour. Prominent in the voters' perception on the electoral process was that they in general view the electoral process as not consistent with the ideals of democracy. The common reservation they showed on the electoral process was that political parties contesting elections made democratic norms the first victim of their campaigns. People interviewed in the five surveyed districts had a common view that the voters' list is defective, identity cards are not properly issued, rigging is common and that the use of money and muscle power by the political parties have invariably influenced the electoral process.

The voters' views are also not exceptional. Even the Chief District Officers (CDOs), judges of the District Court and Deputy Superintendent of Police (DSP) in the surveyed districts were critical of the election process. One CDO lamented that the issuance of the identity card had in fact damaged the credibility of electoral process when they found that the underage people had been issued the card, and in some cases a male's ID card was issued with a female's photo. He further said that as the political system is very much power-centric, it is but natural for the political parties to try their level best to win the elections by any means. One of the most observed features of the electoral process was 'might is right' as a DSP pointed, out suggesting that political parties are always anxious of politicizing the police force by using it for election purposes. Change in the high ranking police official including the Inspector General of Police (IGP) with a change in government has added such trends.

Some examples from Rautahat district where the Muslim

population is in a majority is revealing enough as some local leaders suggest that the Muslim vote on religious grounds does not exceed 10 to 15 per cent even in their dominant constituency. Being a poor and educationally backward community, the Muslims do not enjoy money and muscle power. They are weak at the organizational level as well. Some suggest that the activists of the different political parties and their unlawful activities threaten the Muslim community. As the DSP of the Rautahat district, Mahendra K. Pokharel, revealed 89 per cent of the minorities (Muslims) had never seen the ballot paper but a vote is cast in their name each time. The CDO there also lamented that the political leaders had treated the police and bureaucracy as their agents while administering elections. In the view of the CPN (UML) National Council Member Rajiuddin Alam, election in fact is the use of the sovereign rights of the people to exercise their franchise to elect the candidate of their choice. But in Rautahat both these rights have been denied to the people. Elections are not held without the firing of guns and violence as the political parties have become the new incarnation of the traditional feudal lords denying rights to the minorities for their representation in the national mainstream. The voters in general feel that political pressure from above, local vandalism, booth capturing, and vote buying are some of the critical lapses in the electoral process affecting the psychology of voters. In other words, when elections become a grossly manipulative game, the voters cannot remain untouched by the process.

Then, how are the voters affected? The former Minister of State for Local Development and presently a Politbureau member of the CPN (ML) from Dang district, Mahesh Choudhary, has succinctly summarized the popular feelings in general. According to him, 'Dang has always been manoeuvred to extreme ends. Most of the elections in the past have been characterized with violence, death, abduction, kidnapping, booth capturing, intimidation and coercion of polling agents and voters of the other parties. . . .' He said that the police and the administration under excessive political pressure play a major role and alleged that the prominent leaders of the Nepali Congress as well as the CPN (UML) encourage this trend. As a result, he says that the chances of the smaller political parties competing fairly in elections are denied and the possibility of representation from the minority thus destroyed. Dang is densely populated by the Tharus community and the *Kamaiyas* (bonded labourers), who are now officially liberated. Baitadi district constitutes some 20 per cent of the total population of the Dalits (the un-touchables belonging to the traditional Hindu community). The Dalits being social outcasts and deprived economically have been used by the political parties as their vote bank through both money and muscle power. Yet, open politics has also made them conscious of their social condition urging them to change the situation with an increase in political participation in local as well as general elections. The elections therefore have had a positive impact on the Dalit community of Baitadi, who search their role in society by asserting their candidacy in the local elections and in electing the candidates of their choice in the national elections.

The situation in Kaski district is somewhat exceptional in comparison to the above four surveyed districts. The voters' consciousness as well as their political sense in Kaski is more strongly reflected than that of Kathmandu voters. Like Kathmandu and Dhankuta (another prominent surveyed district), Kaski is also one of the hubs of the *Janajati* movement with rising ethnic assertion. Despite their common concern over money and muscle power, and despite feeling that the *Janajatis* have not been able to improve their lot, the voters have avoided political harassment as well as communization of politics based on ethnic cleavages and voted regularly on the basis of their political preferences and the performance of the political parties. The position of political parties obtained through three national elections is given in Table 5.7.

The data in the table, indeed, reflects the voters' choice in electing candidates of their liking. There was an exception in the 1991 elections when an independent candidate was elected from the Rautahat district who later joined the NC. The 1991 elections were relatively free and fair, held in the post-*Jana Andolan* period. The international observer groups also acclaimed it. The elections held later did not get as much admiration as in the case of the first. Particularly, the mid term elections in 1994 were considered not free. The 'cases of riggings, intimidation, misfeasance, unusual influence of money, muscle and power... [were noted in the 1994 mid term election]. However, the final results of the election were not decisively influenced by the unfair practices of such nature.'[16]

TABLE 5.7: POLITICAL PARTIES' POSITION IN SURVEYED DISTRICTS

(*in percentage*)

District	1991				1994				1999			
	NC	UML	RPP	Indp	NC	UML	RPP	Indp	NC	UML	RPP	Indp
Dhankuta	-	2	-	-	-	1	1	-	-	1	1	-
Rautahat	2	1	-	1	4	-	-	-	1	3	-	-
Kaski	1	2	-	-	1	2	-	-	3	-	-	-
Dang*	2	1	-	-	3	1	-	-	4	-	-	-
Baitadi	3	-	-	-	-	-	2	-	2	-	-	-

Note: * Since 1994 Dang district has four electoral constituencies. Baitadi's constituency was reduced to two.

Source: Election Commission, *Election Results, 1991, 1994 and 1999*, Kathmandu, various documents.

Tremendous expenditures incurred by candidates in the 1999 elections were another facet of unfair electoral practices. In some constituencies, candidates were alleged to have spent Rs.10 to Rs.12 million. Gopal Guragain, the District Secretary of the CPN (UML) who had won the national election from Dhankuta Constituency II during the 1991 elections to the House of Representatives and had lost the subsequent two elections in 1994 and 1999 to the RPP candidate, Surya Bahadur Thapa, said that the latter had defeated him in these elections by spending Rs.10.15 million in 1994 and Rs.10.50 million in 1999. The NC spent Rs. 8 million in the constituency number II whereas his party spent just Rs. 400,000. A *Janajati* women candidate of the Rashtriya Janamukti Morcha in Dhankuta Constituency II fighting elections against Surya Bahadur Thapa (RPP) and Gopal Guragain (CPN-UML) lost the elections miserably because she could not offer any money to voters who demanded payment to them outright in exchange of vote.[17] In the opinion of Ghanshyam Rai, the Mechi-Kosi Regional Secretary of Rashtriya Janamukti Morcha (National Peoples' Liberation Front), the election is a fraud as has been proven by the success of Surya Bahadur Thapa with money and muscle power. Similarly, Mrs. Kamala Pant, a Nepali Congress candidate who won the 1999 election from Gorkha Constituency II, has publicly admitted that she had to spend Rs. 2.7 million to get elected.[18]

Other things remaining the same, perhaps the excessive use of money in buying votes is also one of the crucial reasons why the results of the three general elections are not uniform in determining voting behaviour. In Dhankuta where the CPN (UML) had won in 1991, lost one seat to the RPP in the subsequent elections on the alleged ground of money. The NC improved its position in Rautahat from 2 to 4 seats between 1991 and 1994 but was reduced to one seat in the 1999 elections. The 1999 election results in Kaski overwhelmingly favoured the NC. So was the case in Dang. In Baitadi, the NC regained its lost ground by winning 2 seats in the 1999 elections. The CPN (UML) has bettered its position by winning 3 seats in Rautahat.

These three general elections with certain exceptions, however, have indicated that Nepal is consistently evolving in the direction of the two party dominant systems within the framework of multiparty democracy. Despite 39 registered political parties, the two continued their dominance in all the three elections. Parties with the regional slogans, the NSP, for example, were not favoured even in the Terai. Nor did the parties with a religious tilt, like the Shiv Sena Nepal, which had fielded 25 candidates muster more than 1,756 votes in the name of Nepali version of *Hindutva.* The ultra-nationalist party Rashtra Bachau Abhiyan as well had its image battered as a consequence of its total failure to impress voters in the 1999 electoral contest. The choice of the NC as the pluralist political party shows that ethno-politics has yet to emerge decisively to influence the contours of the Nepali political landscape. Even in places like Dhankuta, known as ethnically entrenched *Khambuwan Chhetra* or the *Kirat Pradesh,* voters are found to have been motivated mostly by other reasons than the ethno-religious cause. The needs and priorities of the voters and their expectations from the candidates are rather focused on the issues of local development (92 per cent), constituency development (84.2 per cent), social reforms (61.2 per cent) at the local level, uplift of disadvantaged (50.8 per cent) as expected from the member of parliament at the national level.

The voters in general assess that the situation has not improved for the people after 1990 while. 71.6 per cent respondents have no clear-cut idea about the governments formed after 1990. Their simple views on the governments are that 'some are good and some are bad'. On the average, 16.6 per cent of the people think that all governments are 'bad and corrupt'. Voters also feel that the elected bodies both at the local and the national level have performed dismally in responding to popular expectations. At the VDCs and Municipalities level, only 20.6 per cent are satisfied with their representatives in working towards fulfilling their expectations, 26.8 per cent have answered in the negative although 51 per cent respondents feel that the local elected bodies have partly fulfilled their expectations. The positive response to the query goes down once you climb up the ladder to DDC level. Only 6.2 per cent respondents have an affirmative answer to the question of fulfilling expectations from the elected local bodies. At the parliament level, the respondents reduce the figure further down to 5.2 per cent and 51 per cent of the voters suggest that the elected Parliament or candidates have failed to respond to their expectation. Their general dissatisfaction with the elected candidates of a particular political party could thus have been a reason for the vote swing.

Political Orientation and Political Choice

The political orientation and political choice of the voters are crucially tied with the context that the political parties have evolved in Nepal. Political parties evolved in Nepal as 'extra-systemic', movement organizations contributing to what Joshi and Rose have stated 'democratic innovation in Nepal'.[19] The people thus have long association with the political parties, particularly with the NC party that had revolutionalized the political system from Ranarchy to democracy. Though the Royal coup in December 1960 had dismantled the fragile democratic exercises introduced in the country in the early 1950s, it could not eliminate the democratic aspirations of the people as well as their political and personal identification with a certain political party functioning, though unlawfully, for the restoration of multi-party democracy in Nepal. The years of oblivion of political parties neither dissipated the popular aspirations nor extinguished their ambitions to struggle for democracy. As this responsibility passed from one generation to another, their struggle for democracy culminated in re-establishing democracy in 1990. Thus both the parties today represent the people as voters. The familiarity of voters with two prominent political parties—the NC and the

Communist Party of Nepal, CPN (UML) in particular—has led to their political orientation either to identify themselves as democrats, that is, sympathizers of the NC or Left parties by becoming a natural supporter of the various Communist groups.

The credit for making democracy possible in Nepal is attributed by the people to the NC for its unflinching advocacy of constitutional monarchy and multiparty system since its inception in 1947. Its leaders attained national status through their untiring struggle and drawing mass attention with open politics courting imprisonment and political harassment even during the Panchayat period. Leaders like B.P. Koirala and Ganesh Man Singh had become icons of democracy even when they were alive. People took pride in calling themselves workers/associates/ sympathizers of the party that B.P. Koirala and Ganesh Man Singh kept afloat. On the other hand, the mass following that the Communist Party of Nepal—established by late Pushpa Lal Shrestha in 1949, which later emerged as the Unified Marxist-Leninist CPN (UML) after the successful completion of *Jana Andolan* led by the Nepali Congress in 1990—is both the cause and consequence of the underground organizational efficiency and the left's successful strategy to penetrate into the panchayat polity between 1960-90. The Communists in Nepal who were bent on eliminating their strongest political rival NC had contributed to re-establishing democracy in 1990 by forming the United Left Front with their deadly rival, the NC at a time when the Leninist extinction occurred all over the world with the collapse of the Berlin Wall. The Communists in Nepal however survived as a force to reckon with after the first ever Communist country—the Soviet Union—disappeared.

The Communists who had managed to win just 4 seats during the elections to the House of Representatives in 1959 at the height of the Cold War, won altogether 82 seats in the parliamentary elections of 1991 showing its meteoric rise as a force. In the three national elections held between 1991 and 1999, the NC and the CPN (UML) had been successful in garnering a large chunk of popular votes. The NC had collected 37.75, 33.38 and 36.14 per cent of popular votes in 1991, 1994 and 1999 elections respectively. Comparable figures for the CPN (UML) were 27.98, 30.85 and 30.74 per cent respectively in these elections. However, a caveat remains. Though the CPN (UML) lost the elections in 1999 on the basis of first-past-the-post system, there is hardly any difference between the 30.85 per cent popular vote it received during the 1994 elections with 88 seats in the parliament that helped it to form the minority government and the 30.74 per cent votes with a reduced 71 seats in the 1999 parliament. If one were to add the 6.38 per cent of the popular vote received by the breakaway CPN (ML) to its total vote of 37.12 per cent, it could have made significant progress in receiving popular votes.

On the basis of the popular votes cast to the two political parties, one can examine the political orientation as well as the political choice of the voters. It would thus be pertinent to recall here the typology of voters. In comparative perspective, in terms of the popular votes cast to the two political parties a majority of Nepali voters can be classified as stable and loyal voters who had voted consistently for the party of their choice. The swing of votes to the two parties, particularly to the NC, is nominal and declined from 37.75 per cent in 1991 to 33.38 per cent in 1994. But the reason for such a decline was not only the voters' dissatisfaction with the NC but also the factional disputes within it creating divisional loyalty of the voters between and on personality lines. In 1999, the NC restored its position by increasing the popular vote by 2.76 per cent, which was 1.61 per cent below the popular level of 1991 election. By contrast, the CPN (UML) has imroved its position on the popular vote from 1991. As said above, had not the party been divided into two, the CPN (UML) position would have been comparable to that of the NC in 1991 in terms of popular votes. Perhaps such popularity of the CPN (UML) is also caused by the entry into the election fray of the new voters in 1999 whose age averaged around 10 years during the first national election in 1991. Also there are party changers whose votes fluctuated between different political parties at different times. The reason why voters fluctuated between different parties will be dealt with shortly. The vote changers can be classified as performance voters who swing their votes on the basis of political parties' performance and response to the popular will.

Data collected during the field survey of five districts subscribe to the voters' typology as discussed earlier. As can be seen in Table 5.8, there are 57 per cent of respondents who had regularly voted in all elections, meaning they had voted in the three general elections and two elections for the local bodies. 57.7 per cent of

TABLE 5.8: VOTE FOR WHOM?

	Total		Ethnicity							
			Hill High Caste	Hill Tribal	Newar	Tarai High Caste	Tarai Other Caste	Taria Tribal	Other	Dalit
	No.	%	%	%	%	%	%	%	%	%
Same party	256	57.7	66.4	65.8	58.8	66.7	29.4	51.6	20.0	51.2
Different parties	169	38.1	30.7	27.9	35.3	27.8	60.8	48.0	80.0	46.5
Some time for party some time for independent	13	2.9	2.2	3.6	5.9	.0	7.8	.0	.0	2.3
Don't know	6	1.4	.7	2.7	.0	5.6	2.0	.0	.0	.0
Total	444	100.0	100.0	100.0	100.0	100.0	100.0	100.0	100.0	100.0

the interviewees had voted constantly for the same political party. The percentage of one time voter is as low as 8.2 per cent. Perhaps the one-timers are the new eligible voters or the marginal ones who did not cast the vote in subsequent elections. The people who voted for the different parties are 38.1 per cent. Castewise, the Tarai people, besides Brahmins and Kayastha, are found to have voted for the different parties at different times (60.8 per cent) in comparison to Dalits (46.5 per cent), Newars (35.3 per cent) and Hill Brahmins and Chhetris (30.7 per cent). If the voting pattern were to be divided along religion were, 65.9 per cent of Buddhists voted regularly for the same party, followed by 57.7 per cent Hindus and 20 per cent Muslims. The respondents voting for different parties are 80 per cent Muslims, 40.9 per cent Hindus and 27.1 per cent Buddhists.

Asked why had they voted for the different political parties having different ideology, 61 per cent of the 111 respondents had identified the performance failure of the political party of their choice had led them to vote differently at different times; 47.3 per cent of the respondents held the leaders responsible for breaking promises and 29.7 per cent for failing to develop the constituencies they were elected from. Ethnically 60 per cent of the Hill Brahmins and Chhetris identified the performance of the party as a crucial reason for vote change, which is followed by the cause of inefficient party leadership (46.7 per cent) and erosion of party ideology (44.4 per cent); 57.1 per cent of the Newar respondents say that inefficient party leadership has been the real cause of vote change. For 60 per cent respondents of the Terai Brahmins and Kayasthas groups, and 65.7 per cent of other Terai caste groups the prominent reason to change vote remains the leadership' failure to fulfil their promises. Another 34.3 per cent of the Terai caste group says the leaders' failure to bring development to the constituencies is the cause of change. Some 47.6 per cent of the Dalit respondents interviewed in the Terai also give the same reason for their change in vote. Religionwise, 100 per cent of the Muslim, 62 per cent of the Hindu and 48.1 per cent of the Buddhist respondents say the performance failure of the party led them to change their vote. Compared to 44 per cent of Hindus and 44.7 per cent of Buddhists, 75 per cent of the Muslims had pointed out the leadership inefficiency as a prominent reason for vote change (see Table 5.9).

TABLE 5.9: REASON FOR BEING CHANGE-VOTERS

	Total		Ethnicity							
			Hill High Caste	Hill Tribal	Newar	Tarai High Caste	Tarai Other Caste	Taria Tribal	Other	Dalit
	No.	%	%	%	%	%	%	%	%	%
Party failure to perform	111	61.0	60.0	42.9	42.9	80.0	77.1	53.3	100.0	71.4
Party leaders' inefficiency	80	44.0	46.7	40.0	57.1	20.0	51.4	40.0	75.0	33.3
Erosion in party ideology	43	23.6	44.4	34.3	14.3	20.0	8.6	13.3	25.0	4.8
Failure to fulfil promises	86	47.3	33.3	57.1	28.6	60.0	65.7	33.3	75.0	47.6
Failure to bring development	54	29.7	26.7	40.0	28.6	.0	34.3	16.7	.0	42.9
Becoming selfish, corrupt and power seekers	38	20.9	15.6	25.7	14.3	40.0	32.9	13.3	25.0	28.6
Insensitivity to women/ backward communities	22	12.1	11.1	5.7	.0	.0	17.1	16.7	.0	19.0
Others	16	8.8	11.1	8.6	14.3	.0	2.9	13.3	.0	9.5
Don't know	2	1.1	.0	2.9	.0	20.0	.0	.0	.0	.0
Total	182	248.4	248.9	257.1	200.0	240.0	280.0	200.0	300.0	257.1

During the field survey, the interviewers had also tried to explore the possible answers to the factors affecting the voting behaviour by raising questions on their localized as well as general interests concerning the country. These questions were first related to the representation pattern in general and the responses of the representatives to their constituencies. Voters of different ethnicity/caste groups were asked about their opinion on representation of tribals, untouchables and women in local bodies' elections. The Hill tribals' response was 68.7 per cent 'adequate', whereas 70 per cent of the Terai Brahmins and Kayasthas considered the representation of tribal-ethnic groups in the VDCs/Municipalities were very 'few' which was endorsed by 64.9 per cent of other Terai groups. Another 53 per cent of the Hill Brahmins and Chhetris also answered in the negative. In the case of DDC, 53.6 per cent of Hill Brahmins and Chhteris said 'no' to the representation followed by 65 per cent of the Terai Brahmins and Khayasthas and 56.1 per cent of other Terai groups for 'few' representation. About the Untouchables' representation, 52.2 per cent of the Dalits say it is 'negligible', followed by 50.9 per cent of the Terai groups, 50 per cent of the Terai Brahmin and Kayasthas and 48.3 per cent of the Hill Brahmins and Chhetris suggesting 'few' representation. Similarly, 43.5 per cent Dalits said the Untouchables' representation at the DDC as 'negligible' compared with 50 per cent of the Terai Brahmin and Kayashas who said their representation are 'few'.

On women's representation inVDCs/ Municipalities, 77.5 per cent of the Hill Brahmins and Chhteris, 51.5 per cent of the Hill Tribals, 61.1 per cent of Newars, 55 per cent of the Terai Brahmin and Kayasthas, 64.9 per cent of other Tarai groups, and 63 per cent of Dalits said it is 'few'. The case of their representation in the DDC just 2.8 per cent of all ethnic/caste groups said it is 'adequate', while 43 per cent of the Hill Brahmins and Chhetris said it is 'negligible'.

On the question of the responses of the representatives to their elected constituencies, a majority of respondents 58.4 per cent (292) out of the 500 interviewed answered negatively. Of 292 respondents, the Hindu constitutes 57.8 per cent, the Buddhist 62 per cent, the Muslim 80 per cent and the others 42.9 per cent. But there are 98 persons suggesting that the elected representatives at least have contributed to raise public awareness in the community. Likewise 67 respondents said that their representatives have provided employment opportunities to the people of their constituencies.

The electorates were also asked about the reason for electoral participation to which 50.6 per cent responded 'just vote casting' particularly during the 1999 elections. Such ritualistic answers of the voters were counterpoised with a question: whom would you vote for in the coming election? (see Table 5.10) Seventy-two per cent of respondents from both rural and urban areas answered that they will vote for the 'able and honest candidate.' Only 19.6 per cent respondents answered they will vote for the party candidate. Just 0.2 per cent of the voters preferred their own relatives to be voted to power in the future. Thus, the chances of parochial voting in the future election are still negligible as the data suggest. The ethnic breakdown of the data suggest 66.9 per cent Hill Brahmins and Chhetris, 64.9 per cent Hill Tribals, 88.9 per cent Newars, 70 per cent Terai Brahmins and Kayasthas, 80.7 per cent other Terai groups, 77.9 per cent Terai tribals, 82.6 per cent Dalits and 83.3 per cent others favoured the able and honest candidates to be their representative in the future. Religiously, 74 per cent Hindus, 63 per cent Buddhists, 80 per cent Muslims and 71.4 per cent others favoured the 'able and honest candidates'.

What then is the basis of political orientation and choice of the Nepali voters? On the basis of the evidence gathered through the primary data, one can say that the Nepali voters are mostly divided into two prominent political parties—the NC and the CPN (UML). The voters are psychologically oriented towards them because of their roles in Nepali politics. The RPP that has come to the foreground as the third largest party after the 1994 mid term election is still far afield in competition. Likewise, the Nepal Sadbhavana Party (NSP)—a Terai based party advocating for the rights of the Terai people—has shown its limits in the mass appeal. The party is not only localized but its organizational inefficiencies were also glaringly demonstrated when the party failed to win elections from several of its own Terai constituencies. There were 68 NSP candidates contesting elections in 1999 of whom only 5 succeeded with altogether 2,78,435 votes (3.13 per cent of the total vote cast) from the Terai region where the Madeshi (Terain) population are in a majority. This shows that

TABLE 5.10: VOTE FOR WHOM IN COMING ELECTION

	Total		Hill High Caste	Hill Tribal	Newar	Tarai High Caste	Tarai Other Caste	Taria Tribal	Other	Dalit
	No.	%	%	%	%	%	%	%	%	%
Party candidate	98	19.6	24.5	20.1	11.1	20.0	17.5	17.6	16.7	10.9
Able and honest candidate	360	72.0	66.9	64.9	88.9	70.0	80.7	77.9	83.3	82.6
To neighbour	7	1.4	.7	2.2	.0	.0	.0	4.4	.0	.0
To own community	4	.8	.0	.7	.0	5.0	1.8	.0	.0	2.2
To relative	1	.2	.0	.0	.0	.0	.0	.0	0	2.2
One who offers personal benefit	2	.4	1.3	.0	.0	.0	.0	.0	.0	.0
Others	16	3.2	3.3	6.7	.0	5.0	.0	.0	.0	2.2
Don't know	12	2.4	3.3	5.2	.0	.0	.0	.0	.0	.0
Total	500	100	100	100	100	100	100	100	100	100

Source: Field Survey 2001.

the regional as well as the populist slogans are alsso not the vote catchers. Thus the political parties like the RPP, NSP and others have their functional role for vote diversion rather than in influencing either the electoral course of shaping public opinion on national issues. The problems with these parties are that their emergence as political organizations under democracy are mainly considered as destabilizers by the people. The RPP, formed by the influential leaders of the erstwhile panchayat regime, has yet to make any dent in the popular perception of its being really different from its previous self. Likewise, the NSP is perceived by the people as having been guided by the extraterritorial interests. On the other hand, these parties are deprived of a historical role in Nepal which the major political parties—the NC and the CPN (UML)—enjoy. Unless other political parties functioning in Nepal bridge this perceptual gap prevalent among the voters in relations to the major political parties, it would be difficult for them either to expand their organizational base or to mobilize people benefiting their interests.

The assertion of the minority rights by the NSP, especially for the people of Terai, either has failed to generate required popular response because other political parties have also made the ethnic clamour. The social, economic, political and foreign policy programmes of RPP and NSP are substantially different from the two major parties' election manifestos except in changes of words and emphasis.[20] The NSP's clamour for constitutional amendment to turn Nepal into a federal state with provincial government has fewer supporters among the voters. Though the voters have urged for local self-government through decentralization, the focus, however, remains distributive justice not bifurcation of national government. Such a mobilization strategy adopted by the NSP backfired due to its failure to give any new agenda to the voters. Similarly, the voters knew that with a total 68 candidate, fielded in the 1999 elections, the NSP would not have been able to form a government even if the party wins all the contested seats. The position for the federal state and provincial government that NSP had taken, therefore, was for public consumption. This makes the NSP's position miserable in the electoral context. Perhaps the reason for the routing of the NSP president Gajendra Narayan Singh from the Saptari Constituency II is evident.

In the same vein, the RPP has no prospect of being an alternative party in the near future. The political programmes it laid in front of the people are not convincing. With the presence of every RPP candidate, the legacy of the 30-years of misrule of the panchayat regime looms large before the voters. The RPP survives just because of the default of major political parties and also due to personality factors. For, the RPP has still retained some prominent leaders with some local influence and electoral knowledge.

But this does not mean that the votes are exclusively driven by their judgement to cast votes. In the case of the gendervote relationship, most women voters are guided by the judgement of either their husbands or of the male family members. This has been observed in the field survey. In the case of no-party voters, the electorate is manipulated by different factors such as the use of money and muscle power. Money, in reality, matters in elections. In this regard, the case of Dhankuta is unique. The RPP candidate Surya Bahadur Thapa, for example, is the most unpopular figure because of the 'Chintang genocide' ordered by him as the prime minister of the country during the panchayat period in 1979. The national security forces had mercilessly 'massacred' some 14 Communist rebels, raped 25 women along with destroying property in the Chintang village in October 1979.[21] But the man managed to win elections twice from the same district in 1994 and 1999.

Thus excessive manipulation of voters with the use of money power could also have considerable impact on electoral outcome. The people in Dhankuta wonder how Surya Bahadur Thapa had won the elections? In reality, Dhankuta has no popular base for the RPP. One can find a sign board of the RPP local office but the door is always locked, as told by the unit president. Besides the signboard, the RPP has no presence in the Dhankuta municipality. Ironically, it wins the elections.

Parochialism and communalism had also influenced the voters. The NC had lost successive elections in Dhankuta district. One of the basic reasons for this has been the organizational bias shown by the party high command towards the district itself. According to Ramesh Shrestha, the unit president of the Dhankuta Municipality, Prime Minister Girija P. Koirala (1991-4) removed all the NC regional offices and shifted them to Biratnagar (the home town of the prime minister). The organizational base of the party was also weakened with adverse impact on the party profile. But this is not the only case why the NC could not make its presence felt in Dhankuta. Parochialism and communalization too play their role in making the NC's profile in Dhankuta miserable. The case of this district also illustrates how a combination of caste, class and locational factors affect voting behaviour despite party affiliation. It is said:

> A Rai candidate of the NC (Hari Kumar Rai) became a victim of caste sentiment of Newars in the 1994 midterm election when he contested the election from the constituency number 1 [where the majority of Rai/Limbus lived]. The Bazzar (market) area was also under this constituency. According to him, the party activists of Newar community showed caste solidarity by concentrating themselves in another parliamentary constituency from where a Newar contested election also as NC candidate. As the voters from Bazzar area declined by 50 per cent in comparison to 1991 election, both the NC candidates were defeated.[22]

On the basis of the above discussion it can be safely concluded that the empirical research and the data analysis are a useful tool to indicate certain trends. But one can never be sure of what societal factors in actuality motivate human behaviour as the voting behaviour study is also a part of investigating human conduct. Analysing human instinct is a difficult task for a political scientist in a country where behavioural studies are a rarity in comparison to the institutional-finctional and structural studies. Thus, the political choice that the voters make in the electoral process of the country cannot be analysed definitively without comprehending the complexities of the electoral process itself.

Some General Observations

The multiparty political dispensation in the country since 1990 has compelled the regime ordering process to fundamentally base its legitimacy on the endorsement of the sovereign people through elections. The process of authority building under democracy has shifted from the use of force to use of ballot.

The behaviour of the Nepali voters in general can therefore be observed as a learning process. The experiences of the three general elections show that the Nepali voters are both retrospective as well as prospective. They are retrospective in the sense that they decide their votes on the basis of the performance of the incumbent governments/candidates. For the non-aligned or independent voters, besides the loyalists, the NC's performance during 1991-4 was not up to their expectation. As an earlier survey report found 87.97 per cent of the people polled were dissatisfied with the role of the political parties. When prioritizing the cause of their dissatisfaction even 69.93 per cent of the partymen belonging to the NC had pointed out that the party management has been damaged, 61.43 per cent were not satisfied with the weak leadership, and 64.71 per cent had found the lacunae between the programme and practice.[23] Others were sensitive to the development within the NC during its first tenure as the party leadership took decision including that of holding the mid term election without any consideration of consequences. When the mid term poll was announced without any convincing explanation for which the voters as well as a majority of the NC partymen were not prepared, the voters found no reason to put the NC again into power and form government.

The Nepali voters are inoptimizing the future in the sense that they learn retrospectively about what had happened, and make their choice. Even if they do not find any concrete reason to be optimistic by electing the NC to power, their bitter experience of the coalition politics may have led them to cast in their lot with the NC in expecting certain changes within it. Another facet of the voting behaviour in Nepal is that the voters had severely punished the miscreants of the parties without electing them to the parliament.

Both in their retrospective as well as prospective contexts, the Nepali voters seem to have related themselves to the promising political party while casting their votes. NC's continued popularity in electoral terms at least is due to the extreme conflict ridden positions of other parties. Though the NC has also not escaped such ills, it has survived the worst disaster of split.

Again, the experiences of three elections demonstrate that none of the contending political parties is a vote catcher. Such a tendency is evident in percentage of popular votes that the NC and the CPN (UML) in particular have had been collecting in the past three elections. Their margin of popular votes has neither swung drastically against each other nor has it improved considerably in these elections. Therefore, the two contending parties are in cut-throat competition. Against these two parties there are none to pose a serious challenge presenting themselves as a viable alternative either to the NC or the CPN (UML) both at national or local levels.

However, there are problems much related to the usual dissatisfaction of the voters towards the performances of the political parties and the government. They would like to see the major political parties to be opened and inclusive of the social demands for representation from the different category of multi-ethnic society. People in general would also like to see the representation of the disadvantaged people in the composition of the highest echelon of the political parties. They would like the end of gender imbalance in political representation. Other problems abound and the major parties are always looked upon with expectations, though people have become highly critical of their overall performance.

NOTES

1. For details on the caste system in accordance with the *Muluki Ain* 1854 see, Prayag Raj Sharma, 'Caste, Social Mobility and Sanskritization in a Tribal-Hindu Society: A Study of Nepal's Old Legal Code', in S. Iijima, ed., *Changing Aspects of Modern Nepal,* Tokyo: ISLCAA, 1977; Krishna Kant Adhikari, *Nepal Under Jang Bahadur 1846-1877,* vol. 1, Kathmandu: BUKU, 1984; Dor Bahadur Bista, *Fatalism and Development: Nepal's Struggle for Modernization,* Hyderabad: Orient Longman, 1991; and for Prithvi Narayan Shah's instruction dealing with government see, L.F. Stiller, s.j., *Prithwi-narayan Shah in the Light of Dibya Upadesh,* Ranchi, India: Catholic Press, 1968.
2. Krishna Kant Adhikari, ibid., p. 50.
3. See Dor Bahadur Bista, 'The Structure of Nepali society', in Kamal P. Malla, ed., *Nepal: Perspectives in Continuity and Change,* Kirtipur: Centre for Nepal and Asian Studies, 1989, p. 178.
4. NSAC, *Nepal: Human Development Report 1998,* Kathmandu: Nepal South Asia Centre, 1998, pp. 145-6.
5. Harka Gurung, *Nepal: Social Demography and Expressions,* Kathmandu: New Era, 1998.
6. *The Constitution of the Kingdom of Nepal, 1990,* Kathmandu: Ministry of Law, 1990.
7. Ibid.

8. Anirudha Gupta, *Politics in Nepal,* Bombay: Allied Publishers, 1964, pp. 146-8.
9. See Dhruba Kumar and Krishna Hachhethu, *Social Movements, Democracy and the Nepali State,* Kathmandu: Centre for Nepal and Asian Studies, Draft Report, March 2001.
10. The Election Commission, 1996.
11. See Krishna Khanal and Krishna Hachhethu, *Aam Nirbachan 2056: Sansad Ra Sarkarka Chunautiharu,* Kathmandu: Centre for Nepal and Asian Studies (CNAS), 1999.
12. See Krishna Khanal and Krishna Hachhethu, ibid.
13. Unless otherwise stated, the data cited are from the field survey conducted for the study in January 2001.
14. For details, see ICIMOD, *Districts of Nepal: Indicators of Development,* Kathmandu: ICIMOD, 1997.
15. Dilli Ram Dahal, 'Nepal's Governing Elite: Their Composition and Role in Constituting the State', in Dhruba Kumar, ed., *Domestic Conflict and Crisis of Governability in Nepal,* Kathmandu: CNAS, 2000, pp. 124-6.
16. NEOC, *Nepal: Election Observation Report, Mid-Term Poll 1994,* Lalitpur: National Election Observation Committee, 1994, p. 56.
17. Personal Communication, January 2001.
18. Ms Kamala Pant disclosed this fact during the seminar deliberation organized by the NCCS 'Workshop on Electoral System and Research Methodology' at Dhulikhel on 23 December 2000.
19. Bhuwan Lal Joshi and Leo E. Rose, *Democratic Innovations in Nepal:* Berkeley CA: University of California Press, 1966.
20. For example see, Krishna Khanal and Krishna Hachhethu, op. cit., pp. 10-20.
21. See *Dhankuta Jillako Kamunist Andolanko Itihas,* Dhankuta: CPN (UML), n.d.
22. Based on an Interview cited in Krishna Hachhethu, 'Party Building in Nepal: The Nepali Congress Party and the CPN (UML)' (unpublished Ph.D. thesis in Political Science, Institute for Humanities and Social Sciences, Tribhuvan University, February 2001), p. 222.
23. For details, see CCD, *Nepal: People, Polity and Governance,* Kathmandu: Centre for Consolidation of Democracy, 1996.

ANNEXURES

ANNEX A: BACKGROUND CHARACTERISTICS OF SAMPLE RESPONDENTS

		Districts					
		Dhankuta	Rautahat	Kaski	Dang	Baitadi	Total
Area							
Rural	No.	80	80	80	79	80	399
	%	80.0	80.0	80.0	79.0	80.0	79.8
Urban	No.	20	20	20	21	20	101
	%	20.0	20.0	20.0	21.0	20.0	20.2
Sex							
Female	No.	38	9	40	15	20	122
	%	38.0	9.0	40.0	15.0	20.0	24.4
Male	No.	62	91	60	85	80	378
	%	62.0	91.0	60.0	85.0	80.0	75.6
Age Group							
18-35	No.	59	49	40	58	39	245
	%	59.0	49.0	40.0	58.0	39.0	49.0
36-54	No.	35	36	45	37	48	201
	%	35.0	36.0	45.0	37.0	48.0	40.2
55 and above	No.	6	15	15	5	13	54
	%	6.0	15.0	15.0	5.0	13.0	10.8
Religion							
Hindu	No.	60	94	37	99	99	389
	%	60.0	94.0	37.0	99.0	99.0	77.8
Buddhist	No.	27	1	62	1	1	92
	%	27.0	1.0	62.0	1.0	1.0	18.4
Muslim	No.	0	5	0	0	0	5
	%	.0	5.0	.0	.0	.0	1.0
Others	No.	13	0	1	0	0	14
	%	13.0	.0	1.0	.0	.0	2.8
Ethnicity							
Hill caste groups	No.	18	3	25	25	80	151
	%	18.0	3.0	25.0	25.0	80.0	30.2
Hill ethnic groups	No.	64	0	67	3	0	134
	%	64.0	.0	67.0	3.0	0	26.8
Newar	No.	10	2	2	3	1	18
	%	10.0	2.0	2.0	3.0	1.0	3.6
Terai high caste groups	No.	0	18	0	2	0	20
	%	.0	18.0	.0	2.0	0	4.0
Terai low caste groups	No.	0	53	0	4	0	57
	%	.0	53.0	.0	4.0	.0	11.4

(*contd.*)

ANNEX A (*contd.*)

		Dhankuta	Rautahat	Kaski	Dang	Baitadi	Total
Terai ethnic groups	No.	0	8	0	60	0	68
	%	.0	8.0	.0	60.0	.0	13.6
Muslim	No.	0	5	0	0	0	5
	%	.0	5.0	.0	.0	.0	1.0
Others	No.	1	0	0	0	0	1
	%	1.0	.0	.0	.0	.0	.2
Dalit	No.	7	11	6	3	19	46
	%	7.0	11.0	6.0	3.0	19.0	9.2
Education							
Illiterate	No.	22	19	11	7	2	61
	%	22.0	19.0	11.0	7.0	2.0	12.2
Literate	No.	21	28	37	20	21	127
	%	21.0	28.0	37.0	20.0	21.0	25.4
Up to school level	No.	24	36	37	40	54	191
	%	24.0	36.0	37.0	40.0	54.0	38.2
Higher education	No.	33	17	15	33	23	121
	%	33.0	17.0	15.0	33.0	23.0	24.2
Occupation							
Agriculture	No.	37	44	30	52	41	204
	%	37.0	44.0	30.0	52.0	41.0	40.8
Labour	No.	4	11	2	7	2	26
	%	4.0	11.0	2.0	7.0	2.0	5.2
Service	No.	21	25	25	19	20	110
	%	21.0	25.0	25.0	19.0	20.0	22.0
Business	No.	25	7	28	12	10	82
	%	25.0	7.0	28.0	12.0	10.0	16.4
Student	No.	9	6	2	2	7	26
	%	9.0	6.0	2.0	2.0	7.0	5.2
Housewife	No.	2	5	12	7	4	30
	%	2.0	5.0	12.0	7.0	4.0	6.0
Dalit occupation	No.	0	1	0	0	16	17
	%	.0	1.0	.0	.0	16.0	3.4
Others	No.	2	1	1	1	0	5
	%	2.0	1.0	1.0	1.0	.0	12
Economic status							
Rich	No.	2	7	1	2	0	12
	%	2.0	7.0	1.0	2.0	.0	2.4
High-middle	No.	6	23	1	6	5	41
	%	6.0	23.0	1.0	6.0	5.0	8.2
Low middle	No.	67	44	88	64	77	340
	%	67.0	44.0	88.0	64.0	77.0	68.0

(*contd.*)

ANNEX A (*contd.*)

			Dhankuta	Rautahat	Kaski	Dang	Baitadi	Total
Poor		No.	25	26	10	28	18	107
		%	25.0	26.0	10.0	28.0	18.0	21.4
Member in								
Political	Yes	No.	10	36	18	41	58	163
Party		%	10.0	36.0	18.0	41.0	58.0	32.6
	No	No.	90	64	82	50	42	337
		%	90.0	64.0	82.0	59.0	42.0	67.4
Party member in								
Nepali Congress		No.	2	10	10	16	23	61
		%	20.0	27.8	55.6	39.0	39.7	37.4
UML		No.	3	12	4	11	18	48
		%	30.0	33.3	22.2	26.8	31.0	29.4
RPP		No.	3	3	3	10	15	34
		%	30.0	8.3	16.7	24.4	25.9	20.9
Sadbhawana		No.	0	9	0	0	0	9
		%	.0	25.0	.0	.0	.0	.9
Rashtriya Janamorcha		No.	0	0	0	2	0	2
		%	.0	.0	.0	4.9	.0	1.2
Others		No.	1	1	0	0	0	2
		%	10.0	2.8	.0	.0	.0	1.2
ML		No.	1	1	1	2	2	7
		%	10.0	2.8	5.6	4.9	3.4	4.3

TABLE A 1: ESSENTIAL COMPONENTS OF DEMOCRACY

	District											
	Dhankuta		Rautahat		Kaski		Dang		Baitadi		Total	
	No.	%	No.	%	No.	%	No.	%	No.	%	No.	%
Periodic election	6	6.0	18	18.0	18	18.0	19	19.0	27	27.0	88	17.6
Stable government	21	21.0	44	44.0	37	37.0	32	32.0	56	56.0	190	38.0
Independent judiciary	20	20.0	40	40.0	12	12.0	23	23.0	25	25.0	120	24.0
Economic development	54	54.0	58	58.0	38	38.0	73	73.0	34	34.0	257	51.4
Social reform/change	52	52.0	65	65.0	29	29.0	31	31.0	39	39.0	216	43.2
Conscious people	48	48.0	33	33.0	45	45.0	66	66.0	65	65.0	257	51.4
Uplift of minorities and disadvantaged group	31	31.0	30	30.0	39	39.0	48	48.0	41	41.0	189	37.8
Others	7	7.0	0	.0	3	3.0	4	4.0	7	7.0	21	4.2
Don't know	15	15.0	4	4.0	16	16.0	0	.0	1	1.0	36	7.2
Total	100	254.0	100	292.0	100	237.0	100	296.0	100	295.0	500	274.8

Note: % based on multiple responses.

TABLE A2: OPINION ON DEMOCRATIC EXERCISE IN NEPAL

		District											
		Dhankuta		Rautahat		Kaski		Dang		Baitadi		Total	
		No.	%	No.	%	No.	%	No.	%	No.	%	No.	%
Constitution is democratic	Agree	19	19.0	42	42.0	37	37.0	33	33.0	49	49.0	180	36.0
	Partly agree	33	33.0	21	21.0	22	22.0	27	27.0	35	35.0	138	27.6
	Disagree	11	11.0	28	28.0	12	12.0	6	6.0	15	15.0	72	14.4
	Don't know	37	37.0	9	9.0	29	29.0	34	34.0	1	1.0	110	22.0
Parties/leaders follow spirit of constitution	Agree	2	2.0	4	4.0	6	6.0	5	5.0	3	3.0	20	4.0
	Partly agree	29	29.0	20	20.0	27	27.0	33	33.0	29	29.0	138	27.6
	Disagree	51	51.0	74	74.0	57	57.0	44	44.0	67	67.0	293	58.6
	Don't know	18	18.0	2	2.0	10	10.0	18	18.0	1	1.0	49	9.8
Government respect public feeling	Agree	2	2.0	4	4.0	6	6.0	5	5.0	3	3.0	20	4.0
	Partly agree	37	37.0	25	25.0	21	21.0	45	45.0	33	33.0	161	32.2
	Disagree	51	51.0	62	62.0	59	59.0	48	48.0	55	55.0	275	55.0

(*contd.*)

TABLE A2 (*contd.*)

		District											
		Dhankuta		Rautahat		Kaski		Dang		Baitadi		Total	
		No.	%	No.	%	No.	%	No.	%	No.	%	No.	%
	Don't know	6	6.0	1	1.0	6	6.0	3	3.0	1	1.0	17	3.4
Good relations between people and representatives	Agree	5	5.0	3	3.0	13	13.0	19	19.0	6	6.0	46	9.2
	Partly agree	28	28.0	35	35.0	24	24.0	33	33.0	26	26.0	146	29.2
	Disagree	64	64.0	60	60.0	59	59.0	48	48.0	68	68.0	299	59.8
	Don't know	3	'3.0	2	2.0	4	4.0	0	.0	0	.0	9	1.8
Development in country	Agree	11	11.0	5	5.0	7	7.0	17	17.0	25	25.0	65	13.0
	Partly agree	58	58.0	60	60.0	53	53.0	74	74.0	48	48.0	293	58.6
	Disagree	29	29.0	34	34.0	37	37.0	8	8.0	26	26.0	134	26.8
	Don't know	2	2.0	1	1.0	3	3.0	1	1.0	1	1.0	8	1.6
Total		100	100	100	100	100	100	100	100	100	100	500	100

TABLE A3: WHAT IS ELECTION?

	District											
	Dhankuta		Rautahat		Kaski		Dang		Baitadi		Total	
	No.	%	No.	%	No.	%	No.	%	No.	%	No.	%
Exercise of people sovereign right	69	69.0	54	54.0	61	61.0	85	85.0	59	59.0	328	65.6
Selection of good representative	74	74.0	71	71.0	63	63.0	84	84.0	59	59.0	351	70.2
Selection of party policy and programme	34	34.0	46	46.0	17	17.0	33	33.0	17	17.0	147	29.4
A legitimate way of capturing power	28	28.0	55	55.0	19	19.0	36	36.0	24	24.0	162	32.4
A game among elites to reach power	34	34.0	29	29.0	36	36.0	22	22.0	40	40.0	161	32.2
Others	6	6.0	1	1.0	1	1.0	3	3.0	2	2.0	13	2.6
Don't know	5	5.0	6	6.0	1	1.0	1	1.0	0	.0	13	2.6
Total	100	250	100	262	100	198	100	264	100	201	500	235

Note: % based on multiple responses.

TABLE A4: EXPECTATION FROM MEMBER OF PARLIAMENT

	District											
	Dhankuta		Rautahat		Kaski		Dang		Baitadi		Total	
	No.	%	No.	%	No.	%	No.	%	No.	%	No.	%
Constituency development	72	72.0	88	88.0	87	87.0	87	87.0	87	87.0	421	84.2
Social reform	51	51.0	78	78.0	63	63.0	42	42.0	43	43.0	277	55.4
Uplift of disadvantaged groups	49	49.0	50	50.0	43	43.0	66	66.0	46	46.0	254	50.8
Make parliament effective	7	7.0	5	5.0	12	12.0	14	14.0	8	8.0	46	9.2
Make government effective	15	15.0	14	14.0	9	9.0	24	24.0	12	12.0	74	14.8
Seeking recommendation for job and others	57	57.0	60	60.0	43	43.0	48	48.0	74	74.0	282	56.4
Nothing	4	4.0	1	1.0	3	3.0	1	1.0	4	4.0	13	2.6
Others	10	10.0	0	.0	3	3.0	5	5.0	8	8.0	26	5.2
Don't know	5	5.0	0	.0	0	.0	0	.0	0	.0	5	1.0
Total	100	270	100	296	100	263	100	287	100	282	500	279.6

Note: % based on multiple responses.

TABLE A5: EXPECTATION FROM REPRESENTATIVES OF LOCAL ELECTED BODIES

	District											
	Dhankuta		Rautahat		Kaski		Dang		Baitadi		Total	
	No.	%	No.	%	No.	%	No.	%	No.	%	No.	%
Local development	89	89.0	97	97.0	92	92.0	94	94.0	88	88.0	460	92.0
Social reform	61	61.0	69	69.0	78	78.0	52	52.0	46	46.0	306	61.2
Uplift of disadvantaged groups	47	47.0	33	33.0	37	37.0	59	59.0	34	34.0	210	42.0
Management of local disputes	15	15.0	48	48.0	13	13.0	28	28.0	50	50.0	154	30.8
Seeking recommendation for job and others	32	32.0	32	32.0	29	29.0	20	20.0	39	39.0	152	30.4
Make police and administration responsible to people	21	21.0	16	16.0	12	12.0	32	32.0	21	21.0	102	20.4
Nothing	0	.0	1	1.0	3	3.0	0	.0	2	2.0	6	1.2
Others	12	12.0	0	.0	4	4.0	2	2.0	4	4.0	22	4.4
Don't know	1	1.0	0	.0	0	.0	0	.0	1	1.0	2	4
Total	100	278.0	100	296.0	100	268.0	100	287.0	100	285.0	500	282.8

Note: % based on multiple responses.

TABLE A6: PERFORMANCE OF VARIOUS LEVEL OF ELECTED BODIES AS EXPECTED BY PEOPLE

		District											
		Dhankuta		Rautahat		Kaski		Dang		Baitadi		Total	
		No.	%	No.	%	No.	%	No.	%	No.	%	No.	%
VDC-Municipality	Yes	22	22.0	5	5.0	21	21.0	30	30.0	25	25.0	103	20.6
	Partly	54	54.0	44	44.0	47	47.0	58	58.0	52	52.0	255	51.0
	No	19	19.0	51	51.0	30	30.0	11	11.0	23	23.0	134	26.8
	Don't know	5	5.0	0	.0	2	2.0	1	1.0	0	.0	8	1.6
DDC	Yes	14	14.0	0	.0	5	5.0	4	4.0	8	8.0	31	6.2
	Partly	40	40.0	42	42.0	32	32.0	46	46.0	49	49.0	200	41.8
	No	24	24.0	54	54.0	36	36.0	20	20.0	40	40.0	174	34.8
	Don't know	22	22.0	4	4.0	27	27.0	30	30.0	3	3.0	86	17.2
Parliament	Yes	4	4.0	1	1.0	8	8.0	11	11.0	2	2.0	26	5.2
	Partly	31	31.0	24	24.0	32	32.0	39	39.0	21	21.0	147	29.4
	No	44	44.0	66	66.0	43	43.0	29	29.0	76	76.0	258	51.6
	Don't know	21	21.0	9	9.0	17	17.0	21	21.0	1	1.0	69	13.8
Total		100	100.0	100	100.0	100	100.0	100	100.0	100	100.0	500	100.0

TABLE A7: ROLE AND FUNCTION OF POLICE AND ADMINISTRATION AT LOCAL LEVEL

	District											
	Dhankuta		Rautahat		Kaski		Dang		Baitadi		Total	
	No.	%	No.	%	No.	%	No.	%	No.	%	No.	%
Cooperative	36	36.0	23	23.0	30	30.0	23	23.0	37	37.0	140	29.8
Deliver quick service	16	16.0	10	10.0	12	12.0	4	4.0	29	29.0	71	14.2
Control crime	13	13.0	20	20.0	16	16.0	13	13.0	20	20.0	82	16.4
Party-line	37	37.0	57	57.0	34	34.0	34	34.0	27	27.0	189	37.8
Bribery	39	39.0	76	76.0	51	51.0	47	47.0	49	49.0	262	52.4
Partiality	32	32.0	79	79.0	50	50.0	49	49.0	50	50.0	260	52.0
Seek *chakari*	35	35.0	25	25.0	22	22.0	23	23.0	25	25.0	130	26.0
Others	4	4.0	0	.0	10	10.0	2	2.0	3	3.0	19	3.8
Don't know	16	16.0	2	2.0	5	5.0	17	17.0	3	3.0	43	8.6
Total	100	228.0	100	292.0	100	230.0	100	212.0	100	243.0	500	241.0

Note: % based on multiple responses.

TABLE A8: ABOUT THE PAST 1990 GOVERNMENTS

	District											
	Dhankuta		Rautahat		Kaski		Dang		Baitadi		Total	
	No.	%	No.	%	No.	%	No.	%	No.	%	No.	%
All good and effective	8	8.0	2	2.0	6	6.0	0	.0	0	.0	6	3.2
All bad and corrupt	20	20.0	34	34.0	12	12.0	9	9.0	8	8.0	83	16.6
Some good, some bad	63	63.0	60	60.0	69	69.0	76	76.0	90	90.0	358	71.6
Don't know	9	9.0	4	4.0	13	13.0	15	15.0	2	2.0	43	8.6
Total	100	100.0	100	100.0	100	100.0	100	100.0	100	100.0	500	100.0

TABLE A9: CHANGES OBSERVED AFTER RESTORATION OF DEMOCRACY

		District											
		Dhankuta		Rautahat		Kaski		Dang		Baitadi		Total	
		No.	%	No.	%	No.	%	No.	%	No.	%	No.	%
Improvement in life standard	Agree	16	16.0	16	16.0	27	27.0	26	26.0	26	26.0	111	22.2
	Partly agree	35	35.0	19	19.0	36	36.0	40	40.0	39	39.0	169	33.8
	Disagree	48	48.0	65	65.0	34	34.0	34	34.0	35	35.0	216	43.2
	Don't know	1	1.0	0	.0	3	3.0	0	.0	0	.0	4	.8
Local development	Agree	15	15.0	4	4.0	22	22.0	24	24.0	22	22.0	87	17.4
	Partly agree	65	65.0	62	62.0	47	47.0	69	69.0	53	53.0	296	59.2
	Disagree	19	19.0	34	34.0	30	30.0	7	7.0	25	25.0	115	23.0
	Don't know	1	1.0	0	.0	1	1.0	0	.0	0	.0	2	.4
Increase employment opportunity	Agree	7	7.0	3	3.0	20	20.0	7	7.0	8	8.0	45	9.0
	Partly agree	41	41.0	20	20.0	31	31.0	47	47.0	38	38.0	177	35.4
	Disagree	4	44.0	73	73.0	45	45.0	44	44.0	53	53.0	259	51.8
	Don't know	8	8.0	4	4.0	4	4.0	2	2.0	1	1.0	19	3.8

(contd.)

TABLE A9 (*contd.*)

		District											
		Dhankuta		Rautahat		Kaski		Dang		Baitadi		Total	
		No.	%	No.	%	No.	%	No.	%	No.	%	No.	%
Decrease social exploitation and untouchability	Agree	25	25.0	44	44.0	31	31.0	39	39.0	23	23.0	162	32.4
	Partly agree	43	43.0	32	32.0	39	39.0	40	40.0	51	51.0	205	41.0
	Disagree	30	30.0	24	24.0	25	25.0	19	19.0	26	26.0	124	24.8
	Don't know	2	2.0	0	.0	5	.0	2	2.0	0	.0	9	1.8
Decrease corruption	Agree	9	9.0	2	2.0	3	3.0	1	1.0	6	6.0	21	4.2
	Partly Agree	15	15.0	6	6.0	11	11.0	5	5.0	33	33.0	70	14.0
	Disagree	62	62.0	90	90.0	70	70.0	78	78.0	58	58.0	358	71.6
	Don't know	14	14.0	2	2.0	16	16.0	16	16.0	3	3.0	51	10.2
Total		100	100.0	100	100.0	100	100.0	100	100.0	100	100.0	500	100.0

TABLE A10: VOTINGS IN THE POST 1990 ELECTIONS

	District											
	Dhankuta		Rautahat		Kaski		Dang		Baitadi		Total	
	No.	%	No.	%	No.	%	No.	%	No.	%	No.	%
One	15	15.0	4	4.0	8	8.0	13	13.0	1	1.0	41	8.2
Two	8	8.0	13	13.0	17	17.0	15	15.0	4	4.0	57	11.4
Three	16	16.0	5	5.0	21	21.0	17	17.0	8	8.0	67	13.4
Four	8	8.0	2	2.0	9	9.0	8	8.0	8	8.0	67	13.4
Five	47	47.0	71	71.0	41	41.0	47	47.0	79	79.0	285	57.0
No-voting	6	6.0	5	5.0	3	3.0	0	.0	0	.0	14	2.8
Don't know	0	.0	0	.0	1	1.0	0	.0	0	.0	1	.2
Total	100	100.0	100	100.0	100	100.0	100	100.0	100	100.0	500	100.00

TABLE A11: IF VOTED MORE THAN ONCE TIME, TO WHOM?

	District										Total	
	Dhankuta		Rautahat		Kaski		Dang		Baitadi			
	No.	%	No.	%	No.	%	No.	%	No.	%	No.	%
Same party	47	59.5	33	36.3	65	73.9	50	57.5	61	61.6	256	57.7
Different parties	31	39.2	52	57.1	18	20.5	32	36.8	36	36.4	169	38.1
Some time for party candidate other for independent	0	.0	5	5.5	3	3.4	3	3.4		2.0	13	2.9
Don't know	1	1.3	1	1.1	2	2.3	2	2.3	0	.0	6	1.4
Total	79	100.0	91	100.0	88	100.0	87	100.0	99	100.0	444	100.0

TABLE A12: REASON FOR BEING CHANGE VOTERS

	District											
	Dhankuta		Rautahat		Kaski		Dang		Baitadi		Total	
	No.	%	No.	%	No.	%	No.	%	No.	%	No.	%
Party's failure to perform	16	51.6	47	82.5	9	42.9	13	37.1	26	68.4	111	61.0
Party leaders are inefficient	12	38.7	32	56.1	0	42.0	7	20.0	20	52.6	80	44.0
Erosion in party ideology	14	45.2	5	8.8	3	14.3	7	20.0	14	36.8	43	23.6
Failed to fulfil promise	14	45.2	38	66.7	11	52.4	10	28.6	13	34.2	86	47.3
Failed to bring about development	11	35.5	17	29.8	7	33.3	6	17.1	13	34.2	54	29.7
Becoming selfish, corrupt and power seekers	6	19.4	14	24.6	5	23.8	4	11.4	9	23.7	38	20.9
Insensitivity to women/ backward communities	3	9.7	8	14.0	2	9.5	5	14.3	4	10.5	22	12.1
Others	4	12.9	0	.0	2	9.5	8	22.9	2	5.3	16	8.8
Don't know	0	.0	1	1.8	1	4.8	0	.0	0	.0	2	1.1
Total	31	258.1	57	284.2	21	233.3	35	171.4	38	265.8	182	248.4

Note: % based on multiple responses.

TABLE A13: REPRESENTATION OF ETHNIC GROUPS, UNTOUCHABLE & WOMEN IN LOCAL ELECTION

		District											
		Dhankuta		Rautahat		Kaski		Dang		Baitadi		Total	
		No.	%	No.	%	No.	%	No.	%	No.	%	No.	%
Ethnic groups	Adequate	67	67.0	2	2.0	66	66.0	43	43.0	0	.0	178	35.6
representation	Few	24	24.0	65	65.0	23	23.0	39	39.00	.0	.0	151	30.2
in VDC-	Negligible	3	3.0	21	21.0	3	3.0	10	10.0	2	2.0	39	7.8
Municipality	No	1	1.0	4	4.0	1	1.0	2	2.0	96	96.0	104	20.8
	Don't know	5	5.0	8	8.0	7	7.06	6.0	2	2.0	28	5.6	
Ethnic groups	Adequate	56	56.0	1	1.0	15	15.0	1	1.0	0	.0	73	14.6
representation	Few	24	24.0	56	56.0	12	12.0	26	26.0	0	.0	118	23.6
in DDC	Negligible	2	2.0	23	23.0	7	7.0	21	21.0	0	.0	53	10.6
	No	2	2.0	7	7.0	1	1.0	7	7.0	97	97.0	114	22.8
	Don't know	16	16.0	13	13.0	65	65.0	45	45.0	3	3.0	142	28.4
Untouchable's	Adequate	1	1.0	3	3.0	4	4.0	0	.0	1	1.0	9	1.8
representation	Few	25	25.0	49	49.0	23	23.0	22	22.0	59	59.0	178	35.6
in VDC-	Negligible	45	45.0	29	29.0	51	51.0	40	40.0	33	33.0	198	39.6
Municipality	No	16	16.0	11	11.0	12	12.0	15	15.0	7	7.0	61	12.2
	Don't know	13	13.0	8	8.0	10	10.0	23	23.0	0	.0	54	10.8

Untouchable's representation in DDC	Adequate	1	1.0	1	1.0	2	2.0	0	.0	0	.0	4	.8
	Few	18	18.0	36	36.0	7	7.0	4	4.0	14	14.0	79	15.8
	Negligible	39	39.0	32	32.0	17	17.0	16	16.0	30	30.0	134	26.8
	No	14	14.0	15	15.0	12	12.0	24	24.0	44	4.0	109	21.8
	Don't know	28	28.0	16	16.0	62	62.0	56	56.0	12	12.0	174	34.8
Women's representation in VDC-Municipality	Adequate	23	23.0	6	6.0	17	17.0	16	16.0	1	1.0	63	12.6
	Few	60	60.0	63	63.0	45	45.0	68	68.0	87	87.0	323	64.6
	Negligible	11	11.0	22	22.0	24	24.0	13	13.0	11	1.0	81	16.2
	No	2	2.0	0	.0	2	2.0	0	.0	1	1.0	5	1.0
	Don't know	4	4.0	9	9.0	12	12.0	3	3.0	0	.0	28	5.6
Women's Representation in DDC	Adequate	10	10.0	0	.0	4	4.0	0	.0	0	.0	14	2.8
	Few	38	38.0	36	36.0	12	12.0	18	18.0	28	28.0	132	26.4
	Negligible	14	14.0	8	8.0	19	19.0	28	28.0	56	56.0	125	25.0
	No	11	11.0	31	31.0	3	3.0	6	6.0	5	5.0	56	11.2
	Don't know	27	27.0	25	25.0	62	62.0	48	48.0	11	11.0	173	34.6
Total		100	100.0	100	100.0	100	100.0	100	100.0	100	100.0	500	100.0

TABLE A14: OPINION ON CONTRIBUTIONS MADE BY ELECTED REPRESENTATIVE FOR INTEREST OF DISADVANTAGED GROUPS

	District											
	Dhankuta		Rautahat		Kaski		Dang		Baitadi		Total	
	No.	%	No.	%	No.	%	No.	%	No.	%	No.	%
Yes	24	24.0	16	16.0	24	24.0	33	33.0	48	48.0	145	29.0
No	60	60.0	82	82.0	56	56.0	43	43.0	51	51.0	292	58.4
Don't know	16	16.0	2	2.0	20	20.0	24	24.0	1	1.0	63	12.6
Total	100	100.0	100	100.0	100	100.0	100	100.0	100	100.0	500	100.0

TABLE A15: TYPES OF CONTRIBUTIONS

	District											
	Dhankuta		Rautahat		Kaski		Dang		Baitadi		Total	
	No.	%	No.	%	No.	%	No.	%	No.	%	No.	%
Increase awareness	12	50.0	11	68.8	14	58.3	20	60.6	41	85.4	98	67.6
Speech/writing	9	37.5	4	25.0	8	33.3	3	9.1	11	22.9	35	24.1
Demonstration	6	25.0	3	18.8	3	12.5	3	9.1	3	6.3	18	12.4
Interest articulation	11	45.8	5	31.3	7	29.2	13	39.4	12	25.0	48	33.1
Negotiation with party leaders	4	16.7	7	43.8	4	16.7	1	3.0	2	4.2	18	12.4
Adopting party policy and programme	9	37.5	0	.0	4	16.7	7	21.2	7	14.6	27	18.6
Providing employment and opportunity	9	37.5	7	43.8	7	29.2	9	27.3	35	72.9	67	46.2
Others	4	16.7	0	.0	2	8.3	11	33.3	4	8.3	21	14.5
Don't know	0	.0	0	.0	0	.0	1	3.0	0	.0	1	.7
Total	24	266.7	16	231.3	24	204.2	33	206.1	48	239.6	145	229.7

Note: % based on multiple responses.

TABLE A16: VIEWS ON ELECTION

		District										Total	
		Dhankuta		Rautahat		Kaski		Dang		Baitadi			
		No.	%	No.	%	No.	%	No.	%	No.	%	No.	%
Voting on the basis of party principle	Agree	21	21.0	58	58.0	59	59.0	34	34.0	28	28.0	210	42.0
	Partly agree	39	39.0	22	22.0	17	17.0	46	46.0	31	31.0	155	31.0
	Disagree	34	34.0	17	17.0	14	14.0	18	18.0	30	30.0	113	22.6
	Don't know	6	6.0	3	3.0	10	10.0	2	2.0	1	1.0	22	4.4
Raising communal feeling by party/candidates	Agree	30	30.0	30	30.0	27	27.0	26	26.0	32	32.0	145	29.0
	Partly agree	21	21.0	36	36.0	22	22.0	30	30.0	19	19.0	128	25.6
	Disagree	38	38.0	33	33.0	31	31.0	36	36.0	47	47.0	185	37.0
	Don't know	11	11.0	1	1.0	20	20.0	8	8.0	2	2.0	42	8.4
Voters will be affected by communal slogans in coming days	Agree	20	20.0	19	19.0	26	26.0	21	21.0	31	31.0	117	23.4
	Partly agree	25	25.0	34	34.0	26	26.0	29	29.0	21	21.0	135	27.0
	Disagree	35	35.0	41	41.0	20	20.0	32	32.0	46	46.0	174	34.8
	Don't know	20	20.0	6	6.0	28	28.0	18	18.0	2	2.0	74	14.8

Will increase representation of ethnic groups in coming days	Agree	34	34.0	27	27.0	38	38.0	37	37.0	37	37.0	173	34.6
	Partly agree	27	27.0	37	37.0	23	23.0	28	28.0	26	26.0	141	28.2
	Disagree	18	18.0	25	25.0	7	7.0	10	10.0	31	31.0	91	18.2
	Don't know	21	21.0	11	11.0	32	32.0	25	25.0	6	6.0	95	19.0
Issues concerning women, untouchable and marginalized sections will be election agendas	Agree	43	43.0	26	26.0	43	43.0	41	41.0	55	55.0	208	41.6
	Partly agree	29	29.0	36	36.0	11	11.0	28	28.0	27	27.0	131	26.2
	disagree	18	18.0	32	32.0	11	11.0	14	14.0	16	16.0	91	18.2
	Don't know	10	10.0	6	6.0	35	35.0	17	17.0	2	2.0	70	14.0
Total		100	100.0	100	100.0	100	100.0	100	10.0	100	100.0	500	100.0

TABLE A17: WHOM TO VOTE COMING ELECTION

	District											
	Dhankuta		Rautahat		Kaski		Dang		Baitadi		Total	
	No.	%	No.	%	No.	%	No.	%	No.	%	No.	%
Party candidate	11	11.0	16	16.0	22	22.0	23	23.0	26	26.0	98	19.6
Able and honest candidate	77	77.0	81	81.0	62	62.0	72	72.0	68	68.0	360	72.0
Neighbour	1	1.0	0	.0	2	2.0	3	3.0	1	1.0	7	1.4
Own community	1	1.0	2	2.0	0	.0	0	.0	1	1.0	4	.8
Relative	0	.0	0	.0	0	.0	0	.0	1	1.0	1	.2
One who offer personal benefit	0	.0	0	.0	2	2.0	0	.0	0	.0	2	.4
Others	4	4.0	1	1.0	7	7.0	1	1.0	3	3.0	16	3.2
Don't know	6	6.0	0	.0	5	5.0	1	1.0	0	.0	12	2.4
Total	100	100.0	100	100.0	100	100.0	100	100.0	100	100.0	500	100.0

TABLE A18: WHAT IS POLITICAL PARTY

	District											
	Dhankuta		Rautahat		Kaski		Dang		Baitadi		Total	
	No.	%	No.	%	No.	%	No.	%	No.	%	No.	%
A group of people committed to particular ideology	31	31.0	42	42.0	40	40.0	60	60.0	55	55.0	228	45.6
One which articulates people demand and interest to government	45	45.0	67	67.0	22	22.0	68	68.0	70	70.0	272	54.4
Indispensable institution of democracy	30	30.0	43	43.0	29	29.0	47	47.0	68	68.0	217	43.4
Institution involved in socio-economic development	37	37.0	55	55.0	18	18.0	41	41.0	40	40.0	191	38.2
Instrument of power and authority	37	37.0	32	32.0	29	29.0	19	19.0	13	13.0	130	26.0
Institution used by leader/ workers for personal interest	27	27.0	24	24.0	24	24.0	10	10.0	19	19.0	104	20.8
Others	2	2.0	1	1.0	1	1.0	0	.0	1	1.0	5	1.0
Don't know	23	23.0	8	8.0	12	12.0	5	5.0	1	1.0	49	9.8
Total	100	232.0	100	272.0	100	175.0	100	250.0	100	367.0	500	239.2

Note: % based on multiple responses.

TABLE A19: BASIS OF CANDIDATE SELECTION FOR GENERAL ELECTION 1999

	District											
	Dhankuta		Rautahat		Kaski		Dang		Baitadi		Total	
	No.	%	No.	%	No.	%	No.	%	No.	%	No.	%
Continuity/seniority	59	59.0	45	45.0	38	38.0	64	64.0	75	75.0	281	56.2
Community/ethnic	22	22.0	19	19.0	31	31.0	20	20.0	10	10.0	102	20.4
Popularity	55	55.0	62	62.0	55	55.0	64	64.0	73	73.0	309	61.8
Rich and influential	32	32.0	48	48.0	18	18.0	19	19.0	18	18.0	135	27.0
Favourite of central leader	37	37.0	61	61.0	24	24.0	41	41.0	36	36.0	199	39.8
Opportunist	14	14.0	15	15.0	6	6.0	5	5.0	6	6.0	46	9.2
Others	0	.0	0	.0	2	2.0	2	2.0	2	2.0	6	1.2
Don't know	13	13.0	10	10.0	17	17.0	16	16.0	2	2.0	58	11.6
Total	100	232.0	100	260.0	100	191.0	100	231.0	100	222.0	500	227.2

Note: % based on multiple responses.

TABLE A20: BASIS OF CANDIDATE SELECTION FOR LOCAL ELECTION 1997

	District											
	Dhankuta		Rautahat		Kaski		Dang		Baitadi		Total	
	No.	%	No.	%	No.	%	No.	%	No.	%	No.	%
Continuity and seniority	49	49.0	27	27.0	42	42.0	46	46.0	72	72.0	236	47.2
Community/ethnic	27	27.0	39	39.0	33	33.0	45	45.0	15	15.0	159	31.8
Popularity	57	57.0	67	67.0	59	59.0	70	70.0	75	75.0	328	65.6
Rich and influential	31	31.0	37	37.0	13	13.0	10	10.0	10	10.0	101	20.2
Favourite of district leaders	30	30.0	54	54.0	13	13.0	35	35.0	21	21.0	153	30.6
Favourite of Central leaders	10	10.0	18	18.0	13	13.0	9	9.0	13	13.0	63	12.6
Opportunist	9	9.0	14	14.0	7	7.0	2	2.0	6	6.0	38	7.6
Others	2	2.0	0	.0	0	.0	1	1.0	0	.0	3	.6
Don't know	16	16.0	5	5.0	14	14.0	13	13.0	3	3.0	51	10.2
Total	100	231.0	100	261.0	100	194.0	100	231.0	100	215.0	500	226.4

Note: % based on multiple responses.

TABLE A21: MAIN ELECTION AGENDA OF 1999 ELECTION

	District											
	Dhankuta		Rautahat		Kaski		Dang		Baitadi		Total	
	No.	%	No.	%	No.	%	No.	%	No.	%	No.	%
Political stability	18	18.0	19	19.0	16	16.0	24	24.0	29	29.0	106	21.2
Infrastructure building	67	67.0	74	74.0	69	69.0	77	77.0	70	70.0	357	71.4
Nationality	3	3.0	10	10.0	11	11.0	12	12.0	10	10.0	46	9.2
Land reform	2	2.0	7	7.0	1	1.0	12	12.0	0	.0	22	4.4
Employment	48	48.0	72	72.0	25	25.0	33	33.0	58	58.0	236	47.2
Security, control of price rise and corruption	78	78.0	78	78.0	63	63.0	83	83.0	78	78.0	380	76.0
Uplift of disadvantaged groups	35	35.0	34	34.0	29	29.0	31	31.0	43	43.0	172	34.4
Others	5	5.0	0	.0	1	1.0	0	.0	3	3.0	9	1.8
Don't know	7	7.0	0	.0	13	13.0	5	5.0	1	1.0	26	5.2
Total	100	263.0	100	294.0	100	228.0	100	277.0	100	292.0	500	270.8

Note: % based on multiple responses.

TABLE A22: STRATEGIES FOR VOTE MAXIMIZATION

	District											
	Dhankuta		Rautahat		Kaski		Dang		Baitadi		Total	
	No.	%	No.	%	No.	%	No.	%	No.	%	No.	%
Party ideology, policy and programme	41	41.0	29	29.0	38	38.0	46	46.0	63	63.0	217	43.4
Leader image	20	20.0	33	33.0	16	16.0	21	21.0	31	31.0	121	24.2
Candidate's personality	35	35.0	44	44.0	36	36.0	21	21.0	47	47.0	183	36.6
Assurance for development	75	75.0	85	85.0	86	86.0	88	88.0	82	82.0	416	83.2
Distribution of development materials	53	53.0	47	47.0	14	14.0	61	61.0	17	17.0	192	38.4
Others	15	15.0	5	5.0	3	3.0	2	2.0	9	9.0	34	6.8
Don't know	11	11.0	6	6.0	8	8.0	5	5.0	2	2.0	32	6.4
Total	100	250.0	100	249.0	100	201.0	100	244.0	100	251.0	500	239.0

Note: % based on multiple responses.

TABLE A23: MEANS OF PARTY/CANDIDATE-VOTERS COMMUNICATION

	District											
	Dhankuta		Rautahat		Kaski		Dang		Baitadi		Total	
	No.	%	No.	%	No.	%	No.	%	No.	%	No.	%
Door to door campaign	62	62.0	94	94.0	79	79.0	91	91.0	92	92.0	418	83.6
Mass meeting/rally	68	68.0	51	51.0	78	78.0	74	74.0	77	77.0	348	69.6
Pamphlet distribution	72	72.0	15	15.0	40	40.0	39	39.0	57	57.0	223	44.6
Newspapers	1	1.0	0	.0	4	4.0	6	6.0	0	.0	11	2.2
Radio, TV	3	3.0	1	1.0	0	.0	1	1.0	0	.0	5	1.0
Village elite	11	11.0	53	53.0	22	22.0	6	6.0	4	4.0	96	19.2
Workers mobilization	67	67.0	74	74.0	49	49.0	55	55.0	59	59.0	304	60.8
Others	1	1.0	1	1.0	2	2.0	1	1.0	0	.0	5	1.0
Don't know	2	2.0	0	.0	1	1.0	1	1.0	1	1.0	5	1.0
Total	100	287.0	100	289.0	100	275.0	100	274.0	100	290.0	500	283.0

Note: % based on multiple responses.

TABLE A24: DEGREE OF ELECTORAL PARTICIPATION

		District											
		Dhankuta		Rautahat		Kaski		Dang		Baitadi		Total	
		No.	%	No.	%	No.	%	No.	%	No.	%	No.	%
General election 1991	Under age	27	27.0	5	5.0	21	21.0	23	23.0	9	9.0	85	17.0
	Public speech	3	3.0	1	1.0	1	1.0	4	4.0	13	13.0	22	4.4
	Campaigning	7	7.0	9	9.0	11	11.0	22	22.0	21	21.0	70	14.0
	Donation	1	1.0	0	.0	0	.0	0	.0	0	.0	1	.2
	Participation in mass meetings	12	12.0	1	1.0	15	15.0	3	3.0	15	15.0	46	9.2
	Just vote casting	36	36.0	68	68.0	35	35.0	31	31.0	38	38.0	208	41.6
	No-participation	12	12.0	13	13.0	16	16.0	15	15.0	3	3.0	59	11.8
	Others	1	1.0	1	1.0	1	1.0	1	1.0	1	1.0	5	1.0
	Don't know	1	1.0	2	2.0	0	.0	1	1.0	0	.0	4	.8
General election 1994	Under age	16	16.0	1	1.0	9	9.0	7	7.0	1	1.0	34	6.8
	Public speech	2	2.0	2	2.0	2	2.0	5	5.0	16	16.0	27	5.4
	Campaigning	10	10.0	8	8.0	11	11.0	24	24.0	22	22.0	75	15.0
	Donation	2	2.0	0	.0	0	.0	0	.0	0	.0	2	.4
	Participation in mass meetings	14	14.0	1	1.0	13	13.0	4	4.0	18	18.0	50	10.0
	Just vote casting	45	45.0	74	74.0	49	49.0	37	37.0	42	42.0	247	49.4
	No-participation	9	9.0	11	11.0	15	15.0	19	19.0	0	.0	54	10.8

(contd.)

TABLE A24 (*contd.*)

		District											
		Dhankuta		Rautahat		Kaski		Dang		Baitadi		Total	
		No.	%	No.	%	No.	%	No.	%	No.	%	No.	%
	Others	1	1.0	1	1.0	1	1.0	3	3.0	1	1.0	7	1.4
	Don't know	1	1.0	2	2.0	0	.0	1	1.0	0	.0	4	.8
General election 1999	Under age	0	.0	0	.0	2	2.0	2	2.0	0	.0		.8
	Candidate	0	.0	0	.0	0	.0	0	.0	1	1.0	1	.2
	Public speech	4	4.0	2	2.0	3	3.0	7	7.0	17	17.0	33	6.6
	Campaigning	11	11.0	11	11.0	13	13.0	35	35.0	21	21.0	91	18.2
	Donation	1	1.0	0	.0	0	.0	0	.0	0	.0	1	.2
	Participation in mass meetings	16	16.0	1	1.0	17	17.0	4	4.0	18	18.0	56	11.2
	Just vote casting	54	54.0	68	68.0	51	51.0	42	42.0	38	38.0	253	50.6
	No-participation	13	13.0	17	17.0	12	12.0	7	7.0	2	2.0	51	10.2
	Others	0	.0	0	.0	2	2.0	3	3.0	3	3.0	8	1.6
	Don't know	1	1.0	1	1.0	0	.0	0	.0	0	.0	2	.4
Local election 1992	Under age	23	23.0	2	2.0	18	18.0	18	18.0	4	4.0	65	13.0
	Candidate	2	2.0	3	3.0	2	2.0	6	6.0	14	14.0	27	5.4
	Public speech	3	3.0	2	2.0	3	3.0	3	3.0	8	8.0	19	3.8
	Campaigning	6	6.0	9	9.0	11	11.0	17	17.0	23	23.0	66	13.2
	Donation	1	1.0	0	.0	0	.0	0	.0	0	.0	1	.2

(*contd.*)

	Participation in mass meetings	12	12.0	0	.0	10	10.0	1	1.0	8	8.0	31	6.2
	Just vote casting	41	41.0	65	65.0	40	40.0	32	32.0	40	40.0	218	43.6
	No-Participation	11	11.0	16	16.0	15	15.0	19	19.0	3	3.0	6	12.8
	Others	0	.0	1	1.0	1	1.0	3	3.0	0	.0	5	1.0
	Don't know	1	1.0	2	2.0	0	.0	1	1.0	0	.0	4	.8
Local election 1997	Under age	10	10.0	0	.0	7	7.0	2	2.0	0	.0	19	3.8
	Candidate	4	4.0	10	10.0	3	3.0	14	14.0	28	28.0	59	11.8
	Public speech	2	2.0	1	1.0	2	2.0	1	1.0	6	6.0	12	2.4
	Campaigning	9	9.0	10	10.0	11	11.0	22	22.0	16	16.0	68	13.6
	Donation	1	1.0	0	.0	0	.0	0	.0	0	.0	1	.2
	Participation in mass meetings	12	12.0	1	1.0	11	11.0	4	4.0	12	12.0	40	8.0
	Just vote casting	48	48.0	62	62.0	50	50.0	43	43.0	34	34.0	237	47.4
	No-participation	12	12.0	14	14.0	15	15.0	12	12.0	3	3.0	56	11.2
	Others	0	.0	0	.0	1	1.0	2	2.0	1	1.0	4	.8
	Don't know	2	2.0	2	2.0	0	.0	0	.0	0	.0	4	.8
Total		100	100.0	100	100.0	100	100.0	100	100.0	100	100.0	500	100.0

TABLE A25: REASONS FOR DECLINING ELECTORAL PARTICIPATION

	District											
	Dhankuta		Rautahat		Kaski		Dang		Baitadi		Total	
	No.	%	No.	%	No.	%	No.	%	No.	%	No.	%
Erosion in party's ideology	1	3.8	4	11.1	6	17.1	2	5.3	3	5.5	16	8.4
Selfish leaders/workers	6	23.1	9	25.0	13	37.1	8	21.1	6	10.9	42	22.1
Lack of internal democracy in party	3	11.5	2	5.6	2	5.7	1	2.6	1	1.8	9	4.7
Ineffective leadership	6	23.1	3	8.3	4	11.4	2	5.3	1	1.8	16	8.4
Lack of proper evaluation	5	19.2	7	19.4	8	22.9	5	13.2	5	9.1	30	15.8
Nepotism/favouritism in party	5	19.2	7	19.4	3	8.6	2	5.3	2	3.6	19	10.0
Political corruption	8	30.8	12	33.3	12	34.3	9	23.7	7	12.7	48	25.3
Others	11	42.3	11	30.6	10	28.6	18	47.4	39	70.9	89	46.8
Don't know	1	3.8	7	19.4	4	11.4	1	2.6	0	.0	13	6.8
Total	26	176.9	36	172.2	35	177.1	38	126.3	55	116.4	190	148.4

Note: % based on multiple responses.

TABLE A26: OPINION ON SOME ISSUES OF ELECTION

		District											
		Dhankuta		Rautahat		Kaski		Dang		Baitadi		Total	
		No.	%	No.	%	No.	%	No.	%	No.	%	No.	%
Respect to public opinion in candidate selection	Agree	47	47.0	44	44.0	38	38.0	40	40.0	49	49.0	218	43.6
	Partly agree	26	26.0	16	16.0	20	20.0	28	28.0	18	18.0	108	21.6
	Disagree	17	17.0	35	35.0	25	25.0	21	21.0	30	30.0	128	25.6
	Don't know	10	10.0	5	5.0	17	17.0	11	11.0	3	3.0	46	9.2
Consultation with party local leader/ workers	Agree	34	34.0	50	50.0	42	42.0	37	37.0	53	53.0	216	43.2
	Partly agree	29	29.0	16	16.0	13	13.0	32	32.0	19	19.0	109	21.8
	Disagree	21	21.0	27	27.0	24	24.0	9	9.0	22	22.0	103	20.6
	Don't know	16	16.0	7	7.0	21	21.0	22	22.0	6	6.0	72	14.4
Do not use money and muscle power	Agree	15	15.0	22	22.0	16	16.0	7	7.0	41	41.0	101	20.2
	Partly agree	22	22.0	14	14.0	24	24.0	10	10.0	19	19.0	89	17.8
	Disagree	48	48.0	62	62.0	41	41.0	75	75.0	37	37.0	263	52.6
	Don't know	15	15.0	2	2.0	19	19.0	8	8.0	3	3.0	47	9.4
Greater mobilization of party worker in 1999 general election victory	Agree	45	45.0	43	43.0	45	45.0	53	53.0	59	59.0	245	49.0
	Partly agree	17	17.0	14	14.0	20	20.0	22	22.0	21	21.0	94	18.8
	Disagree	21	21.0	29	29.0	18	18.0	18	18.0	16	16.0	102	20.4
	Don't know	17	17.0	14	14.0	17	17.0	7	7.0	4	4.0	59	11.8

(contd.)

TABLE 26 (*Contd.*)

		District											
		Dhankuta		Rautahat		Kaski		Dang		Baitadi		Total	
		No.	%	No.	%	No.	%	No.	%	No.	%	No.	%
Party	Agree	2	2.0	4	4.0	2	2.0	2	2.0	1	1.0	11	2.2
candidates	Partly agree	22	22.0	17	17.0	20	20.0	37	37.0	17	17.0	113	22.6
fulfil their	Disagree	72	72.0	77	77.0	74	74.0	59	59.0	80	80.0	362	72.4
promises	Don't know	4	4.0	2	2.0	4	4.0	2	2.0	2	2.0	14	2.8
Total		100	100.0	100	100.0	100	100.0	100	100.0	100	100.0	500	100.0

TABLE A27: DID YOU VOTE IN 1999 ELECTION

	District											
	Dhankuta		Rautahat		Kaski		Dang		Baitadi		Total	
	No.	%	No.	%	No.	%	No.	%	No.	%	No.	%
Yes	85	85.0	84	84.0	84	84.0	87	87.9	93	93.0	433	86.6
No	15	15.0	16	16.0	15	15.0	13	13.0	7	7.0	66	13.2
Don't know	0	.0	0	.0	1	1.0	0	.0	0	.0	1	.2
Totals	100	100.0	100	100.0	100	100.0	100	100.0	100	100.0	500	100.0

TABLE A28: IF NOT, WHY?

	District										Total	
	Dhankuta		Rautahat		Kaski		Dang		Baitadi			
	No.	%	No.	%	No.	%	No.	%	No.	%	No.	%
No entry in voter list	2	13.3	5	31.3	4	26.7	2	15.4	2	28.6	15	22.7
No voter ID card	0	.0	1	6.3	0	.0	0	.0	3	42.9	4	6.1
Proxy voting	1	6.7	1	6.3	0	.0	0	.0	0	.0	2	3.0
Far-distance of polling centre	3	20.0	4	25.0	3	20.0	1	7.7	0	.0	11	16.7
Violence and insecurity in polling centre	0	.0	1	6.3	0	.0	0	.0	0	.0	1	1.5
Lack of proper candidate	2	13.3	1	6.3	1	6.7	0	.0	0	.0	4	6.1
Boycott called by party affiliated	0	.0	1	6.3	0	.0	0	.0	0	.0	1	1.5
Others	11	73.3	5	31.3	7	46.7	10	76.9	5	71.4	38	57.6
Don't know	0	.0	0	.0	1	6.7	0	.0	0	.0	1	1.5
Total	15	126.7	16	118.8	15	106.7	13	100.0	7	142.9	66	116.7

Note: % based on multiple responses.

TABLE A29: OPINION OF RIGGING IN POLLING CENTER

	District										Total	
	Dhankuta		Rautahat		Kaski		Dang		Baitadi			
	No.	%	No.	%	No.	%	No.	%	No.	%	No.	%
Yes	7	8.2	18	21.4	50	59.5	18	20.7	16	17.2	109	25.2
No	77	90.6	66	78.6	28	33.3	69	79.3	77	82.8	317	73.2
Don't know	1	1.2	0	.0	6	7.1	0	.0	0	.0	7	1.6
Total	85	100.0	84	100.0	84	100.0	87	100.0	93	100.0	433	100.0

TABLE A30: NATURE OF RIGGING

	District											
	Dhankuta		Rautahat		Kaski		Dang		Baitadi		Total	
	No.	%	No.	%	No.	%	No.	%	No.	%	No.	%
Booth capturing	0	.0	5	27.8	2	4.0	2	11.1	1	6.3	10	9.2
Vote buying	6	85.7	6	33.3	8	16.0	10	55.6	8	50.0	38	34.9
Use of force and violence	1	14.3	14	77.8	15	30.0	9	50.0	0	.0	39	35.8
Under aged voting	5	71.4	9	50.0	28	56.0	5	27.8	10	62.5	57	52.3
Not allowing agent of other party	0	.0	0	.0	1	2.0	2	11.1	1	6.3	4	3.7
Proxy voting	6	85.7	12	66.7	40	80.0	9	50.0	12	75.0	79	72.5
Partiality by police and administration	1	14.3	4	22.2	9	18.0	10	5.6	5	31.3	29	26.6
Others	1	14.3	0	.0	2	4.0	0	.0	1	6.3	4	3.7
Total	7	285.7	18	277.8	50	210.0	18	261.1	16	237.5	109	238.5

Note: % based on multiple responses.

TABLE A31: MORE EXPENSES ON ELECTION, WHAT SECTORS?

	District											
	Dhankuta		Rautahat		Kaski		Dang		Baitadi		Total	
	No.	%	No.	%	No.	%	No.	%	No.	%	No.	%
Publicity	39	39.0	49	49.0	69	69.0	39	39.0	80	80.0	276	55.2
Mobilization of workers	54	54.0	47	47.0	75	75.0	58	58.0	89	89.0	323	64.6
Distribution of development materials	39	39.0	11	11.0	7	7.0	36	36.0	12	12.0	105	21.0
For brokers	29	29.0	46	46.0	15	15.0	38	38.0	27	27.0	155	31.0
For police and administration	9	9.0	17	17.0	15	15.0	22	22.0	4	4.0	67	13.4
For arm purchase and force	10	10.0	61	61.0	11	11.0	15	15.0	1	1.0	98	19.6
For vote buying and distribution of goods	59	59.0	55	55.0	40	40.0	53	53.0	59	59.0	266	53.2
Others	0	.0	0	.0	0	.0	1	1.0	1	1.0	2	.4
Don't Know	15	15.0	5	5.0	7	7.0	7	7.0	1	1.0	35	7.0
Total	100	254.0	100	291.0	100	239.0	100	269.0	100	274.0	500	265.4

Note: % based on multiple responses.

TABLE A32: LEVEL AND TYPE OF INVOLVEMENT IN VOTE BUYING

	District											
	Dhankuta		Rautahat		Kaski		Dang		Baitadi		Total	
	No.	%	No.	%	No.	%	No.	%	No.	%	No.	%
Involved	5	5.0	7	7.0	1	1.0	7	7.0	7	7.0	27	5.4
Saw	17	17.0	19	19.0	6	6.0	13	13.0	12	12.0	67	13.4
Heard	62	62.0	66	66.0	68	68.0	60	60.0	73	73.0	329	65.8
Don't know	16	16.0	8	8.0	25	25.0	20	20.0	8	8.0	77	15.4
Total	100	100.0	100	100.0	100	100.0	100	100.0	100	100.0	500	100.0

TABLE A33: MEASURES TO REDUCE RIGGING

	District											
	Dhankuta		Rautahat		Kaski		Dang		Baitadi		Total	
	No.	%	No.	%	No.	%	No.	%	No.	%	No.	%
Refined voter list	39	39.0	20	20.0	33	33.0	27	27.0	32	32.0	151	30.2
More power to election commission	16	16.0	35	35.0	11	11.0	23	23.0	40	40.0	125	25.0
Abide by election code of conduct	25	25.0	37	37.0	52	52.0	23	23.0	42	42.0	179	35.8
Introduce voter ID card system	52	52.0	52	52.0	49	49.0	47	47.0	94	94.0	294	58.8
Effective security and management of polling centre	24	24.0	51	51.0	27	27.0	37	37.0	17	17.0	156	31.2
Discourage use of money and force	47	47.0	54	54.0	36	36.0	61	61.0	29	29.0	227	45.4
Impartiality of police/ administration	26	26.0	47	47.0	30	30.0	41	41.0	29	29.0	173	34.6
Others	7	7.0	0	.0	4	4.0	3	3.0	1	1.0	15	3.0
Don't Know	17	17.0	0	.0	5	5.0	6	6.0	1	1.0	29	5.8
Total	100	253.0	100	296.0	100	247.0	100	268.0	100	285.0	500	269.8

Note: % based on multiple responses.

TABLE A34: MAJOR POLITICAL ACHIEVEMENTS AFTER 1990

	District											
	Dhankuta		Rautahat		Kaski		Dang		Baitadi		Total	
	No.	%	No.	%	No.	%	No.	%	No.	%	No.	%
Constitution making	39	39.0	42	42.0	27	27.0	58	58.0	51	51.0	217	43.4
Periodic election	17	17.0	10	10.0	21	21.0	31	31.0	38	38.0	117	23.4
Freedom of speech and writing	70	70.0	67	67.0	69	69.0	75	75.0	91	91.0	372	74.4
Decentralization	43	43.0	48	48.0	19	19.0	17	17.0	28	28.0	155	31.0
Independent judiciary	8	8.0	34	34.0	6	6.0	8	8.0	13	13.0	69	13.8
Change of government according to law	13	13.0	7	7.0	9	9.0	19	19.0	22	22.0	70	14.0
Responsible opposition	4	4.0	6	6.0	3	3.0	8	8.0	13	13.0	34	6.8
Others	5	5.0	1	1.0	3	3.0	1	1.0	2	2.0	12	2.4
Don't know	22	22.0	23	23.0	24	24.0	10	10.0	3	3.0	82	16.4
Total	100	221.0	100	238.0	100	181.0	100	227.0	100	261.0	500	225.6

Note: % based on multiple responses.

TABLE A35: MAJOR ACHIEVEMENT IN SOCIAL AND ECONOMIC SECTORS AFTER 1990

	District											
	Dhankuta		Rautahat		Kaski		Dang		Baitadi		Total	
	No.	%	No.	%	No.	%	No.	%	No.	%	No.	%
Infrastructure development	53	53.0	46	46.0	41	41.0	70	70.0	67	67.0	277	55.4
End of duel ownership in land	8	8.0	9	9.0	1	1.0	22	22.0	12	12.0	52	10.4
Uplift of disadvantaged	27	27.0	32	32.0	26	26.0	20	20.0	37	37.0	142	28.4
Decline of untouchable practices	46	46.0	79	79.0	53	53.0	47	47.0	58	58.0	283	56.6
Land distribution to Sukumbasi (landless)	34	34.0	26	26.0	12	12.0	25	25.0	27	27.0	124	24.8
Abolition of bonded labour (*Kamaiya* system)	26	26.0	28	28.0	12	12.0	56	56.0	37	37.0	159	31.8
Respect to minority languages	21	21.0	5	5.0	25	25.0	24	24.0	8	8.0	83	16.6
Others	10	10.0	1	1.0	3	3.0	1	1.0	4	4.0	19	3.8
Don't know	14	14.0	5	5.0	16	16.0	0	.0	3	3.0	38	7.6
Total	100	239.0	100	231.0	100	189.0	100	265.0	100	253.0	500	235.4

Note: % based on multiple responses.

TABLE A36: MAJOR PROBLEMS EMERGING IN POST 1990 DEMOCRACY

	District											
	Dhankuta		Rautahat		Kaski		Dang		Baitadi		Total	
	No.	%	No.	%	No.	%	No.	%	No.	%	No.	%
Erosion in party's ideology	28	28.0	19	19.0	18	18.0	22	22.0	33	33.0	120	24.0
Erosion of leaders/ workers morality	44	44.0	56	56.0	44	44.0	32	32.0	53	53.0	229	45.8
Corruption	56	56.0	87	87.0	62	62.0	72	72.0	54	54.0	331	66.2
Unemployment	40	40.0	50	50.0	40	40.0	48	48.0	54	54.0	232	46.4
Insecurity	37	37.0	61	61.0	46	46.0	65	65.0	41	41.0	250	50.0
Excessive politicization	40	40.0	16	16.0	29	29.0	22	22.0	27	27.0	134	26.8
Instability	9	9.0	3	3.0	10	10.0	12	12.0	21	21.0	55	11.0
Others	5	5.0	0	.0	6	6.0	5	5.0	2	2.0	18	3.6
Don't know	9	9.0	1	1.0	3	3.0	3	3.0	1	1.0	17	3.4
Total	100	268.0	100	293.0	100	258.0	100	281.0	100	286.0	500	277.2

Note: % based on multiple responses.

TABLE A37: RECOMMENDATIONS FOR CONSOLIDATION OF DEMOCRACY

	District											
	Dhankuta		Rautahat		Kaski		Dang		Baitadi		Total	
	No.	%	No.	%	No.	%	No.	%	No.	%	No.	%
Good governance and clean politics	117	117.0	87	87.0	90	90.0	89	89.0	111	111.0	494	98.8
Social reform and development	37	37.0	43	43.0	25	25.0	20	20.0	13	13.0	138	27.6
Economic development	26	26.0	26	26.0	44	44.0	46	46.0	23	23.0	165	33.0
Free and fair elections	6	6.0	16	16.0	5	5.0	6	6.0	16	16.0	49	9.8
Uplift of disadvantaged groups	16	16.0	7	7.0	7	7.0	17	17.0	45	45.0	92	18.4
Employment	26	26.0	29	29.0	30	30.0	37	37.0	29	29.0	151	30.2
Control of corruption	29	29.0	53	53.0	53	53.0	39	39.0	29	29.0	203	40.6
Security	18	18.0	32	32.0	25	25.0	37	37.0	26	26.0	138	27.6
Others	2	2.0	7	7.0	4	4.0	2	2.0	2	2.0	17	3.4
Don't know	2	2.0	0	.0	0	.0	0	.0	0	.0	2	.4
Total	100	279.0	100	300.0	100	283.0	100	293.0	100	294.0	500	289.8

Note: % based on multiple responses.

Bibliography

BOOKS

Acharya, Narahari, ed., *Bishweshwor Prasad Koirala: Nepali Congress ka Char Dasak,* Kathmandu: Sambatsar Prakashan, 2053 (1997)

———, *Bhabi Nepalko Prastavana* (Proposal for Future Nepal), Kathmandu: Sambatsar Prakashan, 1999.

Adhikari, Krishna Kant, *Nepal Under Jang Bahadur 1846-1877,* vol. 1, Kathmandu: BUKU, 1984.

Aivar, S.U. and S.U. Raju, *When the Wind Blows: India's Ballot-box Revolution,* Bombay: Himalaya Publishing, 1978.

Anderson, Charles W., *Statecraft: An Introduction to Political Choice and Judgement,* New York: John Wiley & Sons, 1977.

Apter, David, *Introduction to Political Analysis,* New Delhi: Prentice-Hall, 1978.

———, *The Politics of Modernization,* Chicago: University of Chicago Press, 1965.

Baral, Lok Raj, *Nepal's Politics of Referendum: A Study of Groups, Personalities and Trends,* New Delhi: Vikas Publishing House, 1983.

———, *Oppositional Politics in Nepal,* New Delhi: Abhinav Publications, 1977.

———, *The Regional Paradox: Essays in Nepali and South Asian Affairs,* Delhi: Adroit, 2000.

———, *Nepal: Problems of Governance,* Delhi: Konark, 1993.

———, ed., *South Asia: Democracy and the Road Ahead,* Kathmandu: POLSAN, 1992.

Bista, Dor Bahadur, *Fatalism and Development: Nepal's Struggle for Modernization,* Hyderabad: Orient Longman, 1991.

Bogdanor, V. and D. Butler, eds., *Democracy and Elections: Electoral Systems and their Political Consequences,* New York: Cambridge University Press, 1983.

Borre, O., Sushil R. Pandey and Chitra K. Tiwari, *Nepalese Political Behaviour,* New Delhi: Sterling Publishing House, 1994.

Brazier, Rodney, *Constitutional Practices* (2nd edn.), Oxford: Clarendon Press, 1994.

Brown, T. Louise, *The Challenge of Democracy in Nepal: A Political History,* London: Routledge, 1996.

Butler, David and Austin Ranney, *Electioneering: A Comparative Study of Continuity and Change,* Oxford: Clarendon Press, 1992.

Butler, David, et al., *Democracy at the Polls: A Comparative Study of Competitive National Elections,* Washington D.C.: American Enterprise Institute for Public Policy Research, 1981.

Casper, Gretchen, *Fragile Democracies: The Legacies of Authoritarian Rule,* Pittsburgh: Pittsburgh University Press, 1995.

Chalise, Suresh, *Sociology of a Legislative Elite in a Developing Country,* Kathmandu: Nepal Foundation for Advance Studies, 1995.

Chatterjee, Bhola, *Nepal's Experiment with Democracy* (2nd edn.), New Delhi: Ankur Publishing House, 1982.

———, *Portrait of a Revolutionary B.P. Koirala,* New Delhi: Ankur Publishing House, 1982.

Chauhan, R.S., The *Political Development in Nepal 1950-70: Conflict Between Tradition and Modernity,* Delhi: Associated Publishing House, 1971.

Chibber, Pradeep K., *Democracy Without Association: Transformation of the Party System and Social Cleavages in India,* New Delhi: Vistar Publications, 1999.

Dahal, Dev Raj, *The Challenge of Good Governance,* Kathmandu: GDS, 1996.

Devkota, Grishma Bahadur, *Nepalko Rajnaitaik Darpan,* Banaras, 1960.

Dhaman, Rajiv, *The Supreme Court and Parliamentary Sovereignty,* New Delhi: Sterling Publishers, 1976.

Dhungel, Surya P. et al., *Commentary on the Nepalese Constitution,* Kathmandu: DeLF, 1998.

Diamond, Larry and Marc F. Plattner, eds., *The Global Resurgence of Democracy,* Baltimore: Johns Hopkins University Press, 1993.

Donald, R., *Party Systems and Elections in Latin America,* Chicago: Markham Publishers, 1971.

DREFDEN, *Reports on the Study and Research on the Local Elections in Nepal,* Kathmandu: DREFDEN, 1992.

Election Commission, *General Election 1991 Fact Sheet,* Kathmandu: EC, 1991.

———, *General Election in Nepal,* Kathmandu: EC, 1992.

———, *Electoral Process in Nepal,* Kathmandu: EC, 1998.

———, *General Election in Nepal,* Kathmandu: EC, 1999.

———, *Kathmandu Declaration for Free and Fair Election,* Kathmandu: EC, 1999.

———, *The Election Code of Conduct, 2053 (1996),* Kathmandu: EC, 1999.

Elster, Jon, and Rune Slogstad, eds., *Constitutionalism and Democracy,* New York: Cambridge University Press, 1988.

Eulau, Heinz, et al., *Political Behavior: A Reader in Theory and Research,* New Delhi: Amerind Publishing Co., 1972.

Ewing, K.D., *Money, Politics and Law: A Study of Electoral Campaign Finance in Canada,* New York: Oxford University Press, 1993.

Flagan, S.C., et al., *The Japanese Voter,* London: Yale University Press, 1991.

Garvey, John H. and Alienikott, T. Alexander, *Modern Constitutional Theory: a Reader,* St. Paul Minn: West Publishing Co., 1991.

Griffith, J.A.G. and Michal Ryle, *Parliament: Functions, Practices and Procedures,* London: Sweet and Maxwell, 1989.

Grover, Verinder, ed., *Elections, Electoral Mechanism and Behaviour,* New Delhi: Deep and Deep Publications, 1989.

Gupta, Anirudha, *Politics in Nepal: A Study of Post-Rana Political Development and Party Politics,* Bombay: Allied Publishers, 1964.

———, *Nepalese Interviews,* Delhi: Kalinga, 1997.

Gurung, Harka, *Nepal: Social Demography and Expressions,* Kathmandu: New Era, 1998.

Hedenius, Axel, ed., *Democracy's Victory and Crisis,* Cambridge: Cambridge University Press, 1997.

Helmore, L.M. *Corrupt and Illegal Practices: A General Survey and a Case Study of an Election Petition,* London: Routledge and Kegan, 1967.

HMG/N Ministry of Law and Parliamentary Affairs, *The Constitution of the Kingdom of Nepal, 1990,* Kathmandu, 1992.

Hoftun, Martin, William Raeper and John Whelpton, *People, Politics and Ideology: Democracy and Social Change in Nepal,* Kathmandu: Mandala Book Point, 1999.

Huntington, Samuel P., *Political Order in Changing Societies,* New Haven: Yale University Press, 1968.

———, *The Third Wave: Democracy in the Twentieth Century,* Norman: University of Oklahoma Press, 1991.

ICES, *Governance and the Electoral Process in Bangladesh,* Colombo: ICES, 1996.

ICIMOD, *Districts of Nepal: Indicators of Development,* Kathmandu: ICIMOD, 1997.

IIDS, *The Second Parliamentary Election: A Study of the Emerging Democratic Process in Nepal,* Kathmandu: IIDS, 1993.

———, *The Third Parliamentary Election: A Study of Evolving Democratic Process in Nepal,* Kathmandu: IIDS, 1996.

INSEC, *Election Reform Recommendation Committee, 1994 Report,* Kathmandu: INSEC, 1994.

Inter Parliamentary Union, *Electoral Systems: A World Wide Comparative Study,* Geneva: IPU, 1993.

JIOG, *Summary of Observations for Nepal National Election 2056,* Kathmandu: UNEAS, 1999.

Joshi, Bhuwan L. and Leo E. Rose, *Democratic Innovations in Nepal: A Study in Political Acculturation,* Berkeley: University of California Press, 1966.

Judge, David, *The Parliamentary State,* London: Sage Publications, 1993.

Khanal, Krishna and Krishna Hachhethu, *Aam Nirbachan 2056: Sanshad ra Sarkar ka Chunautiharu* (General Elections 1999: Challenges of Parliament and Government), Kathmandu: CNAS, 1999.

Khanal, Krishna, et al., *Nepal: People, Polity and Governance: A Survey Analysis of People's Response to the Democratic Experiment (1991-95),* Kathmandu: CCD, 1996.

Koirala, Bishweshwar Prasad, *Jail Journal,* Kathmandu: Jagadamba Prakashan, 2054 (1998).

Kumar, Dhruba, ed., *State, Leadership and Politics in Nepal,* Kathmandu: CNAS, 1995.

———, ed., *Domestic Conflict and Crisis of Governability in Nepal,* Kathmandu: CNAS, 2000.

Kumar, Sushil, *Elections and Electoral System,* New Delhi: Institute of Constitutional and Parliamentary Studies, 1971.

Lane, Jan-Erik, *Constitution and Political Theory,* Manchester: Manchester University Press, 1996.

Laver, Michael and Kenneth A. Shepsle, eds., *Making and Breaking Governments,* New York: Cambridge University Press, 1995.

Legal Research Associates of Nepal, *Constitution of the Kingdom of Nepal, 2047 and Electoral Laws,* Kathmandu: LRAS, 1990.

Lijphart, Arend, *Democracies: Pattern of Majoritarian and Consensus Democracies in Twenty-one Countries,* New Haven: Yale University Press, 1984.

———, *Electoral Systems and Party Systems: A Study of 27 Democracies 1945-1990,* Oxford: Oxford University Press, 1994.

Lijphart, A. and B. Grofman, eds., *Choosing an Electoral System: Issues and Alternatives,* New York: Praeger, 1984.

Mackie, T.H. and R. Rose, *The International Almanac of Electoral History,* London: Macmillan, 1991.

Mainali, C.P., *Bartaman Prajatantrik Andolan ko Sandharva ma* (on the Present Context of Democratic Movement), Kathmandu: Subhakamana Prakashan, 1990.

Maskay, Biswa Keshar, *Development Governance,* Kathmandu: Centre for Development and Governance, 2000.

McDonald, R., *Party Systems and Elections in Latin America,* Chicago: Markham Publishers, 1971.

Mclean, Iain, ed., *Oxford Concise Dictionary of Politics,* Oxford, 1996.

NEOC, *Nepal: Election Observation Report: Mid-Term Poll 1994,* Lalitpur: National Election Observation Committee, 1994.

Nepal Opinion Survey Centre (NOSC), *Political Opinion Survey of Kathmandu Valley 1993,* Kathmandu: NOSC, 1993.

Neupaen, Govinda, *Nepalko Jatiya Prasna: Samajik Banot ra Sajedariko Sambhavana,* Kathmandu: Centre for Development Studies, 2000.

Nohlen, Dieter, *Elections and Electoral Systems,* New Delhi: Macmillan India Ltd., 1996.

NSAC, *Nepal: Human Development Report 1998,* Kathmandu: Nepal South Asia Centre, 1998.

Olle, Tornquist, *Politics And Development: A Critical Introduction,* New Delhi: Sage, 1999.

Pai Panandiker, V.A. (ed.), *Problems of Governance in South Asia,* New Delhi: Konark Publishers, 2000.

Pai Panandiker, V.A. and Ajaya K. Menon, *The Indian Cabinet: A Study in Governance,* New Delhi: Konark Publishers, 1996.

Palmer, N.D., *Elections and Political Development: The South Asian Experience,* Durham, North Carolina: Duke University Press, 1995.

Panday, Devendra Raj and Anand Aditya, eds., *Democracy and Empowerment in South Asia,* Kathmandu: Nepal South Asia Centre, 1995.

Panday, Devendra Raj et al., *Comparative Electoral Processes in South Asia,* Kathmandu: Nepal South Asia Centre, 1999.

POLSAN, *Political Parties and the Parliamentary Process in Nepal: A Study of the Transitional Phase,* Kathmandu: POLSAN, 1992.

———, *The Nepalese Voters: A Survey,* Kathmandu: POLSAN, 1991.

Powell, G. Bingham, *Elections as Instruments of Democracy Majoritarian and Proportional Visions,* New Haven: Yale Press, 2000.

Powell, G.B., Jr., *Elections as Instrument of Democracy,* London: Yale University Press, 2000.

Pye, Lucian W., *Aspects of Political Development,* Delhi: Amerind Publishing Company, 1972.

Pyper, Robert, *Aspects of Accountability in the British System of Government,* Merseyside: Tudor Business Publishing Ltd., 1996.

Rae, D.W., *The Political Consequences of Electoral Laws,* Boston: Yale University Press, 1971.

Rawal, Bhim, *Nepal ma Samyabadi Andolan: Udbhav, Vikas ra Bartaman Abastha* (Communist Movement in Nepal: Origin, Evolution and Recent Development), Kathmandu: Samana Prakashan, 1988.

Redish, Martin H., *The Constitution as Political Structure,* New York: Oxford University Press, 1995.

Regmi, Jagdish Chandra, *Nepalko Baidhanik Parampara* (2nd edn.) Kathmandu: Tanneri Prakashan, 1997.

Reports of the State Affairs Committee (House of Representatives) Kathmandu, 1998.

Robertson, David, *The Penguin Dictionary of Politics,* London: Penguin Books, 1993.

SAP/Nepal, *Governance in the Doldrums,* Kathmandu: SAP/Nepal, 2000.

Science Association of Nepal (POLSAN), 1992.

Sartori, Giovani, *Democratic Theory* (Indian edition), Calcutta: Oxford and IBH Publishing Company, 1965.

———, *Comparative Constitutional Engineering: An Inquiry into Structures, Incentives and Outcomes,* London: Macmillan, 1994.

SEARCH, *The Three District Political Opinion Survey,* Kathmandu: SEARCH, 1994.

———, *Strengthening Democratic Process in Nepal: General Elections Monitoring Program 1991,* Kathmandu: SEARCH, 1991.

Seshan, T.N., *A Heart Full of Burden,* New Delhi: UBS Publications, 1995

Seth, D.L. and Ashis Nandi, eds., *The Multiverse of Democracy,* New Delhi: Sage, 1996.

Shaha, Rishikesh, *Essays in the Practice of Government in Nepal,* New Delhi: Manohar, 1982.

———, *Nepali Politics: Retrospect and Prospect,* New Delhi: Oxford University Press, 1978.

Sharma, Ganesh Raj, *Bishweshwar Prasad Koiralako Atma Britanta.* Kathmandu: Jagadamba Prakashan, 2055 (1998).

Sharma, Sudhindra and Pawan Kumar Sen, *1999 General Election Opinion Poll: How Voters Assess Politics, Parties and Publications,* Kathmandu: Himal Association, 1999.

Shils, Edward, *Political Development in the New State,* The Hague: Mouton, 1962.

Shrestha, Tulsi Narayan, *Concept of Local Government and Decentralization,* Kathmandu: Ratna Pustak Bhandar, 1996.

Stiller, L.F., s.j., *Prithwinarayan Shah in the Light of Dibya Upadesh,* Ranchi, India: Catholic Press, 1968.

Surendra, K.C., *Nepalma Communist Andolanko Itihas,* Kathmandu: Bidyarthi Pustak Bhandar, 2055 (1998).

Tamang, Shyam Bahadur, *Jan-Mukti Sena Euta Nalekhiyeko Itihas,* Kathmandu: Ekta Prakashan, 2056.

Thapa, Ganga Bahadur, ed., *Promoting Participatory Democracy in Nepal,* Kathmandu: POLSAN, 1998

The Constitution of the Kingdom of Nepal, 1990, Kathmandu: Ministry of Law and Justice, 1990.

Thiagarajah, Jeevan, ed., *Governance and the Electoral Process in Pakistan,* Colombo: ICES, 1997.

UNDP, *Public Sector Management, Governance and Sustainable Human Development* (1995).

Ware, Allan, *Citizens, Parties and the State: A Reappraisal,* Cambridge: Polity Press, 1987.

Warwick, Paul V., *Government Survival in Parliamentary Democracies,* New York: Cambridge University Press, 1994.

Weiner, Myron and J.O. Field, *Electoral Politics in the Indian States,* New Delhi: Manohar, 1974-5.

Weiner, Myron, *The Indian Paradox,* New Delhi: Sage, 1989.

World Bank, *Sub-Saharan Africa: From Crisis to Sustainable Growth,* New York: The World Bank, 1989.

———, *Governance and Development,* New York: The World Bank, 1992.

ARTICLES

Acharya, Narhari, 'Rajgaddi Uttaradhikarika Sambandhama Sansadma Chhalphal Awasyak' (Need for Discussion in Parliament), *Kantipur daily,* 26 June 2001.

Aditya, Anand, 'Emerging Ethnicity and Electoral Intervention in a Democratizing State: An Inquiry into the Prospects of Civic Nationalism in Nepal', in Ganga B. Thapa, ed., *Democracy and Decentralization,* Kathmandu: POLSAN, 1996.

———, 'Shifting Votes in a Multipolar Electorate', *Nepali Political Science and Politics,* vol. 5, 1996, pp. 39-48

———, 'Human Rights and Elections in Nepal', in *Human Rights Year Book 2000,* Kathmandu: INSEC, 2000.

Baral, Lok Raj, and Leo E. Rose, 'Democratization and the Crisis of Governance in Nepal' in Subrata K. Mitra and D. Rothermund, eds., *Legitimacy and Conflict in South Asia,* New Delhi: Manohar, 1997.

———, 'Ethnicity and Constitutional Reforms in Nepal', Iftekharruzzaman, ed., *Ethnicity and Constitutional Reforms in South Asia,* New Delhi: Manohar, 1998.

———, 'Graduate Elections: Arena for Opposition', in S.D. Muni, ed., *Nepal: An Assertive Monarchy,* Delhi: Chetna, 1977.

———, 'Nepal: Politics Without Power', *Asian Survey,* 28:2: 1988.

———, 'Parties in Parliament', *Nepali Journal of Constitutional and Parliamentary Exercises,* 1:1, 1993.

———, 'Political Parties and Governance in South Asia', in V.A. Pai Panandiker, ed., *Problems of Governance in South Asia,* New Delhi: Konark Publishers, 2000.

———, 'Nepal: Problems of Constitutional Transition', *Essays On Constitutional Law,* November-December 1997-January 1998.

———, 'The 1994 Nepal Elections: Emerging Trends in Party Politics', *Asian Survey,* vol. 35, no. 5, May 1995.

———, 'The Return of Party Politics in Nepal', *Journal of Democracy,* vol. 5, no. 1, 1994.

Barnes, Samuel H., 'Electoral, Behavioural and Comparative Politics', in M.I. Lichbach and Zuckerman, eds., *Comparative Politics,* Cambridge: Cambridge University Press, 1997.

Bhattachan, Krishna B., 'Ethno-politics and Ethno-development: An Emerging Paradigm in Nepal', in Dhruba Kumar, ed., *State, Leadership and Politics in Nepal,* Kathmandu: CNAS, 1995.

Bista, Dor Bahadur, 'The Structure of Nepali Society', in Kamal P. Malla, ed., *Nepal: Perspectives in Continuity and Change,* Kirtipur: Centre for Nepal and Asian Studies, 1989.

Borre, Ole, 'Election Survey and Voter Types', paper presented at a seminar on Electoral Process in Nepal: Review and Prospects, organized by POLSAN, Kathmandu, 3 August 1990.

Butler, David, Ashok Lahiri and Prannoy Roy, 'India Decides: Elections 1952-1955', in Partha Chatterjee, ed., *State and Politics in India,* New Delhi: Oxford University Press, 1997.

Chari, P., 'Civilian Control over Military in India', *Indian Defence Review,* October 1991, pp. 9-15.

Dahal, Dev Raj, 'Reforms in the Electoral Process in Nepal', in Devendra Raj Panday, Anand Aditya and Dev Raj Dahal, eds., *Comparative Electoral Processes in South Asia,* Kathmandu: Nepal South Asian Centre, 1999.

Dahal, Dilli Ram, 'Nepal's Governing Elite: Their Composition and Role in Constituting the State', in Dhruba Kumar, ed., *Domestic Conflict and Crisis of Governability in Nepal,* Kathmandu: CNAS, 2000.

Dahal, Ram Kumar, 'Candidate Selection in the 1999 Parliamentary Elections', *NCCS Occasional Paper I,* Kathmandu: Nepal Centre for Contemporary Studies, December 2000.

Diamond, Larry, 'Promoting Democracy in the 1990s: Actors, Instruments, and Issues', in Axel Hadenius, ed., *Democracy's Victory and Crisis,* Colorado: Cambridge University Press, 1997.

Eckstien, Harry, 'Introduction: The Impact of Electoral System on Representative Government', in David Apter and Herry Eckstien, eds., *Comparative Politics,* Delhi: Surjeet Publications, 1989 (Indian reprint).

Eldersveld, Samuel J., 'Theory and Method of Voting Behavior Research', in Heinz Eulau, Samuel J. Eldersvald and Morris Janowitz, eds., *Political Behavior: A Reader in Theory and Research,* New Delhi: Amerind Publishing Co., 1972.

Elklit, Jorgen, 'The Choice of Electoral System and the Consequences for the Political Parties', paper presented at a seminar on Electoral Process in Nepal: Review and Prospects, organized by POLSAN on 3 August 1990.

Gaige, Fred and John Scholz, 'The 1991 Parliamentary Elections in Nepal: Political Freedom and Stability', *Asian Survey,* vol. XXXI, no. 11, November 1991.

Gurung, Harka, 'Representing An Ethnic Mosaic', *Himal,* May/June 1992.

———, 'Sociology of Elections in Nepal', *Asian Survey,* March 1992.

———, 'Democracy and Social Development in Nepal: Ethnicity and Regionalism in Nepal Elections', in Ananda Shrestha, ed., *The Role of Civil Society and Democratization in Nepal,* Kathmandu: NEFAS, 1998.

Hachhethu, Krishna, 'Raj Parampara ra Bidhima Byapak Paribartan' (Royal Tradition and Major Changes in Law), *Himal* (Kathmandu), 30 June-15 July 2001.

———,'Reading the Opinion Poll', in Himal Association, *Political Opinion Survey Nepal 2001,* Kathmandu: Himal Association, 2001.

Harriss-White, Barbara, 'Liberalization and Corruption', *IDS Bulletin,* vol. 27, no. 2, April 1996.

Hormens, F.A., 'The Dynamic of Proportional Representation', in David Apter and Herry Eckstien, eds., *Comparative Politics,* Delhi: Surjeet Publications, 1989 (Indian reprint).

Huber, John D., 'The Vote of Confidence in Parliamentary Democracies', *American Political Science Review,* vol. 86, March 1992.

Jha, Hari Bansh, 'Issues of Ethnicity and Regionalism in the Election', paper presented to a seminar on Election as a Vehicle for Promoting Democracy, organized by CETS, 10 November 1994.

Kashyap, Subhash C., 'Institutions of Governance: The Parliament, the Government and the Judiciary', in V.A. Pai Panandiker, ed., *Problems of Governance in South Asia,* New Delhi: Konark Publishers, 2000.

Kraemer, Karl Heinz, 'Elections in Nepal: 1999 and Before', *Human Rights Year Book 2000,* Kathmandu: INSEC, 2000.

Lakeman, Enid and James D. Lanbest, 'Voting in Democracies', in David Apter and Herry Eckstien, eds., *Comparative Politics,* Delhi: Surjeet Publications, 1989 (Indian reprint)

Lardeyret, Guy, 'The Problem with PR', in Larry Diamond and Marc F. Plattner, eds., *The Global Resurgence of Democracy,* Baltimore: Johns Hopkins University Press, 1993, pp. 156-64.

Leftwich, Adrian, 'Governance, the State and the Politics of Development', *Development and Change,* vol. 25, 1994.

Lucas, J.R., 'The Value of Vote', in *Democracy and Participation,* Hammersworth, UK: Penguin Books, 1976.

Maharjan, Pancha N., 'Local Election in Nepal 1997' (Monograph), Kathmandu: CNAS, 1998.

Meyer, Ralph C., 'How Do Indians Vote?' *Asian Survey,* December 1989.

Mitra, Subrata K., 'Indigenisation, Locally Embedded Values and Parties as Instruments for State-Society Relations: An Agenda for Research', paper presented to international workshop on Political Parties in South Asia, in Nottingham, UK, 29 March-1 April 2001.

Nye, J.S., 'Corruption and Political Development: A Cost-Benefit Analysis', *American Political Science Review,* vol. XI, no. 2, 1967.

Oommen, T.K., 'Conceptualising Nation and Nationalty in South Asia', in S.L. Sharma and T.K. Oommen, eds., *Nation and National Identity in South Asia,* New Delhi: Orient Longman, 2000.

Poudyal, Ananta Raj, 'Nation Building in Nepal: A Case Study of the Post Revolution Period (1950-81)' (unpublished Ph.D. thesis, TU, Kathmandu, 1986).

Rahman, Mizanur, 'Governance and Judiciary', a paper presented at an International Seminar on Good Governance, Dhaka, 4-6 August 1998.

Shah, Bishnu Pratap, 'Nirvachan Pranali ra Loktantra ko Sudridhikaran' (Electoral System and the Consolidation of

Democracy), paper presented to a seminar on Consensus Politics and Implementation of Constitution, organized by NCCS, Kartik 26, 2055.

———, 'Nirvachan Pranali ra Loktantra ko Sudridhikaran' (Electoral System and the Consolidation of Democracy), paper presented at a seminar on Politics of Consensus and Implementation of Constitution, organized by NCCS in cooperation with Fredrich Ebert Stifftung, 12 November 1998, Kathmandu.

———, 'Sambaidhanik Nikayaharuko Sudridhikaran, Samasya ra Samadhan' (Consolidation of Constitutional Organs: Problems and Solutions), paper presented at a seminar organized by National Democratic Institute (NDI), Kathmandu, 29 November 1998.

———, 'Swachha ra Nispaksha Nirvachhan Sudhar ka Prayasharu' (Attempts for Reforms for Free, Fair and Impartial Elections), paper presented in Biratnagar seminar organized by NCCS, 1-3, Asadha 28, 2057.

Shaha, Risikesh, 'Parliamentary Monarch in Nepal', *Nepali Journal of Constitutional and Parliamentary Exercise,* vol. 1, no. 1, 1993.

Sharma, Ganesh Raj, 'Bighatanko Adhikar ra Pradhanmantriya Netritwa', *Kanun,* no. 14, Phagun 2055, pp. 3-9.

Sharma, Prayag Raj, 'Caste, Social Mobility and Sanskritization in a Tribal Hindu Society: A Study of Nepal's Old Legal Code', in S. Iijima, ed., *Changing Aspecs of Modern Nepal,* Tokyo: ISLCAA, 1977.

Shrestha, Aditya Man, 'An Overview of Corruption-Control Mechanism in Nepal', A working paper presented for the Transparency International/Nepal, 1997.

Singh, Ganesh Man, *Mero Kathaka Panaharu,* Part I, Kathmandu: Aayam Prakashan, 1998.

Tiwari, Chitra Krishna, 'Electoral Experience and Process in Nepal', in Peter Gundelach and Karen Siune, eds., *From Voters to Participants,* Denmark: Politica, 1992.

Upadhyaya, Biswa Nath, 'Pratinidhi Sabha Bighatan Sipharis: Aouchitya ra Adhar', *Kanun,* no. 14, Baisakh 2056, pp. 3-11.

Weiner, Myron, 'Introduction', in Myron Weiner and Samuel P. Huntington, eds., *Understanding Political Development,* Boston: Little, Brown, 1987.

Whelpton, John, 'The General Election of May 1991', in Michael Hutt, ed., *Nepal in the Nineties,* New Delhi: Oxford University Press, 1993, pp. 48-81.

———, 'Nine Years On: The 1999 Election and Nepalese Politics since the 1990 *Janaandolan*', *European Bulletin of Himalayan Research,* no. 8, 1995.

Woodhouse, Diana, 'Ministerial Responsibility: Something Old Something New', *Public Law,* Summer 1997, pp. 262-82.

Yadav, Yogendra, 'Reconfiguration in Indian Politics: State Assembly Elections 1993-1995', in Partha Chatterjee, ed., *State and Politics in India,* New Delhi: Oxford University Press, 1997.

Contributors

LOK RAJ BARAL is Professor and Executive Chairman, Nepal Centre for Contemporary Studies, Kathmandu, Nepal. He was Professor and Chairman, Department of Political Science in Tribhuvan University during 1977-88. Professor Baral has more than ten books to his credit, both authoured and edited, and has contributed several articles to the edited volumes, national and international journals. Editor of many journals and a member of board of research centres and editorial board of journals, he was a visiting professor in many universities and centres. He also served as Nepal's ambassador to India in 1996-7

RAM KUMAR DAHAL is Professor of Political Science, Tribhuvan University, Kathmandu, Nepal. Dr. Dahal is author of many books and articles.

KRISHNA HACHHETHU is Associate Professor, Centre for Nepal and Asian Studies, Tribhuvan University. His latest publication is *Party Building in Nepal: Organization, Leadership and People.* He is the co-author of *Leadership in Nepal* and *Nepal: Local Leadership and Governance.* He has contributed many articles and occasional papers to various journals.

KRISHNA P. KHANAL is Professor of Political Science, Tribhuvan University. He has served in different capacities, notably as advisor to the Prime Minister and Executive Director, Centre for Nepal and Asian Studies. He is a regular contributor to journals edited volumes and occasional papers.

DHRUBA KUMAR is associated with the Centre for Nepal and Asian Studies. He is author and editor of many books and journals. His major contribution is in the area of strategic studies.

Index